LONGING FOR GOD IN AN AGE OF DISCOURAGEMENT

THE GOSPEL ACCORDING TO
THE OLD TESTAMENT

*A series of studies on the lives
of Old Testament characters, written for
laypeople and pastors, and designed to
encourage Christ-centered reading, teaching,
and preaching of the Old Testament*

IAIN M. DUGUID
Series Editor

LONGING FOR GOD IN AN AGE OF DISCOURAGEMENT

THE GOSPEL ACCORDING TO
ZECHARIAH

BRYAN R. GREGORY

PUBLISHING

P.O. BOX 817 • PHILLIPSBURG • NEW JERSEY 08865-0817

Printed in the United States of America

Library of Congress Cataloging-in-Publication Data

Gregory, Bryan R., 1976-
  Longing for God in an age of discouragement : the Gospel according to Zechariah / Bryan R. Gregory.
    p. cm. -- (The Gospel according to the Old Testament)
  Includes bibliographical references (p.   ) and index.
  ISBN 978-1-59638-142-1 (pbk.)
  1. Bible. O.T. Zechariah--Commentaries. 2. Bible. O.T. Zechariah--Theology. 3. Bible. O.T. Zechariah--Relation to the New Testament. 4. Bible. N.T.--Relation to Zechariah. I. Title.
  BS1665.53.G74 2010
  224'.98077--dc22
                                                    2010039992

For
Christy, Joshua, and Noah

CONTENTS

FOREWORD

The New Testament is in the Old concealed;
the Old Testament is in the New revealed.
—Augustine

Concerning this salvation, the prophets, who spoke of the grace that was to come to you, searched intently and with the greatest care, trying to find out the time and circumstances to which the Spirit of Christ in them was pointing when he predicted the sufferings of Christ and the glories that would follow. It was revealed to them that they were not serving themselves but you, when they spoke of the things that have now been told you by those who have preached the gospel to you by the Holy Spirit sent from heaven. Even angels long to look into these things. (1 Peter 1:10–12)

"In addition, some of our women amazed us. They went to the tomb early this morning but didn't find his body. They came and told us that they had seen a vision of angels, who said he was alive. Then some of our companions went to the tomb and found it just as the women had said, but him they did not see." He said to them, "How foolish you are, and how slow of heart to believe all that the prophets have spoken! Did not the Christ have to suffer these things and then enter his glory?" And beginning with Moses and all the Prophets, he explained to them what was said in all the Scriptures concerning himself. (Luke 24:22–27)

The prophets searched. Angels longed to see. And the disciples didn't understand. But Moses, the prophets, and all the Old Testament Scriptures had spoken about it—that Jesus would come, suffer, and then be glorified. God began to tell a story in the Old Testament, the ending of which the audience eagerly anticipated. But the Old Testament audience was left hanging. The plot was laid out but the climax was delayed. The unfinished story begged an ending. In Christ, God has provided the climax to the Old Testament story. Jesus did not arrive unannounced; his coming was declared *in advance* in the Old Testament, not just in explicit prophecies of the Messiah but by means of the stories of all of the events, characters, and circumstances in the Old Testament. God was telling a larger, overarching, unified story. From the account of creation in Genesis to the final stories of the return from exile, God progressively unfolded his plan of salvation. And the Old Testament account of that plan always pointed in some way to Christ.

AIMS OF THIS SERIES

The Gospel According to the Old Testament Series is committed to the proposition that the Bible, both Old and New Testaments, is a unified revelation of God, and that its thematic unity is found in Christ. The individual books of the Old Testament exhibit diverse genres, styles, and individual theologies, but tying them all together is the constant foreshadowing of, and pointing forward to, Christ. Believing in the fundamentally Christocentric nature of the Old Testament, as well as the New Testament, we offer this series of studies in the Old Testament with the following aims:

- to lay out the pervasiveness of the revelation of Christ in the Old Testament
- to promote a Christ-centered reading of the Old Testament
- to encourage Christ-centered preaching and teaching from the Old Testament

To this end, the volumes in this series are written for pastors and laypeople, not scholars.

While such a series could take a number of different shapes, we have decided, in most cases, to focus individual volumes on Old Testament figures—people—rather than books or themes. Some books, of course, will receive major attention in connection with their authors or main characters (e.g., Daniel or Isaiah). Also, certain themes will be emphasized in connection with particular figures.

It is our hope and prayer that this series will revive interest in and study of the Old Testament as readers recognize that the Old Testament points forward to Jesus Christ.

TREMPER LONGMAN III
J. ALAN GROVES

PREFACE

Though at times neglected by the church, recently the book of Zechariah has been getting more attention. Many are rediscovering its rich theological contribution to the whole counsel of God, as well as its importance in understanding key parts of the New Testament such as the passion of Christ and the book of Revelation.

In preparing to study the book of Zechariah together, I should mention a few housekeeping items. First, all English translations of Zechariah are my own. Translations of other biblical texts are designated as either from the English Standard Version or the New International Version.

Second, I have generally tried to bring together three things in each chapter: an exposition of the text in its original historical context, reflection on how the text points us to the person and work of Christ, and suggestions of how the text refracted through Christ should shape the life of the church in the world. While texts can obviously provide many fruitful lanes of application, I have sought to develop in each chapter one particular avenue that seems to me to be a natural extension of the passage's principle theological trajectory. The avenues of application and New Testament connections that have been left unexplored will undoubtedly be worth the reader's time to trace on his or her own.

Finally, I am of the firm conviction that studying Scripture ought primarily to increase our love for God and for one another. To that end, may we adopt humble hearts, teachable minds, and malleable wills as we seek to be transformed by our triune God through the reading of Zechariah. All glory be to the Father, the Son, and the Holy Spirit, one God, now and forevermore. Amen.

ACKNOWLEDGMENTS

I n his *Four Hundred Chapters on Love*, Maximus the Confessor wrote, "Friends are abundant—that is, in times of prosperity. In time of trial you can barely find one."[1] That is true both in life and in the normal ups and downs of writing a book. Three loved ones deserve special mention for their dedicated involvement in the project.

In extending thanks and appreciation, pride of place goes to my wonderful wife, Christy, for her love, encouragement, support, and thoughtful input. She, along with our two sons Joshua and Noah, made the months of writing all the more enjoyable.

I also owe a huge debt of gratitude to my brother, Brad Gregory, and my close friend, Rick Gilmartin, both of whom read every word of the manuscript and offered numerous insightful suggestions. However, it is their abiding friendship and constant encouragement for which I am most grateful.

The manuscript was written during my time as an associate pastor at Back Creek Presbyterian Church in Charlotte, North Carolina and sincere appreciation goes to the congregation for making the ministry of the Word a true delight. A special word of thanks goes to Paul Griffith, elder emeritus at Back Creek, who's kind and generous comments after a sermon on Zechariah 4 gave me the initial encouragement to pursue this project.

Thanks also to the wonderful library staffs at the University of Notre Dame and Davidson College. They were always readily available with assistance and their helpfulness was outstripped only by their cheerfulness.

Thank you as well to Tremper Longman III and the entire P&R staff for their support of this work at the beginning and for their diligence and helpfulness to print.

And, finally, a word of appreciation goes to the late Al Groves, a man who, in both his life and his death, caused so many—like Zechariah—to "lift up their eyes."

ABBREVIATIONS

AB	Anchor Bible
ABR	*Australian Biblical Review*
ABRL	Anchor Bible Reference Library
ANF	Ante-Nicene Fathers
BST	Bible Speaks Today
CBC	Cambridge Bible Commentary
CBQ	*Catholic Biblical Quarterly*
CC	*Continental Commentaries*
DSB	Daily Study Bible
FOTL	Forms of the Old Testament Literature Series
HAR	*Hebrew Annual Review*
IBC	Interpretation Biblical Commentary
ICC	International Critical Commentary
ITC	International Theological Commentary
JAOS	*Journal of the American Oriental Society*
JBL	*Journal of Biblical Literature*
JSJSup	Journal for the Study of Judaism, Supplement Series
JSOTSS	Journal for the Study of the Old Testament, Supplement Series
JSPSup	Journal for the Study of the Pseudepigrapha, Supplements
JSS	*Journal of Semitic Studies*
NICNT	New International Commentary on the New Testament
NIVAC	NIV Application Commentary
NPNF	Nicene and Post-Nicene Fathers
NTM	New Testament Monographs

OTL   Old Testament Library
RB   *Révue Biblique*
SJOT   *Scandinavian Journal of the Old Testament*
TOTC   Tyndale Old Testament Commentaries
USQR   *Union Seminary Quarterly Review*
VT   *Vetus Testamentum*
VTSup   Vetus Testamentum, Supplements
WBC   Word Biblical Commentary
ZAW   Zeitschrift für die alttestamentliche
           Wissenschaft

PART ONE

AN AGE OF DISCOURAGEMENT

CHAPTER ONE

READING ZECHARIAH

All beginnings are hard. (Chaim Potok[1])

READING ZECHARIAH IN HISTORICAL CONTEXT

As a book of new beginnings, Zechariah is filled with vivid images and enigmatic visions. Within its pages are some of the most memorable passages in all the Old Testament, passages that paint dramatic pictures and offer pointed oracles for a people who—like us—find themselves discouraged by the problems within their own community and the larger geopolitical instability of recent years. Yet understanding these passages can prove difficult without at least a basic grasp of the historical situation in which Zechariah ministered, namely the early Persian period.[2]

Historically speaking, the Persians came to dominate the Near East almost overnight under the leadership of Cyrus the Great. In just two decades (559–539 B.C.), Cyrus had risen to power, assimilated the Median Empire (550 B.C.), marched westward to defeat and acquire Lydia, Lycia, and the Greek states in Asia Minor, taken control of territory extending eastward to India, and conquered the powerful Babylonian Empire (539 B.C.). With the defeat of Babylonia, the Persians inherited all the territory previously under Babylon's control, part of which was Judah. However, appropriating these newly acquired territories would require both an enormous administrative effort and a shrewd sense of diplomacy.

While Cyrus did not overhaul the bureaucratic structure he inherited from the Babylonians, he did implement one very strategic change to win the allegiance of the local populations. He enacted a policy of tolerance under which the conquered peoples were allowed to reconstruct their temples and sanctuaries and return to their traditional religious practices. The benefit to the Persians was twofold: the policy promoted Cyrus as a magnanimous ruler, and at the same time, it generated income for the empire through taxation. Evidence of this policy exists both in the pages of Scripture as well as in a cuneiform document commonly known as the Cyrus Cylinder. The book of Ezra begins as follows:

> In the first year of Cyrus king of Persia, in order to fulfill the word of the LORD spoken by Jeremiah, the LORD moved the heart of Cyrus king of Persia to make a proclamation throughout his realm and to put it in writing:
>
> "This is what Cyrus king of Persia says:
> "'The LORD, the God of heaven, has given me all the kingdoms of the earth and he has appointed me to build a temple for him at Jerusalem in Judah. Anyone of his people among you—may his God be with him, and let him go up to Jerusalem in Judah and build the temple of the LORD, the God of Israel, the God who is in Jerusalem. And the people of any place where survivors may now be living are to provide him with silver and gold, with goods and livestock, and with freewill offerings for the temple of God in Jerusalem.'" (Ezra 1:1–4 NIV)[3]

Similarly, in the Cyrus Cylinder, Cyrus describes his victory over Babylon and declares,

> All the kings who sat in throne rooms, throughout the four quarters, from the Upper to the Lower Sea, those who dwelled in . . . all the kings of the west country who dwelled in tents, brought me their heavy tribute and kissed my feet in Babylon. From . . . to the cities of Ashur and Susa, Agade, Eshnunna, the cities of Zamban, Meternu, Der, as far as the region of the land of Gutium, the holy cities beyond the Tigris whose sanctuaries had been in ruins over a long period, the gods whose abode is in the midst of them, I returned to their places and housed them in lasting abodes. I gathered together all their inhabitants and restored to them their dwellings.[4]

In the specific case of the Jerusalem temple, Cyrus' motivations were undoubtedly more about political and military advantage than heartfelt generosity. The western front of the empire had become problematic and the repopulation and rebuilding of the area would have stabilized the region as well as shored up his resistance to Egypt. Nevertheless, as the Ezra text indicates, the Judeans saw Cyrus' edict (538 B.C.) not just as political maneuvering but also as God's sovereign fulfillment of prophecy and an expression of the Lord's intention to restore Israel. It was more than just an opportunity to return to their land from exile and to begin reconstruction of the temple; it was an indication that the long-awaited restoration was finally underway, and that the Lord was returning to Zion.

In response to the edict, exiles from the "houses of Judah and Benjamin" began returning to Jerusalem and its surrounding area to rebuild the temple (Ezra 1:5–6 ESV). By Persian designation, this area formed the province of Yehud. The province itself was relatively small, roughly circumscribing the land around Jerusalem with a radius of approximately seventeen miles (it included Jericho and Hazor to the north, Gezer to the west, and Beth-Zur and En-gedi to the south, with the Dead Sea and the Jordan River providing the eastern border).[5] In the early days, the population of the entire province might have been no more than fifty thousand people.[6]

To provide the exiles with leadership, Cyrus appointed Sheshbazzar as the first governor of Yehud and charged him with rebuilding the temple and returning to it the gold and silver vessels that Nebuchadnezzar had removed and placed in his own temple in Babylon (Ezra 1:7–11; 5:14–15). The altar was rebuilt immediately so that the people could once again offer burnt offerings (Ezra 3:1–6). Shortly thereafter, preliminary work began on the foundations of the temple in 537 B.C. (Ezra 5:16).[7]

But the work quickly stalled, and over the next seventeen years little happened, due to both internal and external problems.[8] Internally, some argued against rebuilding the temple (Hag. 1:2).[9] It's possible that this resistance was fueled by economic difficulties stemming from high inflation from Persian taxation and the natural instability of an agriculturally dependent economy, which had recently suffered from a drought (Hag. 1:6, 9–11; 2:16). Moreover, with new homes needing to be built to accommodate the returning exiles, the rebuilding of the temple likely would have been a low priority for many (Hag. 1:4). In addition, tensions over property rights between those returning and those who never left probably exacerbated the housing problem further, resulting in considerable strain on the community.[10]

Externally, the Samarian province to the north consistently troubled the Judeans as they tried to reestablish themselves. An appeal to their Persian overlords for help would have been fruitless since at that point "the Persian Empire under Cyrus had not established a sufficiently strong centralized government to allow for the high-level imposition of imperial will."[11] Making matters worse, many in exile were simply unwilling to leave their now prosperous lives in Babylon (and Egypt) to come back to Judah, which sparked shock and resentment among those who were trying to begin the process of reconstruction. Not surprisingly, this constellation of problems—social, economic, and political—produced cynicism and discouragement among the people. In sum, "all indications are, therefore, that life in Yehud was difficult. Its people lived daily with the painful contrast between the glories of the past and the humiliation of the present. Very little of what the returnees had eagerly expected had been realized."[12]

However, winds of change were beginning to blow. During those seventeen years, a number of developments occurred in the Persian Empire. In 530 B.C., Cyrus was killed in battle and his son Cambyses, a widely disliked tyrant, assumed control of the empire. Like his father, he preoccupied himself with military expansion. Though he conquered Egypt in 525 B.C., he died only three years later. Succeeding him was Darius I, a usurper whose reign was to last thirty-six years (522–486 B.C.). When he took command, the empire was in turmoil. To combat this, Darius worked to consolidate the empire by suppressing numerous revolts and reforming its administrative system. He divided the empire into twenty regions called "satrapies," and stationed a Persian official (or satrap) in each one to promote loyalty to the empire, administer the law, and manage effective taxation. Each satrapy was then divided into districts, or provinces, with recognized governors to see after local affairs.

In 520 B.C., Darius appointed Zerubbabel, a descendent of David, as the provincial governor of Yehud, a post he likely held for about ten years. During these years, reconstruction on the temple finally resumed under the leadership of Zerubbabel and the high priest Joshua (Jeshua) and at the behest of the prophets Zechariah and Haggai (Ezra 3:8–11; Hag. 1:1, 14).

Even though temple building was in the best interest of the Persians who wanted to establish a solid provincial infrastructure, local challenges nevertheless surfaced. As the work of reconstruction progressed, adversaries within the province tried numerous strategies to thwart the efforts (Ezra 4:1–5). The conflicts attending the rebuilding seem to have prompted the Persians to send Tattenai, the governor of a neighboring province, along with some associates to Jerusalem to get to the bottom of it (Ezra 5:3–17). After sorting it all out, with Darius confirming Cyrus' decree for the Jerusalem temple to be rebuilt, the construction was allowed to resume, though the builders continued to struggle with their task. At long last, however, the temple was completed "on the third day of the month of Adar in the sixth year of the reign of Darius the king," that is in February of 515 b.c. (Ezra 6:15 esv).

The next sixty-five years were a tumultuous time, both in Yehud and in the larger Persian Empire. As Darius continued to try to extend his domain westward and northward, he was eventually resisted by Greek cities, which openly rebelled against Persia in 499 b.c. The conflict, known as the Greco-Persian wars, lasted for several decades. In 490 b.c., Darius suffered a devastating defeat to Athens at the Battle of Marathon. Four years later, Darius' son Xerxes I assumed the throne and continued the struggle. Though he suffered numerous defeats, he did manage to hold on to several eastern territories.

As events unfolded, with Persian resources being channeled to the war with Greece, other nations within the Persian Empire, such as Egypt and Babylonia, began asserting their independence, with Babylonia apparently becoming a separate satrapy in 481 b.c. On the western front, several revolts by the Egyptians prompted the Persians to march through Yehud's territory in order to deal with the uprisings, some of which occurred during Xerxes' reign and some of which occurred under the reign of Xerxes' son Artaxerxes I, who assumed the throne after his father was assassinated in 464 B.C. Though the Egyptian revolts were defeated, not until the Peace of Callias (449 B.C.) did a temporary truce with Greece prevail.

These critical years (539–449 B.C.) provide the primary historical backdrop for understanding the visions and oracles in the book of Zechariah. The people of Judah and Jerusalem were struggling financially, frustrated politically, and divided socially. More than anything they needed theological spectacles through which to view and understand the events of their day and the difficult situations of their daily lives. Called to address this need, Zechariah brought a theological message that was thematically centered on two foci: the renewal of God's people and the establishment of God's kingdom.

First, Zechariah called for the renewal of God's people. The very first words recorded as given to Zechariah are:

> The LORD was very angry with your fathers. Therefore say to them, Thus declares the LORD of hosts: Return to me, says the LORD of hosts, and I will return to you, says the LORD of hosts. (Zech. 1:2–3)

Past generations were characterized by a hardness of heart. When the Lord had repeatedly sent prophets to urge the people to turn from their wicked ways and to repent for their evil deeds, the people largely ignored them. Eventually, their unrepentant disobedience ended with the judgment of the Assyrian exile of the northern tribes and the Babylonian exile of the southern tribes.

Yet God declared in Zechariah that he was not done with his people. He called them to repent and he promised that if they did he would cleanse them. Though they were filthy from their sins and the stain of exile, God assured them that they would once again be made clean (Zech. 3:1–10). Gone would be the false prophets, the idols, and the spirit of uncleanness (Zech. 13:1–3), as well as theft and false testimonies (Zech. 5:1–4). In their place would be mercy, justice, peace, and prosperity (Zech. 7:1–8:23). Significantly, the book of Zechariah ends with the declaration that Jerusalem will be so holy that even the common and unclean things like horses' bells and cooking pots will be inscribed with "Holy to the Lord," an inscription previously reserved for the gold plate on the high priest's turban (Ex. 28:36; 39:30).

Second, Zechariah envisioned the establishment of God's kingdom. In the section popularly known as the "night visions" (Zech. 1:7–6:8), the first and last vision form an inclusio—a repetition of certain features at the beginning and the end of a unit—with the theme that one day the Lord, the great King, will subdue all his enemies and bring about his sovereign reign upon the earth (Zech. 1:7–17; 6:1–8). The theme is continued in the second half of the book with oracles declaring the coming destruction of Israel's enemies (Zech. 9:1–8; 12:1–9). Nevertheless, the last word is not of destruction but of redemption: he will fight against the nations, subduing them so that they might turn to him as the true and rightful king (Zech. 8:22; 14:1–21). Then the Lord will be exalted as the King of the entire world, and he alone will be acknowledged as the true God (Zech. 14:9).

Moreover, the Lord will return to Zion and will work salvation for his people (Zech. 9:9–17). In fact, the book mentions Jerusalem more than forty times. Zechariah longs for the day when the Lord will return to Zion and dwell in Jerusalem so that they become the "Holy Mountain" and the "City of Truth" (Zech. 8:3 NIV). It will once again be teeming with people and livestock (Zech. 2:4). In 1:16, the measuring line is used not just to plan the reconstruction of the temple as in Ezekiel 40, but of the entire city of Jerusalem. In other words, the Lord plans to restore Jerusalem as the imperial city of his coming kingdom.

A lofty vision no doubt, but one which the people desperately needed to hear. Zechariah had "learned that at a time of calm in the world's history, when the nations believed themselves secure in their own powers alone, the kingdom of God was already prepared in heaven."[13] The book of Zechariah's most foundational purpose is to lift the eyes (a recurring phrase in the book) of the people of God from their discouraging circumstances to see the bigger picture of God's coming kingdom. If they could begin grasping that "the kingdom of God was already prepared in heaven," they would find their discouragement melting away and a renewed motivation to do what the Lord was calling them to do, namely to build the temple, purge the social evils among them, and order their lives and communities around the priorities and expectations of God's coming kingdom.

READING ZECHARIAH IN LITERARY CONTEXT

Understanding the historical backdrop of Zechariah makes for more fruitful reading, but just as important is an understanding of its literary shape. It is widely recognized that Zechariah can be divided into two separate literary halves (Zechariah 1–8 and Zechariah 9–14) because of many important functional differences.

First, Zechariah 1–8 has specific time stamps (Zech. 1:1, 7; 7:1) that locate the visions and oracles in specific historical contexts (520–518 B.C.), while Zechariah 9–14 lacks any such historical notices. Yet it is clear from the oracles in the second half of the book that they presuppose a time after the temple has been completed (515 B.C.) and operations have resumed (see Zech. 11:13; 14:20–21). Moreover, the international turmoil during the early fifth century would explain much of the eschatological thinking in Zechariah 9–14 that forecasts God's turn to shake the nations and upend pagan rule for the benefit of his people and the establishment of his kingdom.[14] The difference between the first and second halves is understandable since the second half has a decidedly different focus. Zechariah

11

1–8 contains visions and oracles that primarily give the people a new way to view their current situation theologically. Thus specific historical markers aid the purpose of those chapters. Zechariah 9–14 tends to focus more on what God has in store for the future and does so using apocalyptic language, thereby making specific historical references unnecessary.

Second, Zechariah 1–8 tends to concentrate on general theological themes cast in mostly idyllic pictures. But Zechariah 9–14 begins to focus God's work in the world more narrowly (and more cryptically) on a significant individual through whom God will accomplish his redemptive purposes. While Zechariah 1–8 does introduce the figure of the Branch (Zech. 3:8; 6:12), the promised individual in Zechariah 9–14 is far more three-dimensional. The reader is told of his humiliation as well as his glory, his suffering as well as his greatness. He is accepted yet rejected, conqueror yet conquered, victor yet victim.

But it would be a mistake to allow the differences between the two halves of the book to eclipse its fundamental unity. Both are concerned with Jerusalem (Zech. 1:12–16; 2:1–13; 9:8–10; 12:1–13; 14:1–21), the cleansing of the community (Zech. 3:1–9; 5:1–11; 10:9; 12:10; 13:1–2; 14:20–21), the inclusion of the nations (Zech. 2:11; 8:20–23; 9:7, 10; 14:16–19), the continuing significance of earlier prophets (Zech. 1:4; 7:4–10; 9:1–8; 11:1–3; 14:1–4), the restoration of the land's fecundity (Zech. 8:12; 14:8), the renewal of the covenant (Zech. 8:8; 13:9), the ingathering of the exiles (Zech. 2:6; 8:7; 10:9–10), the outpouring of God's Spirit (Zech. 4:6; 12:10), and the central role of a coming messiah (Zech. 3:8; 6:12; 9:9–10).[15] Moreover, the unity is not just thematic but organic and progressive. The visions and oracles in Zechariah 1–8 paint a vivid picture of what God's intervention in the world will look like, while the oracles of Zechariah 9–14 set forth the role of a unique individual who would be at the center of this intervention. Thus the book develops along a theological trajectory that increasingly focuses on a particular messianic figure. Considering that Zechariah 9–14 is one of the most drawn upon sources of material for the gospel writers when narrating the passion of Jesus,[16] it shouldn't surprise us that the Gospels depict Christ as the one through whom God's intervention in the world comes. Revelation too makes ample use of the imagery and descriptions in the book of Zechariah when talking about God's final intervention at the end of the age. When read in conversation with the New Testament, Zechariah has much to offer the Christian reader.

READING ZECHARIAH IN A CONTEMPORARY CONTEXT

Reading Zechariah today can be a rich theological and devotional experience. Like the people whom Zechariah addressed, we too face discouragement. Though there are certainly some causes for hope and optimism, it is just as true that when we look around we also see social, political, and economic forces at work that sometimes lead us to despair. A few years ago, I visited a region in Wales that had formerly been one of the world's largest suppliers of coal. Now the industry has largely collapsed, leaving a wake of frustration, hopelessness, and discouragement behind. Unemployment is high, and for some, the horizons look bleak.

Other places in the world are even worse off. Poverty in parts of Asia, Africa, and South America make even the worst neighborhoods in the U.S. and Europe look appealing. Some feel they have no choice but to enter the drug trade, organized crime, or prostitution. Walking through the streets, seeing what some people have resorted to in order to survive is heartrending and overwhelming. One can see vividly how political, economic, and social structures have been hijacked by evil for destructive purposes that leave people living in the rubble. Looking around, the problems of evil, injustice, terrorism, and corruption are so large that it is hard even to know where to begin.

As we turn our attention to the church, we find more reasons for discouragement. Baldly put, if we are God's people then why are we such a mess? Dismissing such a question with the doctrine of indwelling sin doesn't adequately explain the lack of holiness in the church; it only sharpens the question. Didn't Christ come to save us from our sin? No one expects that Christians would be perfect; sin is an inescapable part of this life. But shouldn't we look a *little* more redeemed than we do?

Sadly, even the leaders of churches, seminaries, and para-church ministries do not inspire much more confidence. The number of Christian leaders who have fallen from grace is too long to list. Even outside the purview of the newspapers that report the "high-profile" cases, most people have seen Christian leaders use bullying, manipulation, control tactics, lying, and other ungodly methods for achieving their desired ends.

Perhaps the lack of holiness would be more understandable if there were a widespread zeal among Christians to look a bit more redeemed. But tragically there is an almost apathetic attitude among many in the church toward discipleship and spiritual growth. According to a recent survey, only eighteen percent of believers indicated that spiritual growth was the most serious commitment in their life. When the others were asked why they were not more passionate about discipleship, two-thirds said that they were just too busy, and one-quarter said that they just had a general lack of interest or motivation![17]

No wonder that many outside the church generally have a negative impression of Christians and the faith they claim to hold. As two researchers recently explained, "Christianity has an image problem. . . . Our research shows that many of those outside of Christianity, especially younger adults, have little trust in the Christian faith, and esteem for the lifestyle of Christ followers is quickly fading among outsiders. . . . The term 'hypocritical' has become fused to young people's experience with Christianity."[18]

But even personally, there are reasons for discouragement. Before we point our fingers too quickly at the church's specks, we all would do well to look at the lumberyards in our own eyes. When we do, it isn't pretty. Why haven't we seen more spiritual transformation in ourselves? Why haven't our own hearts shown more spiritual fruit? Why haven't our own lives demonstrated more spiritual growth? Why do we continue to run to our false idols, drink from broken cisterns, and chase after false loves? Why do we look around at the world, at the church, at our communities, and at our families and have so little belief about what God is capable of doing? Perhaps we need the book of Zechariah, with its encouraging visions and convicting oracles, as much as anyone. Perhaps in our discouragement we too need to encounter God's Word in the book of Zechariah.

FOR FURTHER REFLECTION

1. What trends in the church and/or the world do you find discouraging?
2. What has discouraged you in your own life?
3. How do you tend to react to your discouragement?
4. Which discouragements can you prayerfully lay before God as you begin reading the book of Zechariah?

CHAPTER TWO

THE CALL OF ZECHARIAH (1:1–6)

In the eighth month of the second year of Darius, the word of the Lord came to the prophet Zechariah, the son of Berechiah, the son of Iddo, saying, "The Lord was very angry with your fathers. Therefore, say to them, 'Thus says the Lord of hosts, "Return to me," declares the Lord of hosts, "and I will return to you," says the Lord of hosts. "Do not be like your fathers who did not listen or pay attention to me when the former prophets called out to them saying, 'Thus says the Lord of hosts, "Return to me from your evil ways and evil practices," declares the Lord.' Where are your fathers now? And the prophets, did they live forever? But did not my words and my statutes which I commanded my servants the prophets overtake your fathers?" Then they returned and said, "The Lord of hosts has dealt with us according to our ways and practices, just as He purposed to do." (Zechariah 1:1–6)

Even now the fire is burning, the heat of the word is on, the fierce glow of the Holy Spirit. . . . So for the time being treat the scripture of God as the face of God. Melt in front of it. Repent when you hear all this about your sins. And when you repent, when you torment yourself under the heat of the word, when the tears also begin to flow, don't you find yourself rather like wax beginning to drip and flow down as if in tears? (St. Augustine[1])

The book of Zechariah begins with the prophet's call, which is dated to the eighth month of the second year of Darius' reign (October or November 520 B.C.). In the first eight chapters of Zechariah, this is one of three dates given that situate each section historically within the five crucial years of temple reconstruction (520–515 B.C.).[2]

Section 1 (Zechariah 1:1–6)	"In the eighth month of the second year of the reign of Darius" (1:1)	= October / November 520 B.C.
Section 2 (Zechariah 1:7–6:15)	"On the twenty-fourth day of the eleventh month, which is the month of Shebat, in the second year of Darius." (1:7)	= February 15, 519 B.C.
Section 3 (Zechariah 7:1–8:23)	"In the fourth year of King Darius . . . on the fourth day of the ninth month, which is Chislev" (7:1)	= December 7, 518 B.C.

When the word of the Lord came to Zechariah in the fall of 520 B.C., discouragement would have been widespread in and around Jerusalem. First, the city walls lay in ruins. In the ancient Near East, walls were critical to a city because they protected the people from invasion. Thus, for a city's walls to be torn down was a great disgrace to the people who lived there (Neh. 2:17; Prov. 25:28). Second, at the center of Jerusalem was the conspicuous absence of the temple. Seventeen years earlier initial work had begun on the foundations, but that work had stalled and the aborted effort was no doubt an embarrassment to the people. Resumption of the work had begun again in September 520 B.C., but with only a few weeks of work completed, there was certainly no guarantee that this attempt wouldn't also fizzle out. Third, the leadership of the province was in a state of flux. Zerubbabel had been appointed as provincial governor only months before and there must have been questions about what his new leadership would bring. He seemed promising early on, but the people had had their hopes dashed before.

THE LORD CALLS ZECHARIAH (1:1–6)

Into this age of discouragement, the word of the Lord comes to Zechariah son of Berechiah, the son of Iddo.[3] Given the situation, we might expect the Lord to speak a word of great encouragement. We might anticipate something that would lift the spirits of the people. But instead the word that comes is an abrupt and pointed call to repent. Before any visions are given or promises proclaimed, the Lord calls Zechariah to preach a message of repentance to the people. The visions of hope will come, but not for another three to four months. Now is the time for the people to enter into a sustained period of reflection, repentance, and covenant recommitment.[4]

The call to repentance begins by drawing attention to a history of unfaithfulness, of which the current generation has been made heir. Previous generations had repeatedly provoked the Lord to anger (v. 2). The root of the Hebrew word for "anger" (*qtsf*) is used twice in verse 2, once in its verbal form and once in its noun form. Most English translations seek to communicate this "doubling" effect with the rendering "very angry." Years of idolatry, syncretism, hypocritical worship, moral failure, exploitation of the poor, unapproved alliances with other nations, and corrupt leadership had stretched the Lord's patience to its breaking point. Though notable exceptions existed, the nation had a long history of covenant breaking.

Zechariah calls those of his generation to do what their fathers had not done—repent. Verse 3 puts the matter plainly:

19

" 'Return to me,' declares the Lord of hosts, 'and I will return to you.' " Within the historical context it is clear that the double return is externally centered upon the temple. For the people, returning to the Lord in repentance would be demonstrated as they faithfully rebuilt the temple. For the Lord, returning would be marked by his dwelling with the people through his presence in the temple. From this verse, we might be tempted to conclude that God does not move toward us unless we first move toward him. But the text doesn't allow this and instead we are "challenged by the thrice repeated formula, 'thus says the Lord of hosts,' as though we never would have thought of [turning back to God in repentance], had the Lord not drummed the idea into us!"[5] The message of Zechariah 1:1–6 is that the Lord has taken the initiative to come to his people through the prophet Zechariah and call them back into a renewed relationship with him.

Notice that repentance is primarily a relational act. The Lord says to the people, "Return *to me*." It is not first and foremost about "fixing" deviant behaviors or conforming once again to prescribed ethical norms; it is about relationally reconnecting with the Lord. That is why the fathers are not only faulted for walking in evil ways and adopting evil practices but for not listening or paying attention to God (v. 4). For the postexilic community, repentance had to be more than simply rebuilding the temple. Their efforts at reconstruction had to be energized by a heartfelt return to the Lord that sought to live in covenant relationship with him.

Verses 4–6a issue a stern warning: if the people do not return, they will face the same fate as their fathers. Repeatedly, the Lord had sent prophets to former generations urging them to turn from their evil ways and return to him (v. 4). But they refused to listen and continued in their pattern of covenant disobedience. Eventually, after many generations, the warnings of judgment had caught up with the nation and judgment had overtaken them (vv. 5–6a): the northern kingdom was exiled by the Assyrians, and a little more than a hundred years later the southern kingdom was exiled by the Babylonians. The destroyed walls, the absent temple, and the ruined economy that Zechariah's generation inherited were memorials to the evil practices of their ancestors.

This theme of the anger of the Lord toward the fathers and the resulting admonition to return from evil is seen in other prophets as well. It is found especially in Jeremiah, which highlights not only the same concepts but also uses the same vocabulary.

> From the day that your fathers came out of the land of Egypt to this day, I have persistently sent all my servants the prophets to them, day after day. Yet they did not listen to me or incline their ear, but stiffened their neck. They did worse than their fathers.
>
> So you shall speak all these words to them, but they will not listen to you. You shall call to them, but they will not answer you. And you shall say to them, "This is the nation that did not obey the voice of the Lord their God, and did not accept discipline; truth has perished; it is cut off from their lips.
>
> "Cut off your hair and cast it away;
>   raise a lamentation on the bare heights,
> for the Lord has rejected and forsaken
>   the generation of his wrath." (Jer. 7:25–29 ESV;
>   see also Jer. 18:11; 23:22; 25:5; 35:15)

Thus, the opening call to repentance in Zechariah seems designed to build upon the prophecies of Jeremiah in order to teach the postexilic generation not to mimic the obstinacy of their fathers. Their fathers had ignored the warnings of Jeremiah (and others) and had suffered the disaster of the exile as a result.

Zechariah's exhortation to the postexilic community was not to follow in the footsteps of their ancestors, but instead to submit themselves to the Lord's words and statutes. Thus, verses 3–6a form a unified argument to urge the people to return to the Lord. *Return* is the key word of this opening passage, being used four times in only four verses. The Lord's faithfulness had not changed. His promises, though seemingly dormant, were not dead. Even though there were reasons for discouragement all around the people, there was a world of hope lying before them. And the doorway into that world was repentance.

But would they repent? Verse 6b indicates that they did, assuming that it refers to Zechariah's generation. This verse, however, is ambiguous and scholars have been split over whether it refers to the fathers in exile or the contemporaries of Zechariah. In the case of the former, the verse would indicate that when the exile came upon the people they eventually realized that the Lord's warnings were true and his judgment was justified. The latter would indicate that Zechariah's generation had heeded the call of verses 2–6a and had returned to the Lord with their hearts. Though it is impossible to be certain, it is more likely that it was Zechariah's generation who returned, and reflecting on their national history, confessed, "The Lord of hosts has dealt with us according to our ways and practices, just as He purposed to do." This most effectively guards the integrity of verses 4–6a, which seem to focus on the stubborn obstinacy and decidedly unrepentant hearts of previous generations.[6] Though problems that required rebuke remained (Zech. 5:1–11; 7:4–14), the people of Zechariah's generation did heed the call to return to the Lord, which prepared them to receive God's work among them as told in the remaining oracles of the book of Zechariah.

REPENTANCE IS FOUNDATIONAL

Zechariah's ministry among his generation begins with a call to repentance. Everything else that follows is built upon that foundation. This call to repent comes just weeks after the resumption of work on the temple. At this early stage, perhaps the people were tempted to exalt the building project over their love for God. Or perhaps they were tempted to the same fault the people were guilty of in Jeremiah 7—an overreliance on the temple as a talisman without an accompanying inner fidelity to the Lord.

Whatever the situation, Zechariah 1:1–6 drills down to the core need of the people. The fundamental need of the people was not a rebuilt temple; it was a renewed heart. "The temple is being restored, and that is splendid. . . . But, the work on the temple would become a monument to folly, unless it was accompanied by spiritual reconstruction."[7] In this regard, it is telling that the Lord declares to a people who have already returned to the land and who have begun rebuilding the temple (an action closely associated with the Lord's return to Zion) that they still need to return to him. In other words, it is not enough to make a geographical move and to throw up a sacred building; there must be an accompanying internal transformation of the heart. The true foundation of restoration is not the stones laid by Sheshbazzar or Zerubbabel. The true foundation of God's kingdom work is always repentant hearts. It always begins there.

Nowhere is that clearer than in the inauguration of the kingdom of God in the ministry of Christ. At the outset of his public ministry, Jesus tightly links together the advent of the kingdom with a sharp and pointed call for the people to repent:

> Now after John was arrested, Jesus came into Galilee, proclaiming the gospel of God, and saying, "The time is fulfilled, and the kingdom of God is at hand; repent and believe in the gospel." (Mark 1:14–15 ESV)

Sometimes Jesus' announcement is read as if it were narrowly referring to people forsaking their individual sins and deciding to follow Jesus instead. But this misses the fullness of what Jesus was saying; it was a corporate call as well as an individual one. Jesus was declaring that God was at last becoming King of the whole world and since that moment had arrived, those who would follow him (and thus Jesus) must be characterized by repentance.[8] They must corporately turn from their own agendas—whether personal, national, or political—and trust in Jesus and his way of doing things instead.

After some time of preparation, Jesus sends out the twelve disciples in pairs to continue the heralding of the kingdom. As they began their ministry, the heart of their message was also that the people should repent (Mark 6:7–13). And as those acting in the name of their master, their preaching like his was accompanied with signs that the kingdom had arrived, namely exorcisms and healings. After Jesus' resurrection, when it is time for them to spread the good news of the kingdom to the rest of the world, Jesus instructs them "that repentance and forgiveness of sins should be proclaimed in his name to all nations" (Luke 24:47 ESV).

Not surprisingly the church's early days under the apostles' leadership show the same foundational emphasis on repentance. In Jerusalem, Peter in his Pentecost sermon urged those gathered there to "repent and be baptized every one of you in the name of Jesus Christ for the forgiveness of your sins, and you will receive the gift of the Holy Spirit" (Acts 2:38 ESV). The "age of the Spirit" began with a call to repentance. In the following chapters in the book of Acts, the same emphasis is seen again and again in the preaching of Peter (Acts 3:19; 5:31; 8:22). In the second half of the book, as Paul spread the gospel during his missionary journeys, he too consistently led with a call to repentance, though now the corporate dimension of repentance has widened to include the mission to the Gentiles and not just to unrepentant Israel (Acts 13:24; 17:30; 20:21; 26:20)!

The same pattern has continued throughout the history of the church. God's great work always begins with people turning to him in repentance. One of the clearest examples is the birth of the Protestant Reformation, generally assigned to Luther's nailing his Ninety-five Theses on the door at Wittenberg. Luther had become concerned about the medieval practice of indulgences, prompting him to request a disputation. He followed the typical and orderly way of calling for such an academic discussion by posting the requested points of debate on the door of the church. The date was October 31, 1517.

As is well known, the first of those Ninety-five Theses struck at the heart of true spirituality, the continual call to repentance. Luther claimed, "Our Lord and Master when he says, 'Repent,' desires that the whole of life of believers should be a repentance." The second, third, and fourth theses make clear that Luther was attacking the "scholastic view of sacramental penitence, which emphasized isolated, outward acts; while Luther put the stress on the *inward* change which should extend *through life*. As long as there is sin, so long is there need of repentance."[9] Luther could hardly have foreseen the future consequences of such a seemingly innocuous act. However, the simple call to the church that she return to the biblical notion of repentance was to prove a historical shockwave within the Western church, with noticeable effects in both the Protestant and Roman Catholic churches.

The same principle applies to our lives as well. Like the community in Zechariah's day, we easily forget that the true foundation of God's great work is always repentant hearts. For them, the temptation would have been to throw themselves into temple building without the necessary heart-level repentance that should have motivated it. For us, the temptation is similar. When we involve ourselves in kingdom work, we so easily fall into a rhythm of do, do, do, that is detached from a heartfelt relationship with Christ based on repentance and faith. The church's programs and activities need to be kept running. Phone calls must be made. Meetings must be planned. Agendas must be hammered out. Strategies must be drawn up. Details must be handled. We forget that kingdom work is always faulty if it is built upon the wrong foundation. Though many of us know this at a theoretical level, more often than not when it comes to our practice, we attempt much of our kingdom building efforts upon the foundation of self-sufficient execution.

But, just as in Zechariah's day, Spirit-endowed kingdom work isn't rooted in the soil of self-sufficiency, but of repentance and faith. Individually, we must continually examine our words, thoughts, actions, and attitudes, asking the Lord to search the depths of who we are and reveal to us where we need to repent and exercise faith (Ps. 139:23–24). We must even be willing to go beyond identifying the sins that come easily to mind and open ourselves up to the searching and convicting work of the Holy Spirit. As we quiet ourselves in his presence, we find that he will open our eyes to all kinds of subtle sins in the way we think, in the motivations behind what we do and say, and in the roots of our attitudes. We may be rather surprised to find that we are convicted of matters ranging from "doctrinal apostasy, personal iniquity, and tolerating or abetting social injustice."[10]

In one sense, asking God to search us and convict us of our sin is (and should be) a horrifying experience. It is an exposure of who we really are. It is to come to a place where we can confess with St. Augustine, "You, Lord, . . . turned me back towards myself, taking me from behind my own back where I had put myself all the time that I preferred not to see myself. And You set me there before my own face that I might see how vile I was, how twisted and unclean and spotted and ulcerous. I saw myself and I was horrified; but there was no way to flee from myself."[11]

Yet, in another sense, repentance is also the gateway to joy. Like the surgeon's knife that causes pain and exposure in order to heal, repentance opens us up again to the fresh application of God's grace in Christ to our hearts (1 John 1:9). As painful as it is to lay our sins before God by confession and repentance, God uses it to draw our eyes back to our deep and abiding need for Jesus Christ. In addition to being spiritually cathartic, this reinforces the necessity of faith in Christ because only in him do we find forgiveness and true life. In that sense, repentance is not just important for kingdom work but is indispensably foundational.

Though repentance is usually thought to be something individuals do, there is also a sense in which the corporate church must be called back to repentance if it will be effective for the kingdom in this world. The Western church has suffered seemingly endless fragmentation, much of it due to uncharitable dealings and an all-around unwillingness to subordinate minor issues to Jesus' major concern for unity (John 17). Just in American Presbyterianism alone, a chart of the history of divisions and unifications looks like a plate of noodles.

Yet, perhaps even more tragic than the needless divisions themselves is our developed callousness to the situation. We have become so accustomed to living in a fragmented church that "the most manifest mark of the divided Church appears to be its own insensibility to the symptoms of its condition. . . . The Church has ceased to repent. Such is the constriction given birth by a division that ceases to offend."[12] Many churches and denominations seem more willing to quibble over relatively minor governmental issues, shades of doctrinal difference, or even cultural preferences than express the credibility of Jesus Christ through sacrificial unity (John 17:21–23). As a result, the church largely forfeits its ability to speak prophetically to a broken world and cripples its ability to be a signpost of the kingdom of God. Divisions before a watching world sap away the church's saltiness and snuff out its light (Matt. 5:13–16).

But Zechariah 1:1–6, along with the ministry of Jesus, the twelve disciples, Paul, and scores of Christians throughout church history, shows us that the only foundation suitable for Spirit-endowed kingdom work is repentant hearts, both individually and corporately. As we acknowledge our own sin for what it is—grievous and offensive to a holy God—and turn from it with godly contrition, we open ourselves up again to the renewing grace of God in Christ. We find afresh the joy of our salvation and experience God's Spirit upholding and sustaining us (Ps. 51:12). And we find our relationship deepening with the Lord who is always more eager to forgive than we are to confess. As John Chrysostom once preached, "You do not so much desire to be forgiven as he desires to forgive you your sins."[13]

Over time, as we practice heartfelt repentance and turning back to the Lord in faith, we find that we are being transformed from the inside out, being more and more conformed to the image of Christ (Rom. 8:29). St. Ambrose once recounted an episode of a young man who was returning home after an extended journey. During his time away, the man had been set free from his attachment to a prostitute. After he had returned home, he one day ran into the object of his former passion who stopped him and said, "Do you not know me, I am still myself?" "That may be," replied the man, "but I am not myself."[14] Such is the life built on repentance. Over time, the Lord transforms us such that we are no longer our former selves; the old passes, behold all things become new (2 Cor. 5:17). If only we would return to the Lord in repentance, imagine what he might do in our own lives, in our churches, and in the world.

FOR FURTHER REFLECTION

1. How have you seen repentance as something foundational to growth in your own spiritual life?
2. Are you accustomed to thinking of repentance as a habit? Is it something you practice daily?

3. In what areas of your life do you need to repent? Are there specific thoughts, words, actions, or attitudes that you need to turn from?
4. What are ways that your lack of repentance adversely affects the whole church?
5. Is your church a church of repentance? How do you know?

PART TWO

THE NIGHT VISIONS

CHAPTER THREE

LONGING FOR THE PEACE OF GOD: THE VISION OF THE HORSEMAN (1:7–17)

On the twenty-fourth day of the eleventh month, which is the month of Shebat, in the second year of Darius, the word of the Lord came to the prophet Zechariah, the son of Berechiah, son of Iddo: "I saw in the night, and behold, a man mounted upon a red horse. He was standing among the myrtle trees in a ravine. Behind him were red, sorrel, and white horses. Then I said, 'What are these, my lord?' The 'angel who was speaking with me' said, 'I will show you what these are.' Then the man who was standing between the myrtle trees answered and said, 'These are the ones the Lord has sent to roam the earth.' And they reported to the angel of the Lord who was standing between the myrtle trees, 'We have roamed the whole earth and behold all the earth is at peace.' The angel of the Lord answered and said, 'O Lord of hosts, how long will you show no compassion for Jerusalem and the cities of Judah, with which you have been indignant these seventy years?' And the Lord answered with kind and comforting words to the 'angel who was speaking with me.'

Then the 'angel who was speaking with me' said, 'Call out: thus says the Lord of hosts: "I am exceedingly jealous for Jerusalem and for Zion and I am exceedingly angry with the nations who feel secure; I was angry only a little, but they have carried the punishment too far." Therefore, thus says the Lord: "I will return to Jerusalem with tender mercies; my house will be built in it," declares the Lord of hosts. "And a measuring line will be stretched out over Jerusalem." Again, call out: thus says the Lord of hosts: "My cities will again overflow with prosperity; the Lord will again comfort Zion and will again choose Jerusalem."' "
(Zechariah 1:7–17)

When he that is over the Church cometh in, he straightway says, "Peace unto all"; when he preacheth, "Peace unto all"; when he blesseth, "Peace unto all"; when he biddeth to salute, "Peace unto all"; when the Sacrifice is finished, "Peace unto all": and again, in the middle, "Grace to you and peace." (St. John Chrysostom[1])

Zechariah 1:7 begins an extended section of visions commonly called the "night visions." The visions run from 1:7 until 6:8 (sometimes 6:9–15 is also included, but it is best to treat it as an oracular epilogue since 6:1–8 forms an inclusio with 1:7–17), with the first vision coming to Zechariah on the twenty-fourth day of the eleventh month in the second year of Darius, that is February 15, 519 B.C. It is unclear whether the visions were revealed over time with the first one coming on this particular night, or whether the visions came to Zechariah all at once throughout the night of February 15th. However, the lack of any other historical note in the succeeding visions probably suggests the latter.

It is also unclear why the visions come in the night as opposed to the day. Perhaps the detail is included as a literary device of scenic depiction—the night can often symbolize Israel's distress, while the dawn is an image of God's intervening deliverance (e.g., Pss. 30:5; 46:5).[2]

THE VISION OF THE HORSEMAN (1:7–13)

The first vision Zechariah saw would no doubt have resonated deeply with the postexilic community. Throughout their national history, Israel's experience was fraught with the experience of war and conflict. Geographically, Israel was positioned at the crossroads of the ancient Near East. Thus, as a nation, she was constantly getting mixed up in the ups and downs of international power struggles. She had witnessed the rise of Assyria, Babylon, and now Persia. The periodic rise and fall of nations had introduced an inherent instability to their national existence. Now, as a weak nation struggling to rebuild, feelings of anxiety would have been natural. What would future world events mean for them? How could they have assurance and confidence in the midst of a world full of conflict and when each war radically altered their future?

As the people struggle with feelings of anxiety and uncertainty, Zechariah sees a fantastic vision during the night that addresses these very concerns. The vision begins with a man mounted on a red horse (v. 8a), who later we find out is the angel of the Lord (v. 11). Behind him are red, sorrel, and white horses (v. 8b). Though some have tried to assign historical referents to the details of the vision (i.e., the red horse symbolizes X; the sorrel horse symbolizes Y; etc.), the text gives no indication that the vision is to function that way and interpretations of this sort inevitably give way to unfounded speculation. The sounder approach is to interpret the vision for its overall theological meaning.

Since the adjectives, red, sorrel, and white, are all given in the plural, the angel of the Lord on the red horse is followed by a *group* of red horses, a *group* of sorrel horses, and a *group* of white horses. In the ancient Near East, horses were almost always used for military purposes, which indicates this is a war scene. The cavalries represent domination in war (Zech. 10:3) and prestige (1 Kings 10:26) and will feature prominently in the second half of the book as thematic emblems of the Lord's worldwide dominion (Zech. 9:10; 10:3, 5; 12:4; 14:15, 20, 21).[3] Here they function in a supervisory role on behalf of the angel of the Lord on the red horse and thus flank him to the rear.

The groups of horses stand among the myrtle trees in a ravine, perhaps in the Kidron Valley just outside the city of Jerusalem. The scene is ominous: a military cavalry stationed down in a valley, shrouded in the darkness of tree shadows and night. Even in winter, the myrtle tree's thick foliage (the myrtle is an evergreen) would have provided plenty of cover.

At first, Zechariah does not understand what they represent and so the "angel who was speaking with me" steps in to explain the symbolism to the prophet. This angel is distinct from the angel of the Lord who is the protagonist of the vision.[4] As the vision's interpreter, the "angel who was speaking with me" declares that he will offer an explanation, though it is the angel inside the vision, the angel of the Lord, who explains that the horses had been sent out to patrol the earth (vv. 9–10). Zechariah's generation would certainly have heard here an allusion to the Persian administrative system in which delegates on horses were used to keep the king apprised of the affairs in the empire, especially of potential insurrections.[5] In the same way, and to a greater extent, the Lord's martial emissaries patrol the entire world, depicting his sovereign dominion over it.

While the text does not explicitly say that the red, sorrel, and white horses also had riders, it is probably implied in the report of verse 11. When the riders of the patrolling horses returned they reported that they found the whole world to be at peace (v. 11). At this point, several interlocking interpretive difficulties present themselves. First, is the peace the riders report describing the peace brought about by Darius' rule or the peace brought about by the Lord's eschatological rule? Second, is the peace viewed positively or negatively? Third, are the horses returning from war, declaring its resulting peace, or are the horses on a reconnaissance mission, making preparations to go to war?

In attempting to answer this triad of questions, we find that three main positions emerge. First, some hold that the peace being described is that of Darius' Persian Empire, viewed negatively. In this view, the vision portrays the frustration of the people at seeing a pagan empire come into unchallenged rule. It seems to offend the justice of God. Thus, the horses have been sent out to prepare for war against the peaceful pagan world since their self-satisfaction has angered the Lord (v. 15). When the horses have returned and reported the situation, the angel vents his frustration with the cry, "How long?" Then the Lord offers words of comfort and goes on to declare that he will go to war and crush the pagan nations, including the currently peace-establishing Persians.

The difficulty with this view is that the advent of the Persian Empire was largely seen as a favorable event. The Persians liberated Israel from her Babylonian captivity and allowed the people to return to the land and begin rebuilding. Isaiah 45 even portrays Cyrus as a kind of God-ordained "messianic" figure:

> Thus says the LORD to his anointed, to Cyrus,
>   whose right hand I have grasped,
> to subdue nations before him
>   and to loose the belts of kings,
> to open doors before him
>   that gates may not be closed:
> . . . .
> "For the sake of my servant Jacob,
>   and Israel my chosen,
> I call you by your name,
>   I name you, though you do not know me."
>   (Isa. 45:1, 4 ESV)

Second, some also hold that the peace being described is that of Darius' Persian Empire, but instead believe that it is being viewed positively. In this view, the vision portrays the Persian peace as something beneficial for the people of God. They have been permitted to return to their land, and now they can rebuild their city, temple, walls, and lives.

The chief difficulty with this view is that it has trouble making full sense of the Lord's three oracles that follow the vision, which suggest that despite the beneficial conditions of Darius' reign things have still not been set right as they should be. The Persian peace is at best an artificial peace. Better than either of the first two views is the third option, which best accounts for the cosmic scope of the horses' patrol (that of the entire world, not just a province or the empire).

In the third view, the peace being described is the peace of God brought about by his eschatological rule. In this case, Darius' now peaceful Persian Empire serves as the background to the vision, but the vision itself portrays the horses roaming the earth and returning after war to proclaim that God has indeed brought about worldwide peace. This view holds that the vision lifts the people's eyes above and beyond the pagan Persian Empire to see something even greater in the works. Darius had suppressed most of the revolts in his realm such that in Mesopotamia, the world was at peace. But the people are called to long for the coming day when the Lord, the true and great King, will bring about a much greater peace on earth through the subjugation of his enemies.

At this report, the angel of the Lord who is mounted on the red horse can hardly wait for it to become a reality and cries out, "O Lord of hosts, how long will you show no compassion for Jerusalem and the cities of Judah, with which you have been indignant these seventy years?" (v. 12). The seventy years should probably be taken as symbolic. Elsewhere in the Old Testament, seventy years is a designation for the typical lifetime of a human (cf. Ps. 90:10) and such a symbolic description of divine judgment as lasting seventy years was common in the ancient Near East.[6] Thus, it would have been a normal way of denoting the length of divine punishment.

As expressed by the angel's words, the people have grown weary and are ready for the Lord to intervene in the world scene. This first night vision stirs their hopes that such an intervention is not far off. And presumably indicating that he will act soon enough, the Lord reassuringly answers the "angel who was speaking with me" with kind and comforting words (v. 13).

THE LORD'S THREE RESPONSES (1:14–17)

After receiving the kind and comforting words from the Lord, the "angel who was speaking with me" mediates three short oracles (vv. 14–15; v. 16; v. 17; each marked out by the phrase "thus says the Lord [of hosts]") to the prophet and through the prophet to the people. These three oracles unpack the specific implications of the first night vision, and as we will see, the content of the Lord's kind and comforting words in verse 13.

In the first oracle, the Lord makes two declarations. First, he declares that he has an exceedingly great jealousy for Jerusalem and for Zion (v. 14). The text piles up descriptors, which includes a word play, to indicate the Lord's intense emotion on the matter. Literally, the text says that he is jealous (*qine'thi*) with a great jealousy (*qin'ah*). Contrary to what some may have thought, the Lord had not forgotten about Jerusalem or Zion. They were dear to his heart and he was zealously committed to them.

Second, just as the Lord burns with jealousy for Jerusalem and Zion, so he also burns with anger toward the nations (v. 15). As angry as the Lord has been with Israel (Zech. 1:2), he is now angry with the nations and

39

emphatically so. Here the text offers a similar kind of word play as in the first half of the oracle to emphasize the white-hot intensity of the Lord's anger—literally, "I am angry (*qotsef*) with a great anger (*qetsef*)." The reason is that the nations (paradigmatically Babylon and Assyria[7]) have overstepped their limits. God had used them as an instrument of judgment to chasten Israel, but they have taken it too far, being unnecessarily harsh. From the Lord's perspective, they have turned their divinely ordained role as disciplinarian into an opportunity for brutality. As a result, they have become arrogant, feeling smugly secure in themselves (cf. Isa. 47:5–15; Ezek. 25–32; Obad. 15–18; Hab. 1:5–11; 2:6–20).

The second oracle then assures the prophet (and the people) that the Lord will see to it that Jerusalem and Zion are restored (v. 16). Specifically, the Lord will return with tender mercies and the temple will be rebuilt. This is the expected response of the Lord given his promise in the previous passage. The Lord had promised that he would return to the people if they would return to him (Zech. 1:3), which they did (v. 6). Now the Lord announces his intention to fulfill what he promised and return to Jerusalem and Zion.

The city will be reconstructed as builders stretch out a measuring line across it. The imagery is significant. When the Babylonian army had destroyed the city and razed the temple, the people had mourned that God had afflicted his people for their sins. In describing the destruction that God had brought, the measuring line (*qav*) was an instrument of violence: "The Lord determined to lay in ruins the wall of the daughter of Zion; he stretched out the measuring line [*qav*]; he did not restrain his hand from destroying; he caused rampart and wall to lament; they languished together" (Lam. 2:8 ESV). But in Zechariah 1:16, the measuring line (*qav*) becomes an instrument of restoration.

The measuring line specifically refers to the initial step in reconstructing the walls by marking out the wall line with a string. Ezekiel had promised that this would be a sign of God's return to the temple (Ezek. 40:1–4). But the Lord reveals to Zechariah that it will indeed happen not only for the temple but for the mount (Zion) and the city (Jerusalem) as well (cf. Jer. 31:38–39).

The third oracle spells out the full and final result of the restoration. Though naturally some wondered whether the Lord had forgotten his people or had forever rejected them, the Lord reassures them that this is not so. He will renew the election of his holy city Jerusalem and will bring comfort to Zion. The blessing of the Lord will be so great that the cities of Judah (not just Jerusalem!) will once again overflow with prosperity (v. 17). In this one verse, the word *again* is used four times, highlighting how abundant the cities' return to prosperity will be as the proof of the enduring validity of the Lord's ancient promises to his people.

The three oracles are all an expression of the Lord's kind and comforting words in verse 13, structurally indicated by a word connection between verses 13 and 17. The Hebrew word translated "prosperity" here (*mitov*) is the same word in adjectival form used in verse 13 and translated "kind" (*tovim*). In other words, this picture of the cities' prosperity was probably the content of the Lord's kind and comforting words to the angel in verse 13.

Though anxiety, uncertainty, and fear were prevalent within the postexilic community, the vision of the horseman stirred up the people to long for the coming peace of God. The patrol of the horsemen showed them that the peace of the Persian Empire was merely artificial and that God was already preparing true eschatological peace for the world. Moreover, the three oracular responses have spelled out the specifics of what that coming eschatological peace will look like: the Lord's return to Jerusalem and Zion, the subjugation of the nations, and the renewal of the city, temple, and people with overflowing blessings.

THE HOPE OF GOD'S COMING PEACE

In Revelation, John describes the fulfillment of this promised eschatological peace. He vividly portrays a renewed Jerusalem, measured off with a golden measuring rod and aglow with the fullness of the glory of God (Rev. 21:11, 15). Within the city there will be no need for a temple because the Lord and the Lamb will fill it with their presence (Rev. 21:22). One day, this magnificent city will come down from heaven to earth; the old order of things will pass away, and peace will reign forever (Rev. 21:1-2, 10). Not only will there be no more strife in the new order, but it will be characterized by wholeness, harmony, prosperity, and safety.

In the meantime, God's people are often gripped by anxiety, uncertainty, and fear as they watch violent forces beyond their control turn the world on its head. Perhaps the disciples experienced these feelings most intensely in the wake of the crucifixion. At Calvary they witnessed the sword of the Roman Empire leveled against the anointed one. They watched as their Savior was thrown to the political wolves. They saw their Messiah cut down by the powers that be.

Now what would become of them? Jesus had told them that the world's hatred and persecution toward him would also be aimed at them (John 15:18-20). Worried that they would fall to the same fate after Jesus' execution, the disciples huddled together, gripped by anxiety and fear (John 20:19). Significantly, it is in such a setting that Jesus appeared to the disciples in order to commission them out into the world. His first words to them were "Peace be with you!"[8] As he showed them the wounds in his hands and side, the disciples were reassured and overjoyed. The resurrection had transformed the wounds of assault into emblems of God's coming peace. Then, after Jesus reiterated his greeting of peace, he continued with his commission: "As the Father has sent me, I am sending you" (John

20:20–21; cf. Luke 24:36 NIV). To empower them for their task, Jesus breathed upon them and said, "Receive the Holy Spirit" (John 20:22 NIV).

The peace that had been announced at Jesus' advent was not a hollow declaration. When John the Baptist's father ended his prophetic song with the climactic statement that Jesus would guide our feet into the path of peace (Luke 1:79), he was telling the truth. When Jesus was born and a great company of the heavenly host burst into song singing, "Glory to God in the highest, and on earth peace to men on whom his favor rests!" (Luke 2:14 NIV), they were right. And years later, when Jesus was entering into Jerusalem and the crowds spread their cloaks before him and cried out, "Blessed is the king who comes in the name of the Lord! Peace in heaven and glory in the highest!" (Luke 19:38 NIV), they were correctly summarizing his ministry.

As the Messiah, he fulfilled the expectation that peace would characterize God's eschatological intervention (Isa. 9:6–7; 11:6–9). When a sinful woman wet Jesus' feet with her tears, wiped them with her hair, and poured out upon them her alabaster jar of perfume, Jesus forgave her and sent her away with peace (Luke 7:36–50). When a woman who had been hemorrhaging for twelve years stealthily touched his cloak, he healed her and dismissed her in peace (Mark 5:25–34; Luke 8:43–48). And when he was preparing to go to the cross, he warned his disciples that following him would provoke the sword from the world (Matt. 10:32–36; Luke 12:49–53). But he also reassured them that he would leave his peace with them through the ministry of the Holy Spirit (John 14:25–27; 16:31–33), a promise he fulfilled when he appeared to them in that locked room (John 20:22).

Of course, the world has continued its propensity for war, violence, and conflict. Swords have been replaced with automatic weapons and atomic bombs. As history rolls on, nations continue to war against each other in a dizzying spiral of conflict that only allows brief reprieves. The popular historians Will and Ariel Durant calculated in 1968 that in the previous 3,421 years of recorded history only 268 had been free of war![9] One begins to wonder how it is that we have not destroyed ourselves by now. As the Hungarian Reformed theologian Béla Vassady once remarked, "It is indeed a miracle of a long-suffering God that this planet is still in one piece."[10]

In the face of such instability and conflict, it is easy to wonder if there is any sure hope. We too cry out, "How long, O Lord?" (Zech. 1:12; cf. Rev. 6:10). Yet, because Jesus is our peace (Eph. 2:14), we become peacemakers in a world of violence and war (Matt. 5:19). As his ambassadors, we become a community that lives out an alternative vision of humanity. Because we have peace with God through the shed blood of Christ (Rom. 5:1; Col. 1:20), and consequently peace with one another (Eph. 2:11–18), we strive to live out this same reconciling peace in our relationships with all people (Rom. 12:18; 14:19; Heb. 12:14). God establishes peace through the crushing of Satan under our feet (Rom. 16:20) as we obey him.

Just like the disciples who were commissioned to enter the world with God's peace, we too are called to bring an alien peace to a world of conflict and violence. And like Zechariah's generation, we do so in light of God's promised coming eternal peace, not through the various attempts at artificial peace (whether it be ancient Persian rule or modern Western democracy). As Augustine wrote, "the Heavenly City in her pilgrimage here on earth makes use of the earthly peace and defends and seeks the compromise between human wills in respect of the provisions relevant to the mortal nature of man, so far as may be permitted without detriment to true religion and piety. In fact, that City relates the earthly peace to the heavenly peace."[11] In other words, we are called to live with our eyes firmly fixed on the peace of the eternal city, the city of God which is the New

Jerusalem (Rev. 21), and then translate that peace into earthly peacemaking efforts.

David Augsburger describes how a group of women in southern California lived out this calling with courage and conviction.

In the early 1990s, gang violence erupted in Boyle Heights, a section of East Los Angeles. Eight gangs were in conflict in the parish around the Dolores Mission Catholic Church. Killings and injuries happened daily. A group of women who met for prayer read together [a story from the Gospels when one of the women sensed Jesus calling them to "enter the violence."]

That night, seventy women began a peregrinación, a procession from one barrio to another. They brought food, guitars, and love. As they ate chips and salsa and drank Cokes with gang members, they began to sing the old songs of Jalisco, Chiapas, and Michoacán. The gang members were disoriented, baffled; the war zones were silent.

Each night the mothers walked. By nonviolently intruding and intervening they "broke the rules of war." . . .

As the relationships between the women and the gang members grew, the kids told their stories. Anguish over the lack of jobs; anger at police brutality; rage over the hopelessness of poverty. Together they developed a tortilla factory, a bakery, a child-care center, a job-training program, a class on conflict-resolution techniques, a school for further learning, a neighborhood group to monitor and report police misbehavior, and more.[12]

The call is the same for us. As we move out into a tumultuous world as peacemakers gripped by the promise of God's coming peace, we find that our anxiety is replaced by assurance, our uncertainty by security, our fear by confidence, and our apprehension by hope. Like the postexilic community, we wait in eager anticipation to hear the horsemen gather under the myrtles and announce, "We have roamed the whole earth and behold all the earth is at peace. Glory to God in the highest!"

FOR FURTHER REFLECTION

1. What specific things in the world today give you a sense of anxiety, uncertainty, or fear?
2. How can the vision of God's coming peace ease your anxiety, uncertainty, and fear?
3. Where does conflict reign in your own life? In your relationships? In your community?
4. In what ways is God calling you to become a peacemaker?
5. How does God's peacemaking with you through Christ equip and empower you to be a peacemaker?

CHAPTER FOUR

LONGING FOR THE JUSTICE OF GOD: THE VISION OF THE HORNS AND THE BLACKSMITHS (1:18–21)

I lifted up my eyes and looked—and behold—four horns. So I said to the 'angel who was speaking with me,' "What are these?" And he said to me, "These are the horns that scattered Judah, Israel, and Jerusalem." Then the Lord showed me four blacksmiths. And I said, "What are these coming to do?" He said, "These are the horns that scattered Judah so that no man would lift up his head; but these have come to terrify them, to hew down the horns of the nations that lifted a horn against the land of Judah to scatter it. (Zechariah 1:18–21)

All innocence, all modesty, all freedom was in jeopardy under Nero's rule. . . . [Yet] no degree of cruelty can destroy the religion which is founded on the mystery of Christ's cross. (St. Leo the Great[1])

The vision of the horns and the blacksmiths is the shortest of Zechariah's night visions and is organically related to the first vision. The first vision concluded with three oracles promising a reversal of fortunes: Israel

47

would be blessed once again, while the nations would be judged for what they have done. The second aspect of this vision is now developed more fully in the vision of the horns and the blacksmiths. Although it may seem like a continuation of the first vision, it should be understood as a separate vision because it begins with "I lifted my eyes," a recurring marker of a new vision among the night visions (see also 2:1; 5:1; 6:1; cf. 5:5).

THE VISION OF THE HORNS AND THE BLACKSMITHS (1:18–21)

When Zechariah lifts his eyes, he is startled to see four horns (v. 18). Throughout the Old Testament, and within the cultural world of the ancient Near East, horns symbolize the source of strength and power, especially royal power. The symbol comes from the horns of animals, which was the source of their strength. The imagery was applied in royal contexts through the ceremony of anointing a new king by pouring oil from a horn on to the head (cf. 1 Sam. 16:1, 13; 1 Kings 1:39). For instance, after Hannah has been granted a son, Samuel, who would become the "king-maker," she offers a poetically rich prayer that begins and ends with the symbolism of a horn.

Then Hannah prayed and said:

"My heart rejoices in the LORD;
   in the LORD my horn is lifted high.
My mouth boasts over my enemies,
   for I delight in your deliverance.
. . . .
   "those who oppose the LORD will be shattered.
He will thunder against them from heaven;
   the LORD will judge the ends of the earth.

"He will give strength to his king
and exalt the horn of his anointed."
(1 Sam. 2:1, 10 NIV; cf. Ps. 89)

Likewise, when one's horn is cast down, it is a sign of
defeat and disgrace, as when the Lord declares,

I say to the boastful, "Do not boast,"
and to the wicked, "Do not lift up your horn;
do not lift up your horn on high,
or speak with haughty neck."
. . . .
All the horns of the wicked I will cut off,
but the horns of the righteous shall be lifted up.
(Ps. 75:4–5, 10 ESV; see also Jer. 48:21–25)

The image of four horns is an image of royal or national
strength and is the central feature of the vision. In only four
verses, the Hebrew word for "horn(s)" (*qrn*) is used five
times, which clearly focuses the revelation on the strength
of the nations and how they have used their power.

As in the first vision, Zechariah needs help understanding the symbolism of what he is seeing (v. 19a).
Once again, the "angel who was speaking with me" interprets the meaning for him. He identifies the four horns
as the nations that scattered Judah, Israel, and Jerusalem
(v. 19b). Historically, Assyria scattered the northern tribes
("Israel") into exile in 722/721 B.C., after a three year
siege of Samaria (2 Kings 17:1–6). A little over a century
later, the southern tribes ("Judah") fell to Babylon in 605
B.C., with Jerusalem and the temple being destroyed in
587/586 B.C. (2 Kings 24–25).

Other smaller nations were guilty of violence as well.
Edom gloated over the defeat of Judah and even captured
fleeing Judeans during the conquest and turned them back
over to Babylonian officers. After many of the people were
exiled, some Edomites moved into newly vacated Judean

towns, looting the wealth and celebrating until they were drunk (Obad. 1:10–16). Other parts of the land were lost to the expanding Phoenicians and Philistines (Obad. 1:19; Ezek. 26:2) as well as to Ammonites (Jer. 49:1). Sometimes the four horns in Zechariah are assigned to specific nations by correlating them with the four parts of the statue in Daniel 2, the four beasts in Daniel 7, or the horns of Daniel 8, which portray the aggression of the nations. But this is ill advised because Daniel refers to events that will happen several hundred years after Zechariah, whereas this vision is clearly referring to contemporary events.

The use of horns is simply drawing on a well-known motif for aggressive nations. The significance of the horns lies in there being four of them, not in identifying each horn with a particular empire. Just as the four chariots in Zechariah 6 are connected to the four winds of heaven, thereby symbolizing the scope of the whole world, so something similarly comprehensive is likely in view here (Jer. 49:36; Ezek. 37:9). The four horns probably "signify the totality of the hostile nations of the world."[2]

The Lord then shows him four blacksmiths who will oppose the four horns (v. 20). Since horns representing nations were sometimes made of iron (as in Micah 4:13), perhaps blacksmiths were chosen for their ability to cut iron.[3] Or, perhaps the image is chosen because of their skill to fashion weapons of war for use against the nations (1 Sam. 13:19). Whatever the reason, to correctly interpret the passage we must recognize that these are *common* craftsmen. The term is used elsewhere in the Old Testament for jewelry engravers (Ex. 28:11), artisans for the temple furnishings (Ex. 35:35), metalworkers (Deut. 27:15), carpenters (2 Kings 12:11), and stonemasons (2 Sam. 5:11). In other words, they are not from the politically elite, the militarily powerful, or the educationally advantaged. They are not of the upper crust of society; they are patently ordinary figures. By the look of them, there is not much they can do to these powerful horns.

The blacksmith's humble aspect prompts Zechariah to ask what exactly they have come to do (v. 21a). The angel explains that they have come because the horns have scattered Judah such that the people hang their heads in shame and disgrace. The blacksmiths' coming terrifies the horns because their time is now up (v. 21b). What the blacksmiths do to them rings out with both actual and poetic justice. When the nations lifted (*hanos'im*) their horn against the land of Judah, the result was that no man in Judah could lift (*nasa'*) his head because of the dishonor. But now, just as the nations once lifted up their horn, so reciprocally the blacksmiths will hew them down. As a result, the people will once again be able to lift up their heads, following the lead of the prophet who has already lifted (*wa'esa'*) his eyes to see a vision of this coming justice (v. 18). It enhances the poetic and fitting qualities of this passage to realize that all these forms of the word *lift* carry the same meaning in the original language, even though the form is different—lifting, and being unable to lift, heads, eyes, and horns is something of a theme throughout this section.

Some have argued that the blacksmiths can be historically identified as Persia since Cyrus was responsible for conquering Babylon.[4] But even though Persia did produce a largely beneficial environment for the people of Judah, they too could be hostile. Others have suggested that the blacksmiths were the skilled workers who were rebuilding the temple.[5] While that is certainly possible, a better judgment is that "[The blacksmiths] are divine agents carrying out God's will. They can represent, in the past, Babylon or Persia, which each brought to an end an ancient imperial power. And they also can represent an unspecified future divine action against a world power."[6] That is precisely the point to catch. The important thing is not to restrict the identity of the blacksmiths to a particular empire or guild, but to appreciate their function. They are used by God to bring an end to the injustice so evident in the world and commonly seen in various world powers throughout history.

It might have been striking to Zechariah's generation that this promise came without conditions attached. Throughout Israel's history prophets mediated promises to the people, but they were regularly qualified with conditions that they must meet. But in this night vision the promise of God's coming justice is unconditional; it is sure to come in due time.[7] When this will take place is not revealed. What the prophet and his generation need to know is not *when* it will happen, but *that* it will happen. The vision serves to bolster their confidence in God and his commitment to justice despite the oppression and injustice they are experiencing.

Zechariah sees blacksmiths ready to break the horns of the nations responsible for scattering Judah. This vision depicts the justice of God coming to bear on his enemies and his people in a surprising manner. God's justice comes into the world through unassuming, humble blacksmiths. As counterintuitive as it may seem, this is precisely how God topples the horns of injustice.

SEEKING JUSTICE

To varying degrees we have all experienced the frustration and outrage of injustice. Who has not felt the irritation of even relatively trivial acts of unfairness? For instance, who has not sneered at the driver who zooms past everyone else caught in traffic by driving on the shoulder? Some, however, know the more damaging kinds of injustice: losing one's job to someone with clearly inferior qualifications due to nepotism or politicking; watching an obviously guilty defendant acquitted over a minor technicality; seeing an abusive spouse take everything in a divorce settlement; being victimized by social structures set up to allow the rich and powerful to accumulate more and more wealth and power at the expense of the poor and helpless; or facing discrimination because of one's race, gender, or age.

Many of God's people have tragically lost everything, even their lives, to perpetrators of injustice. In just the twentieth century, more Christians have been put to death for no other reason than their faith than in the previous nineteen centuries combined. In 1996 alone, the toll of worldwide martyrs exceeded 100,000.[8] Who will call the oppressors to account? Why do they seem to get away with it? When will the victims be vindicated? How will things be set right again? In the face of such questions, Zechariah 1:18–21 offers hope, encouragement, and perspective as it looks forward to the day when God will intervene and establish justice. God promises to hew down the horns of injustice through his appointed but humble blacksmiths.

The good news is that in Jesus of Nazareth that day has dawned. Through his humble and unassuming servant, God intervenes in an unjust world. Early on in Jesus' ministry, he walked into a synagogue in Nazareth, picked up the scroll of Isaiah and read, "The Spirit of the Lord is upon me, because he has anointed me to proclaim good news to the poor. He has sent me to proclaim liberty to the captives and recovering of sight to the blind, to set at liberty those who are oppressed, to proclaim the year of the Lord's favor" (Luke 4:18–19 ESV; quoting Isa. 61:1–2a). He then rolled up the scroll, handed it back to the attendant, sat down and said, "Today this Scripture is fulfilled in your hearing" Luke 4:21 ESV). In other words, Jesus proclaimed from the outset of his ministry that he had come to overturn injustice.

With this as a ministry theme, Jesus surprised many when he did not establish justice through brute force. "He did not repeat the story of which history has so many illustrations, the story of the victim of oppression who, in the name of justice, dethrones the oppressor and takes his seat on the same throne with the same instruments of oppression."[9] Instead, he brought justice through gentleness and sacrifice. As his work continued, this remained central. Matthew, like Luke, also quotes from Isaiah in describing Jesus' ministry along these lines.

Behold, my servant whom I have chosen,
    my beloved with whom my soul is well pleased.
I will put my Spirit upon him,
    and he will proclaim justice to the Gentiles.
He will not quarrel or cry aloud,
    nor will anyone hear his voice in the streets;
a bruised reed he will not break,
    and a smoldering wick he will not quench,
until he brings justice to victory;
    and in his name the Gentiles will hope.
                (Matt. 12:18–21 ESV; quoting Isa. 42:1–4)

His gentleness and sacrifice for the sake of justice came to its climax at the end of his life when he was personally crushed under the full weight of the world's injustice on Calvary. Though entirely without guilt or fault, he was convicted and crucified. The bringer of justice was victimized by the greatest injustice the world has ever seen. But the injustice of the cross was vindicated by the resurrection, which paradoxically transformed this very act of paramount injustice into an irruption of God's justice into history!

It was a grand announcement that the time was up for the perpetrators of injustice. It declared that their days were numbered and that one day, on the last day, all things really will be set right and justice will prevail. The perpetrators of injustice will face the judgment and justice of the unjustly crucified King of kings and Lord of lords; the systems of injustice will forever be dismantled and replaced with the righteous rule of the Lion of Judah (Acts 17:31; Rev. 19:11).

According to the New Testament, our response to this should be decidedly Christlike. We often fall into the trap of seeking justice by taking our turn on the throne of oppression. We resort to manipulation, power plays, and heavy handed leveraging in order to accomplish what we want. We soothe our consciences with reassurances that the ends justify the means. But Zechariah's vision shows that God works out his justice in our world through unassuming blacksmiths. As God's great blacksmith, Jesus has shown in his ministry, death, and resurrection that God topples injustice through gentleness and sacrifice. To us such a notion seems counterintuitive, but then again, the gospel always is.

In the image of Christ, we too are called to pursue justice in nonviolent ways, characterized by gentleness and a willingness to sacrifice. As we prayerfully engage our world, we should work against injustice in whatever ways God gives us. Today, we are his blacksmiths in the world and we join with Christ in the horn-toppling works of establishing justice wherever and however we can. We work whatever anvils God puts before us, ultimately seeking reconciliation in the name of Christ. A recent and powerful example is the life and ministry of John Perkins.[10] As a black man growing up in Mississippi, he experienced much racism and injustice. On February 7, 1970, he and several others were almost beaten to death by a group of policemen who had ambushed them. Incredibly, Perkins recalls, "It was as I was being beaten that I heard and accepted God's call to a ministry of reconciliation between blacks and whites."[11] Since then he has been a driving force in working to topple the horns of racial and economic injustice.

In particular, he encourages Christians to adopt a three-fold strategy. First, he challenges Christians to relocate where they live so that they can be in touch with and minister to those who are victims of injustice. Knowing that God himself took on human flesh to come and redeem our broken world, Christians ought to be pouring into areas with crime and poverty, seeking to be God's blacksmiths for justice where it is most needed. Second, he encourages Christians to be God's ambassadors for reconciliation, seeking out opportunities to love those who are different than we are. Third, he encourages Christians to pursue avenues of redistribution, making the allocation of wealth, goods, and power more equitable. Specifically, he suggests simplifying our families' economic lifestyles and our churches' economic lifestyles as well as focusing on community development through education, leadership development, vocational training, and business development.[12]

All of us have been placed strategically by God in certain geographical areas, socioeconomic environs, and occupational spheres of influence. The question is, how can we go about working on the anvils God has put before us, hammering out incremental changes right where we are? What are the humble and unassuming ways that we can work for justice in the places we live our lives? What horns of injustice are we in a God-ordained position to attack? And perhaps even more challenging, what radical changes in our lives might God be calling us to embrace in order to be the blacksmiths he has called us to be?

As we work whatever anvils God has given us, we must also remember that ultimate justice will always lie in God's hand. Working for justice in our societies, our cities, and our neighborhoods can often be a frustrating and tiresome task. Moreover, some injustices seem unable to be righted, at least in this life. But Paul makes clear that we need not despair because we can trust patiently in the sovereign justice of God to settle all accounts in his timing. "Beloved, never avenge yourselves, but leave it to the wrath of God, for it is written, 'Vengeance is mine, I will repay,' says the Lord." (Rom. 12:19 ESV)

Helmut Thielicke, the great German theologian and preacher, learned afresh this perspective during a formative conversation with a former New Testament professor.

> During the Second World War, shortly before I was banned from travelling and speaking in public, I saw [my former professor] Schniewind again in Halle—it must have been 1941—and spent a day at his house. This meeting gave me great support in the difficult years that lay ahead.

Literally the whole day consisted of people arriving to report some terrible event to him. Former students brought news from the front of fellow students who had been killed in action. Clergy wives reported that their husbands had been arrested or that a pastor had been transferred to the "suicide squad" of a punishment battalion or had been given a particularly rough time by the Gestapo. And so it continued the whole day long. On hearing the report of a particularly brutal case, Schniewind uttered with great emphasis a sentence that reminded me of the New Testament concept of "Exousia" (power): "The Lord will scatter them in a single moment."

I have never forgotten this prophetic moment. In those days just about everything Hitler did seemed to meet with success. We felt that the noose around our neck was slowly being pulled tighter and tighter. There was no end in sight. And then in such circumstances to hear this statement on the fall of titans! From then on I was able to follow the story of Hitler's terror with the calm certainty that his tyranny would one day come to an end.[13]

Both the pursuit of justice and patient trust in God are necessary. As God's blacksmiths in the world today, we are to work the anvils God has given us but always within the context of a larger trust in the God who will hew down the horns of injustice in his own time and in his own ways.

FOR FURTHER REFLECTION

1. What specific injustices have you experienced? How did you react?
2. In our world today, which wrongs that need righting arouse the most passion within you?

3. What are some avenues where you can address those wrongs and seek justice?
4. What are the humble and unassuming ways that you can work for justice in whatever trade God has given you to do?
5. In what relationships have you experienced personal injustice? How have you tended to react in your emotions, thoughts, words, and behaviors?
6. How might you react in a way that expresses the truth(s) of Zechariah 1:18–21 seen in light of the New Testament?

CHAPTER FIVE

LONGING FOR THE PRESENCE OF GOD: THE VISION OF THE MAN WITH A MEASURING LINE (2:1–13)

I lifted up my eyes and looked—and behold—a man with a measuring line in his hand. So I asked, "Where are you going?" And he said to me, "To measure Jerusalem, to see how wide and how long it should be." Then, behold, the "angel who was speaking with me" was going out and another angel was going out to meet him. And he said, "Run and tell this to the man: 'Jerusalem will be like a city without walls because of a multitude of people and cattle in it. And I will be,' declares the Lord, 'an encircling wall of fire and I will be the glory inside it.'"

"Hey! Hey! Flee from the land of the north," declares the Lord, "though I have scattered you like the four winds of heaven," declares the Lord. "Hey! You who are dwelling with the daughter of Babylon: escape to Zion!" For thus says the Lord of hosts: "After glory [he] sent me, with regard to the nations which plundered you: he who touches you touches the apple of my eye for behold, I am raising my hand against them and they will be the spoil of those they have enslaved. Then you

59

will know that the Lord of hosts has sent me. Cheer
and rejoice, O daughter of Zion, for behold I am coming
and I will dwell among you," declares the Lord. In that
day many nations will join themselves to the Lord—
"They will be my people and I will settle among you."
Then you will know that the Lord of hosts has sent me
to you. And the Lord will inherit Judah as his portion
in the holy land and will again choose Jerusalem. Be
silent, all flesh, before the Lord! For he has roused from
his holy dwelling. (Zechariah 2:1–13)

The One Only-begotten God, ineffably born of God,
entered the Virgin's womb and grew and took the
frame of poor humanity. . . . He by Whom man was
made had nothing to gain by becoming Man; it was our
gain that God was incarnate and dwelt among us, making all flesh His home by taking upon Him the flesh of
One. We were raised because He was lowered; shame
to Him was glory to us. He, being God, made flesh His
residence, and we in return are lifted anew from the
flesh to God. (St. Hilary of Poitiers[1])

The scars of abandonment were still visible, the wounds
still fresh. Many of Zechariah's contemporaries were old
enough to remember the exile firsthand. For all that the
exile represented for the people of God, nothing was more
traumatic than the sense that God had possibly abandoned
them. The sense is captured with intensity in the book of
Lamentations. The writer laments that the Lord seems to
have afflicted, rejected, and even disowned his people (Lam.
1:5, 15; 2:7; 5:20; cf. Isa. 54:7). Likewise, the Lord himself
declared through Jeremiah, "I have forsaken my house; I
have abandoned my heritage; I have given the beloved of
my soul into the hands of her enemies" (Jer. 12:7 ESV; see
also Jer. 7:29). It would only be natural for the people to
wonder whether God would remain aloof or whether he
would reestablish his presence among them now that the
exile was over. Would he once again dwell in Jerusalem?

If they did rebuild the temple, would he return? And if he did, what might they expect from his renewed presence among them?

The third night vision, designed to answer these questions, follows naturally from the first two. The first night vision concluded with three oracles from the Lord, in which the Lord declared that he would do two things. First, he would bring judgment upon the nations, and second, he would restore Jerusalem and the other cities of Judah (Zech. 1:14–17). The second night vision (1:18–21) then developed the first theme, that of God's anger and assured judgment upon the nations. Now, the third night vision (2:1–13) picks up and develops the second theme in the oracles, that the Lord will return to Jerusalem with tender mercies, choosing her again and stretching out a measuring line over the city.[2] The vision of the man with a measuring line in his hand falls into two parts. The first part is the vision proper (2:1–5); the second part is an oracle (2:6–13).

A POPULATED AND PROTECTED CITY (2:1–5)

The vision proper begins like the second night vision with Zechariah lifting up his eyes, looking out, and seeing something. This time it is a man with a measuring line in his hand (v. 1). The measuring line is usually associated with building a structure, such as the new temple (Ezek. 40:3), the new city walls (Ezra 3:7), the new city (Jer. 31:38–39), or even the foundation of the earth (Job 38:5). Beginning a vision with this image would naturally arouse expectations of reconstruction, especially for a city still lacking walls and with only the early stages of temple construction finished. But the man with the measuring line receives some surprising instructions.

Apparently the man is already on the move because Zechariah asks him, "Where are you going?" He replies,

"To measure Jerusalem, to see how wide and how long it should be" (v. 2). The sense of his statement is ambiguous. The man could either be saying that he intends to see how wide and long the city already is or how wide and long it ought to be. The Hebrew lacks the verb and the translator must make a decision on which to supply. The question is whether the man is measuring a Jerusalem that is already rebuilt or whether he is making measurements in preparation for the rebuilding. Given the future sense of verses 4–5, as well as the fact that measuring lines are used in the initial construction phases, it is probably better to understand the man as measuring what the dimensions of the future Jerusalem should (or will) be.

As in the previous two visions, the 'angel who was speaking with me' appears. He goes out and encounters a second angel and says, "Run and tell this to the man: 'Jerusalem will be like a city without walls because of a multitude of people and cattle in it' " (v. 4).[3] The first angel seems excited and urgent since his command begins with consecutive imperatives (literally, "Run! Tell!").[4] He wants the man holding the measuring line to abort his preconstruction surveying for the rebuilding of the walls since Jerusalem is to be a city without walls.

Rather surprisingly, the angel seems excited about the prospect of a Jerusalem without walls. Normally this would be a city's disgrace, but in this vision it is the source of glory because of its overflowing numbers of people and cattle. Part and parcel with such a scenario is that the city would be considerably prosperous. Common to the restoration picture that the prophets painted was an eschatological Jerusalem bursting at the seams from the number of people (and animals) streaming back from exile.

> Surely your waste and your desolate places
>   and your devastated land—
> surely now you will be too narrow for your
>   inhabitants

and those who swallowed you up will be
    far away.
The children of your bereavement
  will yet say in your ears:
"The place is too narrow for me;
  make room for me to dwell in."
      (Isa. 49:19–20 ESV)

Thus says the Lord GOD: On the day that I cleanse
you from all your iniquities, I will cause the cities to be inhabited, and the waste places shall be
rebuilt. . . . Thus says the Lord GOD: This also I
will let the house of Israel ask me to do for them:
to increase their people like a flock. Like the flock
for sacrifices, like the flock at Jerusalem during her
appointed feasts, so shall the waste cities be filled
with flocks of people. Then they will know that I am
the LORD. (Ezek. 36:33, 37–38 ESV)

The vision, then, has taken something normally dishon-
orable and transformed it into something wonderful and
full of hope.

It might be asked how this vision fits with the Lord's
oracle in 1:16 in which he declares that a measuring line
would be stretched out over Jerusalem. Why would he now
stop the man with the measuring line who only seems to
be following through on the previously given oracle? Barry
Webb explains that

[the revelation of verses 3–4 is given to] enable [the
man] to understand the will of God more fully. God
is more committed to the protection and future prosperity of Jerusalem than he himself can ever be. But
(and here is the point) that security and prosperity
will not be achieved by man-made walls, or indeed
by any human activity at all, but by the promised
presence of God. . . . In other words, now is not the

time to be rebuilding the walls. The priority at present is to rebuild the temple (as the following visions will confirm), and God himself will defend the city while that work goes ahead.[5]

The Lord declares that he will be an encircling wall of fire for Jerusalem as well as the glory inside it (v. 5). The image is probably an allusion to the royal Persian city, Pasargadae, which was built by Cyrus and was later the site of his tomb. Instead of walls, the city was outfitted with fire altars inside and outside it, symbolizing the presence of the god Ahura Mazda.[6] The image is adopted and transformed to speak of a day when Jerusalem would not need walls for protection because the Lord would be there with his presence. Inside Jerusalem, his presence will fill the city with glory. The Lord's glory had withdrawn from Jerusalem on the eve of its destruction (Ezek. 10:18–19; 11:22–24). But, Ezekiel had promised that when God began restoring the nation, his glory would return (Ezek. 43:4; 44:4). Now, after years of waiting, the Lord is returning to Jerusalem and will once again fill it with glory. It will once again become a place of surpassing sanctity and honor.

With this new understanding, two reasons for the absence of walls emerge. First, walls are counterproductive because of the swelling of the population. When the Lord repopulates Jerusalem with his people and their livestock during the postexilic period, they will overflow the boundaries of the city. Second, walls are unnecessary because of the Lord's presence. When the Lord is among his people, they cease to be vulnerable; he is their safety and protection.

A MAGNETIC CITY (2:6–13)

As in the vision proper, the presence of the Lord is the energizing element of the oracle section. The oracle breaks down into a command given to the Jews who have not returned from exile, but are still living in Babylon (vv. 6–10), and a promise of the Lord's intentions for the nations (vv. 11–13). Both sections base the commands and promises on the presence of the Lord (vv. 10, 11). The speaker switches from the angel to Zechariah. The prophet begins by trying to grab the attention of those who are still living in exile ("Hey! Hey!"). Through Zechariah, the Lord declares that even though he has scattered them into exile like the four winds of heaven, they should leave Babylon ("the land of the north;" cf. Jer. 6:22; 10:22; 31:8) and return to Zion (vv. 6–7).

The reason for this command is that the Lord is turning the tables on the Babylonians (vv. 8–9).[7] In treating Judah harshly, they have acted violently toward the Lord himself (they have poked him in the most sensitive part of the eye). Though they were once powerful, exiling many people as spoil and plundering their lands, now the Lord has brought about events such that their land has been plundered, and their people are becoming the spoil (that is, of the Persians). Because of the Lord's retribution, they have gone from the top of the ladder to the bottom. In contrast to the securely protected Jerusalem, Babylon had become vulnerable to disaster. So, compelled by the glory of the Lord, Zechariah is sent to declare that there is no reason for Jews to continue staying in a land whose national "stock" is plummeting.

Back in Jerusalem, there is to be great rejoicing because the Lord is coming soon to dwell again in Jerusalem (v. 10). The longing of God's people should always be to dwell in the presence of the Lord (cf. Ps. 84). Naturally, his presence among his people prompts cheerful shouting, joyous singing, and jubilant celebration (cf. Isa. 12:6; Zeph. 3:14–17; Zech. 9:9). But the oracle produces great surprise with the Lord's plan for the nations.

In the first two night visions, the Lord's attitude toward the nations was singular. He was angry with them and promised coming judgment for their oppression, cruelty, and arrogance. Yet, here, a new aspect is introduced. In the coming eschatological day ("in that day" is the typical prophetic formula for the eschatological day of the Lord), many nations will join themselves to the Lord, such that the Lord will call them "my people" (v. 11). For the Lord to call the nations "my people" involves bringing them into a covenant relationship with him, just as he would do with Israel in the promised new covenant (Jer. 31:33; 32:37–38). Likewise, the nations will stream into Jerusalem, as the Jews had done when returning from Babylon, and they too will know the Lord (as in Pss. 22:27–28; 67:1–7).

Implied is that they will forsake their own gods and ways and give exclusive covenant loyalty to the Lord, adopting his ways. For instance, a similar passage in Isaiah, which also addresses the postexilic situation, declares,

> And the foreigners who join themselves to the LORD,
>   to minister to him, to love the name of the LORD,
>   and to be his servants,
> everyone who keeps the Sabbath and does not
>   profane it,
>   and holds fast my covenant—
> these I will bring to my holy mountain,
>   and make them joyful in my house of prayer;
> their burnt offerings and their sacrifices
>   will be accepted on my altar;
> for my house shall be called a house of prayer
>   for all peoples. (Isa. 56:6–7 ESV)

Such is the magnetic effect of the Lord's presence in Jerusalem on the rest of the world.

Lest anyone think this is too lofty an idea, since Jerusalem was in such a humble place at the time of the oracle, the Lord offers the reassurance that he will indeed inherit Judah as his portion and will again choose Jerusalem (v. 12). Therefore, all flesh should be silent before the Lord who is rousing from his holy dwelling (v. 13; cf. Hab. 2:20;

Zeph. 1:7). The only proper response to the advent of God's powerful presence is reverent awe.

GOD'S TRANSFORMING PRESENCE

The vision of the man with the measuring line is saturated with reassurances that God would once again be present among his people. Three times the Lord promises that he will come and dwell in their midst (vv. 5, 10, 11). For the postexilic community, his promise to dwell among them meant that he would change the people from forsaken and abandoned to welcomed and empowered. He would change the city from pitiable to glorious. He would change the community from vulnerable to protected. He would change the nation's barrenness to prosperity. He would change Judah from irrelevant to significant. In other words, God had declared that he would change the world by *entering* the world.

This promise was kept in the incarnation of his Son. In Jesus Christ, God truly came to be present among his people. Thus, upon Mary's conception from the Holy Spirit, the angel of the Lord announced that the Messiah's name would be Immanuel—which means "God with us." (Matt. 1:23). In him, God's glory entered into our world (John 1:14; 2 Cor. 4:6; cf. Zech. 2:5). And even when a jealous King Herod unleashed his assaults on the male children of Bethlehem, baby Jesus, God-incarnate, could not be touched. The presence of God among his people could not be thwarted. Like the Jerusalem of Zechariah's vision, Jesus was the embodiment of God's glorious presence, and though a picture of vulnerability, he was nevertheless unassailable. That is, he was unassailable until the proper time.

In the person of Jesus, God took to himself human flesh that he might walk among us, live beside us, and suffer with us and for us. When the time was right, Jesus dropped his defenses and allowed the assaults to come.

He had said that he was the true temple, the true dwelling place of God on earth (John 2:19–22). He had declared that the physical temple had become corrupt and the city had become a center of apostasy (Mark 13:1–37).[8] He backed up these claims with dramatic action, driving out the money changers and turning over tables (Matt. 21:12–13; Mark 11:15–17; Luke 19:45–46). His point was obvious: he was the locus of God's indwelling presence on earth; the Jerusalem Temple wasn't any more. He was the means through which God's kingdom would come; a politically empowered Judah wasn't. He was the source of renewal; the establishment wasn't.

Sufficiently infuriated, the chief priests, the teachers of the law, and the leaders of the people began plotting to kill him. As they carried out their plans, he allowed himself to be bound and dragged into an exile far greater than those of Israel's history. When he walked out of Jerusalem, it was not to go to Babylon or Assyria, but to Calvary. Though it was a much shorter walk, it left him so much farther away. Though there were people all around, he was never so lonely. And in that darkest of hours, the most hellish part was the abandonment of God: "My God, my God, why have you forsaken me?" (Matt. 27:46; Mark 15:34).

But with the resurrection, the presence of God among us is renewed and sealed forever. When the resurrected Jesus appeared to his disciples in Galilee at the end of Matthew's Gospel, his last words conclude with the promise, "And behold, I am with you always, to the end of the age" (Matt. 28:20 ESV). Even upon his ascension, when he would have to leave them, he had told them that he would send another, the Holy Spirit, which he did at Pentecost (John 16:7; Acts 2).

Poured out on Jesus' followers, the Holy Spirit binds them together, indwelling them. Thus, the church becomes the temple of God and the dwelling place of God on earth (1 Cor. 3:16; 6:19–20; Eph. 2:19–22; 1 Pet. 2:4–5). Through the ministry of the Holy Spirit, his people incarnate God's presence in the world, working as ambassadors on his behalf and seeking to transform it with the gospel (2 Cor. 5:11–21). As a community, the church becomes an outpost of the new creation and a picture to the world of what a people should be like when God dwells among them (Col. 3:1–17).

But more than just what should be, the church points to what *will* be (Heb. 13:14). The church, as a community of the new creation, should give the world a foretaste of its destiny. "God's creation reaches its eschatological fulfillment when it becomes the scene of God's immediate presence. This, in the last resort, is what is 'new' about the new creation. It is the old creation filled with God's presence."[9]

In Revelation, we are promised that such a day is coming when the world will be thus filled. The New Jerusalem will descend from heaven and a loud voice will call out from the throne, " 'Now the dwelling of God is with men, and he will live with them. They will be his people, and God himself will be with them and will be their God . . . for the old order of things has passed away.' He who was seated on the throne said, 'I am making everything new!' " (Rev. 21:3–5 NIV). On that day, there will be no need for a temple in the Holy City because the Lord Almighty and the Lamb will be its temple. And just as Zechariah said would happen, nations will gather there and the glory and honor of them will be brought into it. The glory of God in her midst will shine so brightly that its gates will remain perpetually open without fear of attack (Rev. 21:22–27; cf. Zech. 2:11).

What would it mean for the church to live as a foretaste of the new creation, to embody for the world the presence of God in her midst, to point the world to her glorious destiny when she will be filled with God's immediate presence? What would it mean for us as individuals to "incarnate" the presence of God to those around us and into the institutions we serve and the callings we fulfill? N. T. Wright sums it up well:

We need Christian people to work as healers: as healing judges and prison staff, as healing teachers and administrators, as healing shopkeepers and bankers, as healing musicians and artists, as healing writers and scientists, as healing diplomats and politicians. We need people who will hold on to Christ firmly with one hand and reach out with the other, with wit and skill and cheerfulness, with compassion and sorrow and tenderness, to the places where our world is in pain. We need people who will use all their god-given [sic] skills . . . to analyze where things have gone wrong, to come to the place of pain, and to hold over the wound the only medicine which will really heal, which is the love of Christ made incarnate once more, the strange love of God turned into your flesh and mine, your smile and mine, your tears and mine . . . your joy and mine.[10]

God had promised through Zechariah that he would change the world by *entering* it, and his promise hasn't changed. He began changing things when he entered the world through Christ; he will permanently transform the world when the New Jerusalem descends and soaks this "old" creation with his immediate and concrete presence; and he continues to change the world by entering it now. How does he enter our world today? He enters through the indwelling of the Holy Spirit in the church. He enters through his followers who "make Christ incarnate once more." Through us he transforms the world, and that is when we see his glory!

FOR FURTHER REFLECTION

1. Have there been times in your life when God seemed to have abandoned you?

2. How might Zechariah's vision of God's indwelling and transformative presence reassure you?
3. How does the incarnation of Christ give us perspective on God's commitment to change the world by entering it?
4. What are some ways that you can "make Christ incarnate" to the world around you? Who needs to sense God's presence through you?

CHAPTER SIX

LONGING FOR THE RIGHTEOUSNESS OF GOD: THE VISION OF THE HIGH PRIEST AND THE PURE VESTMENTS (3:1-10)

Then he showed me Joshua the high priest standing before the angel of the Lord, and the Accuser standing at his right hand to accuse him. Then, he said to the Accuser, "May the Lord rebuke you, O Accuser! May the Lord who has chosen Jerusalem rebuke you! Is not this burning stick being plucked from the fire?" Now Joshua was clothed in filthy garments and was standing before the angel. And he said to those standing before him, "Take away the filthy garments from him." Then he said to him, "See, I have removed your iniquity from you, in order to clothe you with festal robes." Then I said to him, "Let them put a clean turban on his head." So they put the clean turban on his head and they clothed him with garments while the angel of the Lord stood by.

Then the angel of the Lord solemnly charged Joshua, saying "Thus says the Lord of hosts: if you walk in my ways and keep my requirements, then you will also govern my house and have charge of my courts. And

I will give you a place among these who are standing here. Hear now, O Joshua the high priest, you and your associates who are sitting before you, for these men are a sign that, behold, I am going to bring my servant, the Branch. For behold, the stone which I have set before Joshua—a stone with seven pairs of eyes—behold, I will engrave an inscription on it, declares the Lord of hosts, and I will remove the iniquity of this land in a single day. In that day, declares the Lord of hosts, every one of you will invite his neighbor to come under his vine and fig tree." (Zechariah 3:1–10)

Justified by faith is he who, excluded from the righteousness of works, grasps the righteousness of Christ through faith, and clothed in it, appears in God's sight not as a sinner but as a righteous man. (John Calvin[1])

With Zechariah 3, we enter into the heart of the night visions. The eight visions form a concentric pattern with Zechariah 3 and 4 at the all-important center section that focuses on the temple and its personnel:[2]

A. Vision 1: Universal in Scope; Focused on God's Omniscience (1:7–17)
  B. Vision 2: International in Scope; Focused on Judah among the Empires (1:18–21)
    C. Vision 3: National in Scope; Focused on Jerusalem's Territory (2:1–13)
      D. Vision 4: Local in Scope; Focused on Jerusalem's Leaders (3:1–10)
      D' Vision 5: Local in Scope; Focused on Jerusalem's Temple (4:1–14)
    C' Vision 6: National in Scope; Focused on Self-Rule of Yehud (5:1–4)
  B' Vision 7: International in Scope; Focused on Yehud within Persia (5:5–11)
A' Vision 8: Universal in Scope; Focused on God's Omnipotence (6:1–8)

The vision of the high priest and the pure vestments falls into two main sections. Verses 1–5 picture a heated exchange over Joshua's suitability for high priestly ministry; verses 6–10 follow with a charge to Joshua given by the angel of the Lord.

INSIDE THE DIVINE COURTROOM (3:1–5)

The vision opens with a glimpse inside the divine courtroom. The divine council is in attendance, and on trial is Joshua the high priest, the grandson of the final high priest of the temple before its destruction (2 Kings 25:18; 1 Chron. 6:14–15; Ezra 3:2). Playing the part of the prosecutor is the Accuser[3] who is standing at Joshua's right side ready to accuse him (cf. Job 1:6–2:7). In Joshua's defense is the angel of the Lord. Interestingly, the dialogue begins with a rebuke to the Accuser, not with a report of the accusations. Either the Accuser had already made his accusations before the vision began or else he is cut off before he can verbalize them. Nevertheless, we can infer what the accusation would have been.

Presumably the Accuser had come to lay blame on Jerusalem but more specifically on the high priest, Joshua (vv. 1–2). The accusations apparently were not baseless since Joshua appears in court dressed in soiled garments, an image of great scandal to those familiar with the sacrificial system. Every year on the Day of Atonement, the high priest would enter into the Holy of Holies in the temple and offer sacrifices for himself, his household, and for all the people (Lev. 16). Before the high priest could enter into the sacred presence of God in the very inner compartment of the temple, he would put on clean, sacred linen garments in order to symbolize the need for the mediator to be holy (Ex. 28:42–43; cf. Ps. 24:3–4). Consequently, for Joshua to be dressed in filthy clothes was a grave situation. In fact, the Hebrew word for "filthy" (*tso'im*)

75

is derived from the root for human excrement (cf. Deut. 23:13; Ezek. 4:12), leaving the reader with a particularly graphic image of the uncleanness.

No doubt these soiled garments referred to his time in Babylon, implying that he had been contaminated by the exile and was therefore unfit for service in the new temple. When the Accuser then presents his charges against Joshua, the pressing question is whether or not God can cleanse the past, even one soiled by the Babylonian exile. The answer was not only important for Joshua, but for the whole community who had gone through the exile too and were now dependent upon a high priest like Joshua to represent them before God.

The angel of the Lord defends Joshua with a declaration of his power to redeem. He points out that Joshua was a "burning stick plucked from the fire."[4] The phrase is an echo of Amos 4:11, which tells of some Judeans who were narrowly rescued from God's destructive judgment. They were a burning stick snatched from the fire, pulled out at the last possible moment before being consumed by the flames. In the same way, though the judgment of the exile and the defilement of the people may have lead some to think that all was lost, God took action before it was too late. God was plucking Joshua (and the people) out from the fire and restoring them.

The angel of the Lord then dramatically acts out the Lord's intention to cleanse Joshua (and the people) from their soiled past. Joshua's filthy garments are taken away and replaced with a ceremonially clean turban and festal robes. These garments are the clothing of the high priest, as described in Exodus 28, when he represented the people before the Lord. The four items named are the ephod, the breastpiece, the special robe, and the turban. Fastened to the turban was a gold plate engraved with the words "Holy to the Lord." It was to be on the high priest's forehead when he bore the people's guilt involved in the consecration of their sacred gifts (Ex. 28:36–38). Therefore, the replacement of Joshua's filthy clothes with a festal robe and a clean turban symbolizes the removal of guilt, both his and the people's (cf. Lev. 16:3–22), and the reinstatement of a purified priesthood.

Significantly, it is the Lord (working through the angel) who performs the plucking and the replacing. Joshua is not told to do anything; the Lord himself graciously does it to Joshua for his sake and the sake of the community. As a result, God's relationship with his people would be renewed through a restored priesthood ministering in a soon-to-be-built temple. The impurity of the people's past would be gone and righteousness would take its place.

ORACULAR RESPONSES (3:6–10)

Now that Joshua is dressed in his clean priestly garments, the angel of the Lord relays oracular messages to him. Grammatically, verse 7 can be understood in two ways. On one hand, the oracle could present Joshua with four conditions and one resulting promise—if you walk in my ways, keep my requirements, govern my house, and keep charge of my courts, then I will give you a place among those standing here. Alternatively, the oracle could be presenting Joshua with two conditions and three promises if these two conditions are met—if you walk in my ways and keep my requirements, then I will see to it that you govern my house, keep charge of my courts and have a place among those standing here. The grammar allows for both though the latter seems slightly preferable.[5]

The exhortation to "walk in my ways" recalls the recurring admonitions in the book of Deuteronomy to remain faithful to God's covenant laws and to administer justice within the community. The other condition to "keep my requirements" is focused more narrowly on specific services within the temple (Lev. 8:35; 18:30; 22:9; cf. Ezek. 44:16), particularly those that maintain purity. If Joshua fulfills these conditions, the Lord promises him that he will govern the Lord's house. In other words, Joshua will be invested with the power to rule. Formerly a royal responsibility, it is now transferred to the high priest. Furthermore, he will be granted the authority to have charge over the Lord's courts. Within the domain of the temple, Joshua will be the unprecedented authority over not just sacred acts, but many public affairs as well. "Unlike the temple itself, which was off limits to the general public, the temple courtyards were the places where the people interacted with the priesthood and came closest to God's presence. The charge to Joshua concerning the courts apparently represents his responsibility for all the business and activities in connection with the public."[6]

Finally, if Joshua meets the conditions outlined, the Lord promises him something altogether shocking. He will have a place among those standing in the divine assembly. Within the temple system, the high priest had the most intimate access to God, he alone being permitted to enter the Holy of Holies. Yet the Lord promises Joshua here an even greater access than that; he will be privy to the divine council itself. He will have uninhibited access to God himself, as only a few others had been granted (1 Kings 22:19; Isa. 6:1–13; Jer. 23:18; Ezek. 1:1).

Building on this great promise, the angel of the Lord paints a hopeful picture of the future in verses 8–10 to Joshua and his colleagues. Joshua and his priestly associates are a sign of what is to come, namely that the Lord will bring his servant, the Branch. Isaiah and Jeremiah had spoken in earlier times of the Branch as a righteous Davidic ruler who would come in the future. For instance, Jeremiah says,

> Behold, the days are coming, declares the Lord, when I will fulfill the promise I made to the house of Israel and the house of Judah. In those days and at that time I will cause a righteous Branch to spring up for David,

and he shall execute justice and righteousness in the
land. In those days Judah will be saved and Jerusalem
will dwell securely. And this is the name by which it
will be called: "The LORD is our righteousness." (Jer.
33:14–16 ESV; cf. Jer. 23:5–6; Isa. 11:1)

Some have argued that the Branch refers to Zerubbabel,
but this is unlikely. For one, Zerubbabel was a contemporary
of Joshua, yet verse 8 indicates that the Branch would arrive
sometime in the future. Better is the view that continues the
trajectory of the prophets and understands the Branch as
a messianic figure who will inaugurate a new eschatological age (the description of which follows in verses 9–10;
cf. Zech. 6:9–15). On that day, the Lord will take a stone
with seven pairs of eyes and engrave an inscription on it.
Though we are not given the words of the inscription, it is
clear that it has something to do with the iniquity of the
land being removed. The nature of the stone has been the
subject of intense debate and has produced two main positions. The first position is that the stone is related to the
temple building project, perhaps either the cornerstone or
the stone for the foundation deposit (cf. Zech. 4:6b–10a).
On this reading, the rebuilding of the temple will be the
catalyst for the messianic age of the Branch when the iniquity will be finally removed from the land.

The second position, which seems to have fewer problems and takes the immediate context more seriously, is
that the stone is related to the high priest's garments already
mentioned in the visionary portion of the passage. In verses
4–5, Joshua is dressed with festal robes and a clean turban,
but strangely, the ephod and the breastpiece are not mentioned. However, since both have stones set in them, an
attractive suggestion is that the stone with seven pairs of
eyes in verse 9 is an allusion to the high priest's ephod and
breastpiece, which together hold fourteen stones.[7] On this
reading, the image of the engraved stone fills out the full
dressing appropriate for the high priest when he performs his

atoning work—verses 4–5 reference the robes and the turban, while verse 9 references the ephod and the breastpiece.

Within the historical context, this can only mean that God is signaling a fresh redemptive work on behalf of his people; the new age is preparing to dawn. Joshua becomes a picture of what the messianic age of the Branch will be like. Just as his filthy garments were removed and replaced with clean vestments so the same will be true of the land as a whole. The removal of iniquity and its replacement with righteousness will be characteristic of everyone's condition when the promised Davidic Branch comes. Once that happens, there will be widespread joy and reconciliation in the community of God's people (v. 10; cf. Mic. 4:4), reminiscent of the idealized golden age of Solomon's unified kingdom (cf. 1 Kings 4:25).

CLOTHED IN A ROBE OF RIGHTEOUSNESS

As one who was soiled by the Babylonian exile, Joshua was unfit for priestly service in the soon-to-be-built temple. The implications were grave not only for him, but for the whole postexilic community whom he represented. In the process of rebuilding the temple, the need to have a purified priesthood must have been a major concern. Was the exile too great of an obstacle to overcome? Had it soiled the priests and the people beyond repair? Could they be made clean again? Was there any hope left for a nation that had been soiled as they had?

We too ask the same kinds of questions. We have all done shameful things, and we struggle to understand why we did them. We all have things in our past that haunt us with a guilt we cannot seem to get rid of. Perhaps that deep sense of regret leaves us feeling as though we are forever soiled by indelible marks on our record. So we ask ourselves in the privacy of our own hearts, is my past too corrupted to move ahead? Can I really be clean again? Is there still hope for me?

In answer to these questions, Joshua appears in the divine courtroom. He wears his vocational garments, which are soiled with his and the people's uncleanness. But, in a work of purifying grace, God has the filthy garments removed and then cloaks Joshua in pure vestments, symbolizing that he is clean and fit for priestly service. The significance of that should not be overlooked. God can cleanse any past, no matter how soiled. He can replace filthy garments with clean robes. No history, whether national or personal, is beyond the reach of his redemptive work.

As much as this was manifested in the high priesthood of Joshua, it was climactically embodied in the person and work of Jesus, *the* great high priest (Heb. 9:11–28). Unlike Joshua, however, Jesus himself was entirely spotless and without sin (Heb. 4:14–15). As the high priest for sinners, Jesus takes our uncleanness upon himself in order to effect an astonishing transfer. As Paul succinctly puts it, "God made him who had no sin to be sin for us, so that in him we might become the righteousness of God" (2 Cor. 5:21 NIV; cf. Phil. 3:9). As Zechariah's vision had portrayed, our uncleanness is removed and we are clothed in righteousness through the ministry of our great high priest, Jesus (Gal. 3:26–27; Eph. 4:20–24). Consequently, because of our righteousness in Christ, our great high priest, we are given uninhibited access to the presence of God (Heb. 4:16; 10:19–22).

In the early church, this imagery was employed with great power in baptismal rituals. During the first two centuries, elaborate preparations for catechumens gradually developed as part of the preparation for baptism, which took place on the night before Easter. Preparations included instruction, fasting, and questioning by the bishop. When the time arrived, the catechumens were led to a small pool enclosed by curtains. They entered the water naked, leaving behind their old garments, and were baptized. Afterwards, they were anointed with oil and clothed in a fresh white linen garment (as in Rev. 3:4–5; 7:9–17; cf. Rev. 4:4; 6:11).

For the rest of the Easter week, they attended services in their newly-given white linens.[8] Baptism for the early Christians represented a deep and lasting spiritual cleansing in Christ, and therefore it seemed natural that once the catechumens had emerged from the cleansing waters their purified state be symbolized with a cloaking in pure white vestments, just as in Zechariah's vision (cf. Gal. 3:27).

Sometimes, because of our past we believe that there is no future for us, that God cannot (or will not) use us because it is simply too late. We are haunted by a soiled past. But we must remember that we have a high priest who has interceded and continues to intercede on our behalf. And because of his faithfulness in our place, we know that God can cleanse any past, no matter how soiled it is—even our past. After all, our God is a God who plucks burning sticks from the fire (cf. Jude 23), who removes filthy garments and replaces them with pure vestments, who gives us a future so unlike our past, who washes us clean and purifies us from impurity so that we are immune from any indictment by the Accuser. So "what, then, shall we say in response to this? If God is for us, who can be against us? . . . Who will bring any charge against those whom God has chosen? It is God who justifies. Who is he that condemns? Christ Jesus, who died—more than that, who was raised to life—is at the right hand of God and is also interceding for us" (Rom. 8:31, 33–34 NIV). Amen and amen.

FOR FURTHER REFLECTION

1. What things in your past continue to haunt you?
2. How does the astonishing transfer pictured in Zechariah's vision and fulfilled in Jesus address your guilt and shame?
3. How might your life be different if you lived with a heart that is assured of being clothed in a robe of righteousness not of your own?

CHAPTER SEVEN

LONGING FOR THE PURPOSES OF GOD: THE VISION OF THE GOLDEN LAMPSTAND AND THE TWO OLIVE TREES (4:1–14)

And 'angel who was speaking with me' returned and woke me, like a man who is roused from his sleep. And he said to me, "What do you see?" I said, "I see, and behold, a lampstand all of gold, with a bowl on top of it, and seven lamps on it, with seven lips on each of the lamps that are on top of it. And there are two olive trees by it, one on the right of the bowl and the other on its left." And I said to the 'angel who was speaking with me,' "What are these, my lord?" Then the 'angel who was speaking with me' answered and said to me, "Do you not know what these are?" I said, "No, my lord." Then he said to me, "This is the word of the Lord to Zerubbabel: Not by might, nor by strength, but by my Spirit, says the Lord of hosts. Who are you, O great mountain? Before Zerubbabel you shall become level ground. For he shall bring forward the top stone amid shouts of 'Grace! Grace!'" Then the word of the Lord

came to me, saying, "The hands of Zerubbabel have
laid the foundation of this house and his hands shall
also complete it, that you may know that the Lord of
hosts has sent me to you. Who is he who despises the
day of small things? They all shall rejoice when they
see the stone of distinction in the hand of Zerubbabel.
"These seven are the eyes of the Lord, which range
throughout the whole earth." Then I said to him, "What
are these two olive trees on the right and the left of the
lampstand?" And a second time I answered and said to
him, "What are these two branches of the olive trees,
which are beside the two golden pipes from which the
golden oil is poured out?" He said to me, "Do you not
know what these are?" I said, "No, my lord." Then he
said, "These are the two sons of oil who stand by the
Lord of the whole earth." (Zechariah 4:1–14)

We have to grasp the unusual and difficult thought that
all heaven is indeed opened, that all the fulness of the
light of eternity streams down, that all the angels and
heavenly choirs are assembled at this point of irruption, that they permeate the heavenly radiance with
their song of praise, and yet that this incursion of eternity which fulfills all hope and longing is concentrated
at a single point, namely, where the child lies in its
crib, where the love of God is so big that it gives itself
in what is smallest, where the eternity of God is so
mighty that it enters a feeble and despised body. For its
strength is not in size and greatness.
(Helmut Thielicke[1])

A DAY OF SMALL THINGS

In the fragile postexilic years in which Zechariah ministered, many were nostalgically remembering Judah's former
glory. With the awe-inspiring palace for the king and the
utterly magnificent temple structure that towered toward the
sky in the heart of Jerusalem, the people had lived under

the Davidic dynasty for more than four hundred years. But then, in 587 or 586 B.C., the nation was conquered by the mighty and powerful Babylonian army. They destroyed the temple, carted off the wealth stored there, and dragged scores of Judeans into exile. Many others scattered across the Jordan or down to Egypt or into Syro-Phoenicia. When the dust settled after the siege was over, the holy city lay in utter ruins. Those left behind, now impoverished and homeless, tried to piece their lives back together. Naturally, Israel's future looked bleak, if not entirely hopeless.

Yet during those exilic years, the people began thinking about why this tragedy had happened. What was God doing in all of it? Prophets like Ezekiel began to help people make sense of the catastrophe by offering new words of hope about what God would do in the future. Even in exile there were stirrings of a work of God that would begin undoing the awful suffering and calamity of the Babylonian exile. It would be like a new exodus when people would march back from their captivity and enter into the Promised Land once again. Once there, they would rebuild a new temple from the ashes. So the people began praying, singing, and reading their sacred texts together. Hope began to break through the bitter soil and flower into renewed expectations—expectations that God would do something beyond their wildest dreams. He would not just put Israel back on the map, but would use her to heal the brokenness of the whole world.

Then suddenly their Babylonian rulers were conquered by the Persians, which led to the announcement of good news. The Persian ruler Cyrus issued an edict in 538 B.C., allowing those in exile to return to their land and begin reconstruction on their temple. Shortly thereafter, work began on the foundations in 537 B.C.[2] Among the people, expectations soared. Optimism raged. Excitement was palpable. It looked as if the renewal might actually have begun.

But the work quickly stalled and over the next seventeen years little happened, due to a number of reasons.

Disillusionment and cynicism set in among the people. Under the leadership of the prophets Haggai and Zechariah, the high priest Joshua, and the governor Zerubbabel, things finally got moving in 520 B.C., though on a much smaller scale than some had hoped. Some looked back and wept at how the new temple fell far short when compared with the original (Ezra 3:12–13; Hag. 2:3). Others looked forward and scoffed at the rebuilding efforts as pathetic when compared to the worldwide vision of restoration that had been birthed during the exilic years (Zech. 4:10).

On December 18, 520 B.C., when the refoundation ceremony for the new temple was held, many ridiculed it. They derided the efforts, contemptuously calling it the "day of small things." Quite possibly, this was a play on words. The prophets were fond of heralding the "Day of the Lord" when God would return and set things right again. Perhaps the scoffers were alluding to this "Day of the Lord" when they mocked what was happening with derision as the "day of small things."[3] To them it looked pitiful and meager with little potential to accomplish the purposes of God within the world.

It is just this attitude that God addresses in this fifth night vision given to Zechariah. The structure of this vision is vital to understanding it. In verses 1–6a, an angel comes to Zechariah, shows him a vision, and asks him if he understands it. The explanation however does not come until verses 10b–14. Inserted in between is the application of the vision to the specific historical situation of the temple reconstruction efforts (vv. 6b–10a).

THE VISION OF THE GOLDEN LAMPSTAND AND THE TWO OLIVE TREES (4:1–6A, 10B–14)

In verses 1–2, the angel comes to Zechariah and asks him, "What do you see?" Zechariah says, "I see, and behold, a lampstand all of gold, with a bowl on top of it, and seven lamps on it, with seven lips on each of the lamps that are on top of it."

The structural configuration of the lampstand is not entirely clear. The Hebrew term for "lampstand" (*menorah*) calls to mind a seven-armed lampstand with a single lamp at the end of each arm. However, the syntax of verse 2 leaves open the possibility that the seven lamps are actually situated on top of the bowl.[4] In either case, the bowl situated on the lampstand functioned as an oil reservoir, which fed a continuous supply of oil to the wicks of the lamps. In verse 3, Zechariah sees two olive trees, one on each side of the lampstand. These two olive trees functioned to supply oil to the reservoir bowl and keep it from running dry, thus ensuring that the lamps burned continuously.

The lampstand being made of gold associates it with the furniture of the tabernacle and temple. Within the symbolic world of the tabernacle, the tree-shaped lampstand was a reminder of the Tree of Life in the garden of Eden (Ex. 25:31–39). The tabernacle as a whole with all its furniture was "a renewed version of the garden of Eden," the place where God would be present among his people.[5] The burning of the lamps would presumably represent the Lord's presence among his people (cf. 2 Sam. 22:29; Rev. 21:23; 22:5).[6] Just as those lamps continued to burn night and day (Lev. 24:1–4), so in the same way the Lord by his Spirit would be among his people continually.

The meaning of the vision confuses Zechariah initially (vv. 4–5). To clear things up, in the ensuing dialogue of verses 10b–14, the angel unpacks the meaning of the lampstand and the two olive trees. The seven burning lamps are "the eyes of the Lord, which range throughout the whole earth." Within the Old Testament, the phrase "eyes of the Lord" often broadly refers to the Lord's omnipresence and omniscience (e.g., Prov. 15:3), but can also more narrowly refer to the Lord's benevolent care for his people (e.g., Ps. 34:15). Furthermore, when his eyes range throughout the earth (as in 2 Chron. 16:9), it carries the added meaning of upholding and strengthening his people, particularly in times of difficulty. Within late sixth-century Yehud, this was good news! The Lord will be with his people, strengthening and upholding them even during the difficult and tumultuous time of temple reconstruction.

The guarantee that the Lord's presence will remain among his people comes from "the two sons of oil who stand by the Lord of the whole earth," which in the vision are symbolized by the two olive trees (vv. 11–14). Though most translators render verse 14 as "these are the two anointed ones," it is probably better to retain the literal reading, "the two sons of oil." Had Zechariah wanted to emphasize anointing, he likely would have used the term *shemen*; instead he uses *yishar*, a term associated with agricultural abundance. The sense is not that these two figures were formally anointed, but simply that they were instruments of the Lord's abundant blessing for Yehud.[7] Just as the two olive trees ensure that the lamps continue to burn, the two "sons of oil" are the key to ensuring that the Lord's presence and work continue among his people. Standing by him, they are his agents (cf. 1 Kings 22:19). Naturally, the two olive trees are referring to the high priest, Joshua, and the governor, Zerubbabel, who are spearheading the reconstruction of the temple. The symbolism of the vision powerfully legitimates them as God's representatives and validates their efforts in rebuilding the temple as the divinely ordained means through which God will continue his work among his people and in the world.

THE HISTORICAL APPLICATION (4:6B–10A)

Despite God's clear validation of rebuilding, these early stages of temple reconstruction were the object of derision by some, who were calling it a "small thing." Accompanying the vision therefore is the oracular pronouncement in verses 6b–10a. Zerubbabel receives the word of the Lord:

"Not by might, nor by strength, but by my Spirit." One of the best-known verses from the book of Zechariah, this declaration sums up the heart of the vision's message. *Might* and *strength* should be taken as a hendiadys, together referring to the use of martial force. The point is that God's restoration program will not be advanced through political or military struggles against Persia, but through the small but God-ordained efforts in rebuilding the temple. These efforts may be scorned as lacking "might" and "strength" in the world of Persian controlled Yehud. They may appear weak and impotent to many. But the Lord says emphatically that even though the temple restoration project may be "small," it will nevertheless accomplish his purposes through the power of his Spirit.

The oracle continues with a description of exactly how this will take place, beginning with the leveling of a "great mountain." Within the cultural world of the ancient Near East, the first task in building a new temple was to clear a level piece of land that would be suitable for the foundation of the building. This was often done on a mountain or an artificially constructed plot of elevated land in order to depict the typological relationship between the earthly temple and the heavenly temple on God's cosmic mountain. So too, Israel viewed the temple as symbiotically related to a typological mountain, namely Zion (e.g., Pss. 24:3; 48:1–2; 87:1–2; 99:9; cf. Isa. 2:2; 66:20). "The Temple on Zion is the antitype to the cosmic archetype,"[8] meaning Zion alone was the legitimate place for a temple to be built. In the case of Zerubbabel, the declaration that the mountain (Zion) would be prepared to receive the foundation of the new temple was a validating sign from the Lord. It was a confirmation that the Lord's Spirit would bless his efforts and ensure his success.

Following the preparation of the platform, according to the oracle, the top stone would be brought forward. Again, the ancient Near Eastern background is illuminating.[9] In rebuilding a temple, continuity was one of the highest values. Great effort was taken to build the new temple in precisely the same spot as the old temple. This geographical continuity was matched with a desire for material continuity as well, enacted by the bringing forth of the top stone. The presentation of the top stone was a ceremonial act in which a stone from the former temple became the first laid stone of the new temple. The purpose was to symbolize the continuity between the old temple and the new one; just as the deity dwelled among the people in the former temple, so also would he dwell among them in the new temple. In response to the presentation of the top stone, the people will let out great shouts of "Grace! Grace!"[10] They will recognize that what is happening is really due to the work of God among them. The repetition of "Grace!" underscores the intensity of the people's joy over what the Lord is doing.

While the first part of the oracle addressed Zerubbabel, the second part addresses Zechariah himself. The word of the Lord now comes to him, assuring him that the project will indeed see completion at the hands of Zerubbabel. In light of that fact, the question rings out: "Who is he who despises the day of small things?" No one should dismiss these small beginnings as inconsequential or unimportant. Bound up within these early stages of temple reconstruction are the purposes of God for his people and derivatively for the whole world. Hidden inside the apparent weakness of this "small thing" is the power of God's Spirit.

Consequently, disdain would be replaced with rejoicing, as the people see the stone of distinction in the hand of Zerubbabel. The nature of this stone is not entirely clear.[11] It may, like the top stone, have a ceremonial function or it may have a much more pragmatic one, serving as a kind of plumb line for the building. Alternatively, it may not even be a stone at all but a kind of metal deposit, symbolically significant for the temple. Whatever its function, it likely refers to a later phase in the foundation laying ceremony and not to the completion of the entire temple structure. Even at such an early stage in the building process, it will nevertheless spark joyful acclamation among the people when they see it in Zerubbabel's hands. Through the lens of faith, what once appeared weak is now shown to be strong. What once appeared to be impotent is now shown to be the instrument of the Spirit's power. What once appeared to be merely a "small thing" is now shown to hold within it the purposes of God for Israel and the world.

A GOD OF THE SMALL THINGS

Isn't that the way God often works? When Elijah found himself so discouraged he wanted God to take his life, God brought him out of the cave at Mount Carmel and had him stand on the mount before the Lord (1 Kings 19:9–12). The wind shattered the rock into pieces, but the Lord was not in the wind. And after the wind an earthquake, but God was not in the earthquake. And after the earthquake a fire, but God was not in the fire. Then, after the fire came the sound of a gentle whisper. "The abrupt refusal of Yahweh to appear as in the traditional theophany at Sinai marked the beginning of a new era in his mode of self-disclosure."[12] From then on, God would especially be seen "in the still small voice."

Not only was that true in Elijah's day and Zechariah's day, but it was true in Jesus' day as well. In a world of imperial power, where Caesar sat on the throne in Rome controlling the affairs of the world, what could be more insignificant than a baby being born fourteen hundred miles away, off in a corner of the empire? What could be smaller than a crying infant in swaddling clothes, tucked away in a dirty, smelly manger? What could be more unimpressive than an unknown teenage girl giving birth in a stable because there was no room at the inn? If there has ever been a day of small things, this was the day.

As the Gospels recount the public ministry of Jesus, it is clear that the disciples and Pharisees alike expected a Messiah who would do big things—a political revolutionary, a circus-show miracle worker, or a Maccabean-style warlord. The disciples believed Jesus was that Messiah and thus seemed to expect him to lead a revolution against Rome, complete with "might" and "strength" (Matt. 16:21–23; Acts 1:6). The Pharisees did not believe Jesus was that Messiah and thus challenged him to prove himself with one flashy miracle after another (Matt. 12:38; Mark 8:11–12; cf. John 2:18). The Jewish crowds did the same (John 2:18; 6:25–40). They all expected a Messiah who would make a big splash. And because of that, many of them missed the "day of small things" in a wandering itinerant prophet from Nazareth. They didn't hear the still small voice of the vagabond rabbi because they thought that when God came among them it would surely be with great apocalyptic upheaval.

Jesus offered hints of this in his teaching, most notably the parable of the mustard seed: "The kingdom of heaven is like a grain of mustard seed that a man took and sowed in his field. It is the smallest of all seeds, but when it has grown it is larger than all the garden plants and becomes a tree, so that the birds of the air come and make nests in its branches" (Matt. 13:31–32 ESV). No one would have been surprised that Jesus compared the kingdom of God to a tree large enough for birds to roost in it; that had already been done by the prophets (e.g., Ezek. 17:22–24; Dan. 4:12). But to compare the kingdom of God to something as small and insignificant as a mustard seed was utterly shocking. No one could have imagined that God's great kingdom work would begin that way, that the "kingdom of God is at work not with heavenly armies, but with earthly disciples—not in the victory over the Romans, but in hidden exorcisms and healings."[13]

The apostle Peter certainly didn't seem to imagine it. Even hours before Jesus' crucifixion, when the mob sent from the chief priests and the elders arrives to arrest Jesus in the garden of Gethsemane, Peter draws the sword. But Jesus rebukes him sharply saying, "Put your sword back in its place . . . for all who draw the sword will die by the sword. Do you think I cannot call on my Father and He will at once put at my disposal more than twelve legions of angels? But how then would the Scriptures be fulfilled that say it must happen this way?" (Matt. 26:52–54 NIV). The way was not through martial force but through the smallness and weakness of the cross.

It is common to think of the crucifixion of Jesus as a major world event, but for people at the time it was just another failed prophet being executed in some far-flung corner of the empire. Its mention by only a handful of ancient historians is minimal at best (and even then largely derogatory).[14] But the resurrection reveals that this small and horrible event was actually the hinge of history. While the world failed to notice, God was changing the course of history. And that is precisely how God works. God changed the world through the "smallness" of the incarnation, an itinerant prophet, and a bloody death on the outskirts of Jerusalem.

Today God continues to work in the same way. It is easy to think that the best way to change the world is to elect a certain person president, overturn Roe v. Wade, or launch some other political or social cause. Certainly those efforts are worthwhile, but the simple fact is that the empire—Roman or otherwise—has never been spiritually transformed, turned upside down and inside out, simply through the rise of a Constantine or the coronation of a Charlemagne. The world was changed when a bunch of radical followers of Jesus did the "small things," like taking care of the poor around them, taking in an orphan, or feeding the hungry. By themselves these actions were not dramatic and often seemed to have few results, but that was how the Roman Empire was turned upside down—through the small things that believers did in radical obedience to Jesus and the gospel.

In the third century, a devastating and widespread plague erupted within the Roman Empire. Dionysius, the bishop of Alexandria, wrote,

> Most of our brother Christians showed unbounded love and loyalty, never sparing themselves and thinking only of one another. Heedless of danger, they took charge of the sick, attending to their every need and ministering to them in Christ. . . . Many, in nursing and curing others, transferred their death to themselves and died in their stead. . . . The heathen behaved in the very opposite way. At the first onset of the disease, they pushed the sufferers away and fled even from their dearest, throwing them into the roads before they were dead and treated unburied corpses as dirt, hoping thereby to avert the spread and contagion of the fatal disease; but do what they might, they found it difficult to escape.[15]

In the scope of the whole world, putting oneself at risk to care for the contagiously sick may seem like a small thing—even a foolish thing—but it is that kind of small thing that God uses to transform empires and change the course of civilization.

Like those in Zechariah's day, we are also tempted to dismiss the small things, to presume that God only works through the big and the flashy, the important and the impressive, or the noticeable and the noteworthy. We are just as likely to overlook what at first glance seems insignificant, assuming that it cannot make much of a difference in the world. As a result, we too need to listen to the word of the Lord through the prophet Zechariah, "Who is he who despises the day of small things? Not by might, nor by strength, but by my Spirit."

For instance, we should not despise the prayer closet. Prayer may seem like a small thing, hardly something that could change the world, but the vision of the lampstand

and the two olive trees reminds us that we have a God who works through the small things. Likewise, we should not despise the thankless work of volunteering at a soup kitchen or an AIDS clinic. Perhaps those things seem like drops in the bucket in light of how great the problems of hunger and disease are in the world. But we must remember that we have a God who works through the small things.

Our lives are full of opportunities to follow Jesus in the "small" ways: keeping the nursery at church, taking flowers to a shut-in, writing a note to someone who is depressed, bringing a meal to someone who is sick, inviting a college student to share a holiday in our home, visiting the hospitalized, serving at a crisis pregnancy center, caring for our families in what can feel like monotonous daily tasks, or having a simple conversation about God with a friend or coworker. All those may seem small, unless we remember that we have a God who works not by might nor by strength but through the power of his Spirit. We have a God of lampstands and olive trees; we have a God of mangers and crosses; we have a God of the small things.

FOR FURTHER REFLECTION

1. How would the Judeans have been tempted to rely on "might and strength" in the early postexilic period?
2. The early efforts of temple reconstruction looked like a "small thing." What would the eyes of faith have seen when it looked at those early efforts?
3. How would the vision of the lampstand and olive trees have strengthened the faith of those living in the early postexilic period?
4. What things do you tend to dismiss as "small things?"
5. How might the vision of the lampstand and olive trees strengthen your faith in God's ability to accomplish his purposes through the "small things" in your life?

CHAPTER EIGHT

LONGING FOR THE AUTHORITY OF GOD: THE VISIONS OF THE FLYING SCROLL AND THE WOMAN IN THE BASKET (5:1–11)

Again I lifted my eyes and looked—and behold—a flying scroll. And he said to me, "What do you see?" I answered, "I see a flying scroll; its length is twenty cubits and its width is ten cubits." And he said to me, "This is the curse which is going out upon the face of the whole land. For everyone who steals according to it has gone unpunished and everyone who swears falsely according to it has gone unpunished. 'I have sent it out,' declares the Lord of hosts, 'and it will enter into the house of the thief and into the house of the one who swears falsely by my name. It will lodge inside his house and will destroy it, both its wood and its stones.'"

Then the 'angel who was speaking with me' went out and said to me, "Now lift your eyes and see what else is going out." Then I said, "What is it?" And he said,

"This is the basket which is going out." And he said,
"This is their appearance in the whole land." And
behold, when the lead cover was lifted, there was a
woman sitting inside the basket. And he said, "This is
Wickedness!" Then he threw her down into the inte-
rior of the basket and threw down a lead weight on
its opening. Then I lifted up my eyes and looked—and
behold—two women were going out and the wind
was in their wings (they had wings like the wings of a
stork). They lifted up the basket between the earth and
the heavens. Then I said to the 'angel who was speaking with me,' "Where are they taking the basket?" And
he said to me, "To build a house for her in the land of
Shinar. Once it is established, she will be set down on
its base." (Zechariah 5:1–11)

[The Word of God] is not something which is under our
control, but something which exercises control over us.
(Karl Barth[1])

Zechariah 5 consists of two separate visions: the vision
of the flying scroll in verses 1–4 and the vision of the woman
in the basket in verses 5–11. Both visions are thematically
connected, and they both address the problem of continuing iniquity among the people. The exile had the potential
to cleanse the people (Isa. 48:10), but even after the exile
was over impurity remained in the community (Jer. 6:29).
More specifically, the community was presumably experiencing serious moral and social problems such as theft
and swearing falsely by the Lord's name.

THE FLYING SCROLL (5:1–4)

Once again Zechariah lifts up his eyes and sees a vision.
This time it is a large flying scroll, one that measured twenty
cubits by ten cubits (about 30 feet by 15 feet). According to
the angel, the scroll symbolizes a curse being sent out over

the land to deal with the social evils. The Hebrew word for "curse" is used in Deuteronomy to designate the consequences for breaking God's covenant law: "But if you will not obey the voice of the LORD your God or be careful to do all his commandments and his statutes that I command you today, then all these curses shall come upon you and overtake you" (Deut. 28:15 ESV). The covenant of Sinai always held out the promise of blessing for obedience, but it also held out the threat of curse for disobedience. The people were deceiving themselves if they thought that merely rebuilding the temple would automatically lead to God pouring out his blessing upon them. They must not only rebuild the temple but they must return wholeheartedly to the covenant itself.

Consequently, out comes a flying scroll, unrolled and very large, so that God's covenant demands are in plain view and easy to read.[2] It is a picture of God's authority that hangs over his people and calls them to account for their social evils, specifically thievery and perjury. The terms are given with the definite article suggesting that these are not referring to people with occasional offenses, but to those whose offenses are so habitual that they can be summarily characterized as "thieves" or as "perjurers."

Perhaps the perpetrators would have excused or rationalized what they were doing with the dire conditions of the day. In the early Persian period, the economy was in the tank because inflation was financially crippling the community.[3] Basic subsistence could be difficult and some undoubtedly resorted to extreme measures to make ends meet. Yet, even if such difficult circumstances made stealing and lying more understandable (from the perspective of human empathy), it did not make them any less destructive to the welfare of the community. As violators of the public good, the thieves and perjurers had become a cancer to the wider community by compounding the widespread financial problems.

Moreover these are serious offenses against God, both being prohibited by the very core of the Sinai covenant, the

Ten Commandments.[4] The intentional allusion to the covenant at Sinai is further strengthened by the Hebrew word used for "curse." It is not the more common word (*'arar*) for curse, but is actually the word more typically translated as an oath (*'alah*). In Deuteronomy 29, it is used as the solemn oath between God and his people in ratifying the covenant (Deut. 29:12–13, 18–19; cf. Ezek. 17:13) as well as the curses guaranteed upon those who break it (Deut. 29:20–21). The crimes of the thieves and perjurers are not merely against other people; they are an affront to the God with whom they are supposed to be in covenant. They are not sins against humanity only but covenant transgressions against God himself (cf. Ps. 51:4).

Though it is impossible to be certain, perhaps that is also why the flying scroll has the unusual dimensions it does. Typically a scroll's length would be much longer than its width. But this scroll is only twice as long as it is wide. The strange dimensions happen to correspond precisely to the dimensions of the portico in the front of the main hall of Solomon's temple (1 Kings 6:3). The apparent allusion is particularly significant since the portico was where priestly justice was likely administered.[5] The implication seems to be that as the people rebuilt the temple and reestablished right worship, they also needed to do something about the unjust social evils among them. They cannot rebuild the temple and expect God to be present among them in covenant relationship (as he was in Solomon's temple) if they continue to tolerate blatant covenant breaking in their community (cf. 1 Kings 8:22–61). Right worship must always translate into right living. If it does not, God's renewed presence among them will not be one of covenant blessing, but of covenant cursing.

Thus, the flying scroll is sent out across the whole land (i.e., the province of Yehud) in order to deal with social ills present. Verse 3 is difficult. The word *niqah* can have the sense of "to be cleaned out" or alternatively "to be cleared from guilt" or "exempted from punishment." Most

English translations opt for the former with the sense being that verse 3 explains what the flying scroll will do: it will cleanse the land by purging out the thieves and perjurers. The latter option would mean that verse 3 explains why the scroll is being sent out: because the community has left thieves and perjurers unpunished for their crimes. This alternative option seems better since *niqah* is in the perfect, making it more probable that a past action (e.g., "has gone unpunished") rather than a future action (e.g., "will be purged") is in view.[6] God will not tolerate such blatant injustice. The law courts may have become perverted and the judicial process may have broken down, but God's judgment will ensure accountability. In an aggressive act of storming the criminals' houses, God will send his curse upon those responsible so that they will finally receive their just desserts.

This promised judgment alludes to two passages in the priestly law: Numbers 5:11–28 and Leviticus 14:44–45.[7] In the first passage, when a woman is suspected of adultery the priest writes the curses for false swearing in a book, washes them off into the "water of bitterness," and then gives the concoction to the woman to drink. If she is guilty, the water will cause bitter pain when it enters her, even making her insides swell and "fall away."

In the second passage, regulations are given for dealing with houses contaminated by rot or mildew. If the priest finds that the house is indeed unclean, then he is supposed to destroy the house, including its stones and timber. The double allusion makes the point even more dramatically. The thieves and the perjurers within the postexilic community are like the guilt of an unfaithful wife or the devouring rot in an unclean house. For the good of the community, God must mete out his covenant judgment, completely eradicating the cancerous evil that threatens to contaminate the rest of the community.

As the thieves and perjurers would discover, when God's judgment on sin comes, there is no safe place to hide, even in the privacy and seclusion of one's own home. Moreover, the consumption of both the timber and stone of the houses shows that God's judgment is utterly exhaustive. Nothing will escape it. In God's economy, transgressing the covenant is a debt that is never left unpaid.

THE WOMAN IN THE BASKET (5:5–11)

The second vision is closely related to the first in that it is also concerned with removing evil from the community. In the first vision, judgment removes the evil, while in this vision, expulsion is used to do the job. The vision begins with the angel showing Zechariah a basket that was "going out in the whole land." Like the scroll in the previous vision, the basket is much larger than normal and is moving about the land. Sitting inside the basket is a woman, who becomes visible once the lid is removed. The angel informs Zechariah that she symbolizes wickedness. The widespread movement of the basket seems to indicate the pervasiveness of the iniquity among the people. The woman being initially hidden inside the basket may symbolize that the evil being condemned among the people is largely hidden from the public's sight as well.[8]

But what kind of evil is in view? In the previous vision, the specific offenses of theft and perjury were named, but in this vision there is no explicit declaration of the social evils in view. There is however a subtle clue. The vision begins with a picture of a measuring basket, literally an ephah. Elsewhere in the Old Testament, the ephah is a normal part of commerce. It was used to measure flour, barley, or grain quantities (e.g., Lev. 6:13; Ruth 2:17; Isa. 5:10), and thus was sometimes tampered with by dishonest merchants in order to cheat buyers. Amos complained that people were making the ephah small and the shekel great and so cheating buyers with false balances (Amos 8:4–6; cf. Lev. 19:36; Ezek. 45:10). The only appropriate description for such people is "wicked" according to the prophet Micah.

> Am I still to forget, O wicked house,
> your ill-gotten treasures
> and the short ephah, which is accursed?

> Shall I acquit a man with dishonest scales,
> with a bag of false weights? (Mic. 6:10–11 NIV)

The woman inside the basket, then, is a picture of the wickedness that is present in their dishonest commercial transactions.

After Zechariah is shown the woman inside the basket, the angel throws her back into the basket and slams the lid shut. Then, two female figures with wings like storks enter the picture, lift the basket, and carry it off. A play on the Hebrew word for "stork" is used to intensify the point. The people were at fault for their covenant unfaithfulness, but God's own faithfulness (*khasid*) to his people would be seen through the two women with wings like storks (*khasidhah*) that remove the iniquity.

When Zechariah asks where the two women are taking the basket, the angel tells him that they are heading for the land of Shinar. The land of Shinar is another designation for the land of Babylon (cf. Gen. 10:10; 11:2; Dan. 1:2). This is an ironic jab at Babylon. Apparently, it is the only suitable home for wickedness. But why opt for the name Shinar instead of the more common name Babylon? Most likely, the reference to Shinar is an intentional allusion to the Tower of Babel account in Genesis 11 where the arrogant presumption of humanity is on vivid display. They build a tower (in all likelihood a ziggurat or temple) in an attempt to reach heaven. It is a blatant denial of God's authority over them. In the same way, for the postexilic community to begin building a temple while social evils like dishonest commerce go unaddressed is an arrogant presumption on God and ultimately mocks his sovereign authority over them.

This interpretation is strengthened by the claim that the basket is being taken to Shinar because a house is being built for it. An equally plausible translation would be "a temple is being built for it," inferring that it will occupy the central function, set up on its base, just as a pagan idol would. In other words, the basket is being transferred to a new religious setting that is more appropriate for it. Dishonest commerce is nothing less than idolatry and thus it belongs not in Yehud but in Shinar, its rightful home.

This also may help to explain why wickedness is personified as a woman. Some have suggested that the symbol of a woman is used simply because the Hebrew word for "wickedness" (harish'ah) is feminine in gender. But, given the overtones of idolatry in the vision, it would not be unreasonable to see here an allusion to the long legacy of goddess idolatry in the history of Israel. Archaeological evidence has shown a longstanding, grassroots propensity in Israel to supplement legitimate worship of the Lord with folk-style religious worship involving terracotta fertility goddess figurines, statues of a Philistine goddess from Ashkelon, and even a cult stand picturing a "Mistress of the Animals" flanked by two lions.[9] Within the pages of the Old Testament, the prophets repeatedly condemn the syncretistic appropriation of the Canaanite goddess, Asherah, as the Lord's consort (e.g., 1 Kings 14:5; Isa. 17:8; Mic. 5:14) and the worship of the "Queen of Heaven" (Jer. 7:18; 44:17–25). With such a history of idolatrous worship involving foreign goddesses, the personification of wickedness as a woman in the vision of the basket seems all too appropriate, and reveals her removal to be long overdue.

The only way to deal with evil (and idolatry in particular) is to eradicate it completely. It must be "sealed up" and "sent far away." There is no such thing as partially getting rid of sin; it cannot simply be managed. The only solution is complete expulsion. What good news for the postexilic community. God will not indefinitely tolerate sin among his people, nor will he give up on them. Through these two visions, God shows that he will not abandon his people in their wickedness, but that he will exercise his covenant authority and eradicate sin through judgment and removal.

THE COVENANT AUTHORITY OF GOD

Like the postexilic community, the church is just as indictable for a lack of holiness among its people. Many today are as guilty as those in Zechariah's day of disconnecting their worship from their ethics. It is easy for us to do many religious things, to participate in corporate worship, even to pray, read Scripture, and participate in the sacraments, and yet keep other parts of our lives hermetically sealed off. Like some in the postexilic community, we try to justify dishonest gain in the marketplace with statements like, "it's not personal, it's business." We can rationalize half-truths and fill our lives with our idols of choice.

Unfortunately the immorality doesn't stop there. Statistics continue to show that morality among professing Christians in the U.S. is little better than the surrounding culture, and sometimes worse.[10] Numerous studies have demonstrated that conservative evangelical Christians in the U.S. have an equal rate of divorce as that of non-Christians, with some studies indicating that it may be even higher. Just as alarming are statistics showing that conservative Protestant husbands are just as likely to commit domestic abuse as the general population. In the area of sexual morality, "born-again" adults cohabitate before marriage and use pornography at rates only a little lower than the national rates. Finally, conservative Protestants are significantly more likely to harbor racist attitudes than the rest of the population.

No wonder many non-Christians look at the church and find it so difficult to believe in Christ. Friedrich Nietzsche's character Zarathustra quipped, "Better songs they will have to sing for me before I learn to believe in their redeemer; more redeemed his disciples would have to look!"[11] Clearly he has a point.

As for Christians, the lack of holiness among God's people can produce serious doubts about their faith as well as despondency and frustration with the church. Someone I know once remarked that if he ever decides to leave the faith (not that he plans to!), it would be because of the apparent lack of godliness in the church. I suspect that he is not alone.

To such a condition among God's people, the visions of the flying scroll and the woman in the basket remind us that God will not indefinitely tolerate sin among his people—whether in the postexilic community or in the church today. There will come a day when he will fully and finally eradicate it and purify the community of his people.

We continue to wait for that day to arrive. Until it does, Jesus himself clearly indicates that the pure and the impure are hopelessly mixed together in this world. That is why Jesus compares the kingdom to a field with both wheat and weeds (Matt. 13:24–30, 36–43). Though the Son of Man is busy sowing wheat in the field, the evil one is also busy sowing weeds alongside them. In the field (which is the world), the sowing of the seed (the preaching of the gospel) causes a mixed crop to spring up (true disciples and false ones). The phrase "all the causes of sin and all evildoers" (v. 41) is very similar to a phrase applied elsewhere in the Gospel to those who take the name of Jesus upon themselves but do so falsely (Matt. 7:23), which is the same problem corrupting the postexilic community.[12] But that is the nature of God's people in this world. Weeds always grow alongside the wheat, and during this present age, they are very difficult to separate. To expect otherwise is to misunderstand the nature of the kingdom in this world and to set ourselves up for disillusionment.

But there will come a day—as both Zechariah and Jesus indicate—when God himself will permanently root out sin from among his people. At the end of the age the Son of Man will send out his angels to separate the weeds from the wheat, the wicked from the righteous. And just as the vision of the flying scroll indicated, the guilty will be judged and they will have nowhere to hide. On that day,

> the kings of the earth and the great ones and the generals and the rich and the powerful, and everyone, slave and free, [will hide] themselves in the caves and among the rocks of the mountains, calling to the mountains and rocks, "Fall on us and hide us from the face of him who is seated on the throne, and from the wrath of the Lamb, for the great day of their wrath has come, and who can stand?" (Rev. 6:15–17 ESV)

Upon judgment, they will be permanently removed from God's presence. Christ will say to them, "Depart from me; I never knew you" (Matt. 7:21–23; cf. Matt. 25:31–46). But for all those who are in Christ, God's work of judgment won't happen *to* them because it has already happened *for* them. Jesus substituted himself for all who place their faith in him, receiving the just penalty for their sins through his death (Rom. 3:25; 1 John 2:2). In doing so, he exhausted the judgment of God that his people might be delivered from the covenant curse they deserve (Gal. 3:13–14).

Consequently, God's work of expulsion doesn't happen *to* them either; it happens *in* them. In the ministry of the Holy Spirit, God works even now to purge sin from his people, just as was pictured in the vision of the woman in the basket (Zech. 5:5–11). He does this by enabling his people to put to death the deeds of the flesh (Rom. 8:13) and producing within his people the fruit of holiness (Gal. 5:22–23).

St. John of the Cross described this purifying work of the Holy Spirit upon the soul with the helpful image of fire acting on a damp log of wood.[13] Initially, the flame assaults the wood, causing it to sweat, smoke, and sputter. Eventually, the flame dries out the wood, thus preparing the wood to receive the flame itself. That is, after purging out the water from the wood, the wood is readied to become inflamed itself with the fire acting upon it. In the same way, the Holy Spirit acts upon the soul to purge it of its impurities. Just as in the case of the log, such a work is often painful for the Christian, but it is necessary. The more the Spirit expels sin from the heart, the more ready it is to be inflamed and illumined by his presence within it. Just as the fire pushes out the water from the log and then penetrates it in order to inflame it, so the Holy Spirit pushes out the impurities of our hearts in order that he might fill it and inflame it with his presence.

As we wait for God to intervene with his purifying covenant authority at the end of the age, our responsibility in the meantime is to pursue holiness. Personally, we must continually flee to Christ who has spared us from judgment and rely on the Holy Spirit who continues to expel sin from our hearts and lives. Corporately, we must encourage one another to do the same, which sometimes requires the spurs of loving and godly discipline (Matt. 18:15–20; 1 Cor. 5:1–5). Though in all of it we must exercise humility and patience. "The church is made up of all sorts of people; it always has been. . . . Even the most discerning are not always good at making judgments; one does not know the heart. The weeds and the wheat look very much alike. . . . The judgment will take place at the end, supervised by Christ. Let that be sufficient."[14]

With that in mind, we do not have to give in to discouragement or disillusionment over remaining sin among God's people. Like the postexilic community, we are reassured that God will not indefinitely tolerate sin among his people; there will be judgment and purification. At the same time, we are given hope because we know that he has not given up on his people; he continues his work of rooting out sin from our hearts and lives even now. That is a great hope—for the church certainly, but also for each one of us individually who continues to struggle against sin and longs for God to remove it from us as far as the east is from the west (Ps. 103:12), as far as Shinar is from Yehud.

FOR FURTHER REFLECTION

1. Which social evils were both common and tolerated among the postexilic community?
2. What social evils are particularly common among God's people today? Which are often tolerated?
3. How does Christ transform the concepts of God judging and purging sin among his people?
4. How do the vision of the flying scroll and the vision of the woman in the basket protect us from both unbridled optimism on the one hand and despondent resignation on the other?

CHAPTER NINE

LONGING FOR THE VICTORY OF GOD: THE VISION OF THE FOUR CHARIOTS (6:1–8)

Again I lifted up my eyes and looked—and behold—four chariots were going out from between the two mountains; the mountains were mountains of bronze. With the first chariot there were red horses, with the second chariot black horses, with the third chariot white horses, and with the fourth chariot spotted horses—all of which were strong. Then I answered and said to the 'angel who was speaking with me,' "What are these, my lord?" The angel answered and said to me, "These are the four winds of heaven going out from before the Lord of all the earth. The one with the black horses is going out to the land of the north; then the white ones went out to the west; then the spotted ones went out to the land of the south." When the strong ones went out, they sought to go range over the earth. So he said, "Go; range over the earth." So they ranged over the earth. Then he called out to me, "See! Those who are going out to the land of the north have caused my Spirit to rest in the land of the north." (Zechariah 6:1–8)

"Who will enter into judgment against me? Let him
stand up and face me. I have set the condemned free.
I have given the dead life. I have raised up the one
who was entombed. Who will speak against me? I," he
says, "am the Christ. I have dissolved death, I have triumphed over the enemy and trodden down Hades and
bound the strong man and carried off humanity into
the height of the heavens. I," he says, "am the Christ."
(St. Melito of Sardis[1])

The final night vision shows obvious similarities with
the first vision (1:7–17). Both focus on groups of colored
horses that go out to patrol the whole earth and both end
with a picture of worldwide rest as the product of God's
sovereign control over world events. Nevertheless, there
are some differences as well. The more incidental ones
involve the presence or absence of chariots, the order of the
horses, and whether the horses are coming in or going out.

However, there are some important differences as well.
The first vision is set in a shaded valley under the cover of
night, whereas the final vision takes place in the mountains
at dawn.[2] The movement from evening to sunrise is an
image of Israel's own journey from darkness to light, from
despair to hope, from being overwhelmed by a nighttime
of defeat to the dawning of a new day of victory. The night
visions have carried Zechariah along, both literally and
figuratively, through the long night of discouragement and
brought him out into a new day where hope is breaking
through with bright rays on the horizon.

THE VISION OF THE FOUR CHARIOTS (6:1–8)

The vision begins with Zechariah once again lifting his
eyes and beholding something surprising. This time he sees
four chariots going out from between two bronze mountains. Chariots immediately evoke martial connotations.

Though they were used for royal travel, they are most often associated with military strength. With the capability of moving swiftly and allowing a soldier to shoot arrows or throw a javelin, chariots gave an army a significant strategic advantage in battle as well as imposing considerable psychological intimidation.

Consequently, the image of a chariot is often used to depict God as the Divine Warrior (Isa. 66:14–16; Jer. 4:13; Hab. 3:8). The royal and military aspects are fused together such that God is pictured as the Great King in battle. For example:

> Bless the LORD, O my soul!
> O LORD my God, you are very great!
> You are clothed with splendor and majesty,
>   covering yourself with light as with a garment,
> stretching out the heavens like a tent.
>   He lays the beams of his chambers on the waters;
>   he makes the clouds his chariot;
> he rides on the wings of the wind. (Ps. 104:1–3 ESV)

The Lord is pictured as the Divine King in royal robes, and the Divine Warrior riding upon the clouds as chariots. God is ready to fight for his people with a heavenly army well stocked with horses and chariots (cf. 2 Kings 6:8–23).

As in many of the night visions, the reconstruction of the temple is the historical backdrop to the imagery invoked. In the vision of the flying scroll (Zech. 5:1–4), the dimensions seem to allude to the dimensions of the portico in Solomon's temple; in this final vision, the bronze mountains seem to allude to the pillars erected there. When Solomon began construction on the first temple, he commissioned Hiram to craft two bronze pillars for the portico, one pillar to the north and one to the south (1 Kings 7:13–22). The two pillars were given the names Jakin, which probably means "he establishes," and Boaz, which probably means "in him is strength." The pillars of bronze were an image of the Lord's stable strength, which emanated from his throne in the temple.

Naturally, this is a fitting allusion for the mountains between which the chariots go out. The image is that of the heavenly temple entrance that leads into the presence of the Lord (see v. 5). From the rebuilt temple, which is the earthly shadow of the heavenly temple, God will exercise his imperial sovereignty over the whole earth in strength and power.

Against its ancient Near Eastern background, the imagery is a strong polemic against the worship of the Mesopotamian sun god in particular. Within the Babylonian-Assyrian pantheon, horses and chariots were iconic for the god Shamash, who was artistically represented as appearing between mountains mounted with gates and adorned with lions.[3] Following the Assyrian conquest of much of Judah, horses and chariots to be dedicated to the sun had been welcomed into the Jerusalem temple, probably by Manasseh and Amon. The implication was political as well as religious: Assyria and her god were the true sovereigns of the world. When Josiah began his reforms, he removed the horses and chariots from the entrance to the temple (2 Kings 23:11), not only as a sign of exclusive worship to the Lord but also as a symbolic denouncement of Assyria's claim to sovereignty.[4]

Zechariah's final vision goes a step further. The imagery is adopted in order to show that the Lord alone is the true sovereign. He is the one who truly has heavenly horses and chariots at his disposal. Power and strength and might are in his hand. Shamash, or any other god for that matter, has no rightful claim of dominion in the world. The Lord alone is in control, and his martial sovereignty will be made known to all as he dispatches his horses and chariots to go out into the world. In fact, the Hebrew word meaning "to go out" (*yts'*) is used seven times in the vision, which "given the symbolic quality of [the number] seven to indicate completion or totality, contributes to the sense of God's total control over the world scene."⁵ Moreover, the designation "the Lord of all the earth" (v. 5), as well as the picture of the horses stampeding out in the four directions of the compass (see below), highlight the spatial comprehensiveness of the Lord's sovereignty.

First, the black horses set off for the land of the north. In the vision of the man with the measuring line, it was clear that the land of the north was a reference to Babylon (2:6; cf. Jer. 6:22; 10:22; 31:8). Though Babylon was not geographically to the north, the availability of water in the Fertile Crescent required advancing armies from the east to attack Israel from the north. Thus, it was the north that became paradigmatic of the place from which Israel's conquerors came since both Assyria and Babylon had advanced from that direction. Moreover, the metaphor of four winds was used to describe the dispersion of the exiles. Now, however, the imagery is used not to describe the humiliation of God's people but to encourage the postexilic community of God's sovereign reign over the entire earth, Babylon included.

Next, the white horses are sent out. Some scholars hold to a straightforward reading of the text that has the white horses being sent out after the black ones. In this reading, the white horses apparently follow the black horses to the land of the north. This would fit well with verse 8, which has the land of the north as its complete focus. Other scholars prefer a slight emendation to the text such that the white horses are sent out to the west. This seems slightly more preferable since the four winds are clearly meant to describe the four directions of the compass, and the horses are sent out specifically to range over all the earth.⁶

Finally, the spotted horses are deployed to the south. Just as the north had certain connotations to the community of God's people, so did the south. The on-again, off-again world power to the south was Egypt. Over the years, Egypt had sometimes been an ally as it was in the days of Solomon (e.g., 1 Kings 3:1). But, the main association in the nation's memory was the Egypt of the exodus, which had become a paradigmatic example of an oppressive adversary (e.g., 1 Kings 8:51). Even just before the exile, the Egyptian Pharaoh Neco was responsible for killing the reforming King Josiah, subordinating Judah under his control for the next four years, and exacting tribute from the people (2 Kings 23:29–35). The announcement that God's martial agents were being dispatched to both the north and the south would have been a signal to the people that God was beginning to fight on their behalf against their traditional enemies.

The deployment of the horses in verses 5–6 presents a couple of oddities. First, the red horses are not mentioned as going out, and the east direction is entirely absent. Yet, clearly the implication of the image is that four chariots drawn by four different colored horses are going in the four different directions. Secondly, as Joyce Baldwin and several other commentators have noted, verse 6 begins with *which*, a word that normally begins a dependent clause and is only rarely found at the beginning of a sentence. The solution that makes the most sense of both peculiarities is that a phrase in the original Hebrew text must have been accidentally dropped in transmission, with the lost phrase being something like "the red horses went towards the east."[7]

After the horses have ranged over the earth, the angel announces their effect. Those who have gone out to the land of the north have caused the Lord's Spirit to rest there. By listing the first country to which the horses are deployed, the angel indicates that if even the most dominant world power (as the Babylonians had previously been) can be conquered, then all other lesser world powers will certainly fall to the Divine Warrior in due time. In other words, "God's subjugation of Babylon and bringing home of many exiles are only a foretaste of the complete and worldwide victory which is to come."[8] When that victory comes, it will be so final that God's Spirit will be able to rest from all military activity.

To the postexilic community such a vision would have given immediate encouragement. The land of the north had painful associations attached to it. The way that the Assyrians and Babylonians had marched into Israel and humiliated the people, looted the land, and razed the cities was not quickly forgotten. Even the mention of it must have opened up mental and emotional wounds. The same would have been true with Egypt to the south. Egypt had been responsible for the enslavement of their forefathers (Ex. 1:11) and the death of their reforming preexilic king, Josiah (2 Kings 23:29). In other words, throughout Israel's history, she had been surrounded by hostile forces from one direction or another. But in the vision of the four chariots, God announces the whole world will come under his dominion. He will subjugate Israel's enemies, reversing the evils that have been perpetrated against his people and bringing about the long-awaited victory.

In the meantime, the postexilic community could go about their tasks of temple construction and community rebuilding free from intimidation. Their history had been replete with examples of Israel being on the losing end of military struggles. They simply were not able to stand up to the firepower of the Assyrians or the Babylonians by their own strength. The Persians had been much more benevolent, but if push came to shove, the postexilic community knew that they had no chance against the military might of the Persian army either. Their reconstruction efforts could be quashed as soon as it was advantageous for the Persians to do so. Yet, they did not have to rely on their own strength, nor did they have to measure their futures by the yardstick of their military might. What they needed to know in their vulnerable hour was that the Divine Warrior was on their side and he had promised to conquer all their enemies in due time. From the divine throne room, he is even now sending out his agents into the world to accomplish his ends. The Persians (or any other military power) did not have the last say in this world; God does. He is sovereign and since his victory is guaranteed, the people could proceed with confident assurance in the temple work God had called them to do.

THE GREAT BATTLE AND
THE GOSPEL OF VICTORY

For half a millennium after Zechariah's night visions, the people of God continued to live in the grip of pagan political powers and their military might. Eventually the Persian regime gave way to the Greeks, and the Greeks gave way to the Romans. Through the centuries, the people grew tired of being ruled by foreign powers. They longed for their God, the Great King, to intervene in the world, conquer the pagans, and set up his everlasting kingdom.

In the early second century B.C., these feelings reached a boiling point during the Maccabean crisis. Pressure mounted for the priest Mattathias to offer sacrifices to pagan gods. In response, he and his sons fled to the Judean hills and organized a movement of freedom fighters ready to resist violently the royal imperative. One of his sons, Judas (the "Maccabee," which likely meant the "Hammer"), took over leadership and after engaging in extensive guerilla warfare, eventually defeated the Syrian forces and restored proper temple service (1 Macc. 2–4).

Under the Roman regime, similar revolts occurred. Judas of Galilee, in the year 6 A.D., rebelled against the Romans for requiring a census tax. Among the extremists, a group which eventually became known as the Zealots, emerged as insurrectionists. Another group, the Sicarii, would often hide daggers in their garments and mix themselves into the crowds during festivals. After getting close to those collaborating with Roman officials, they would attack them and then vanish in the crowd.[9]

For some who believed Jesus was the long-awaited Messiah, such desires shaped their expectations for him and his ministry among them. Many wanted him to pull together a God-empowered militia and overturn their pagan overlords (Matt. 16:21–23; Luke 19:11; Acts 1:6; cf. Luke 17:20). Perhaps that is what initially attracted Simon the Zealot to Jesus. Even the local powers showed apprehension that he might lead a similar revolt to try to overthrow the current power structure (Luke 23:1–3).

Jesus did come to overturn the powers and principalities of this world, but in a way that was unexpected to many. The Gospel of Mark begins with the words, "The beginning of the gospel about Jesus Christ, the Son of God." *Gospel* (*euangellion*) means "good news," but what kind of good news? The answer comes from two important backdrops to the New Testament's usage. One backdrop is the Old Testament and the other is the cultural context of the Roman Empire.[10]

First, in the book of Isaiah, the good news is the announcement that the Lord as King has delivered his people and conquered evil. For instance, "How beautiful upon the mountains are the feet of him who brings good news (*euangelizomenou*), who publishes peace, who brings good news (*euangelizomenos*) of happiness, who publishes salvation, who says to Zion, 'Your God reigns' " (Isa. 52:7 ESV; cf. Isa. 40:9; 60:6; 61:1). In other words, the good news is not a generic message, but a specific and comforting one: God would return to Zion and deliver his people from the hands of their oppressors. It was about the victory for Israel and the defeat of the pagans.

Second, in the Roman world, the good news (*euangelion*) was a term used for one of three things, the declaration of a great victory, the birth of an emperor, or the anniversary of the emperor's accession to the throne. Many times the first and third usages were both in play since an emperor frequently assumed the throne after a military victory.

To say that Jesus' life, ministry, death, and resurrection are a gospel is to say something quite decisive. It means that in Jesus God's victory in the world was at hand. In

Jesus, evil had finally met its match. In Jesus, all the pagan powers were being conquered.

Such a declaration far exceeded the myopic hope of merely a political coup d'état over the Romans. His sights were higher and his mission was cosmic. In his life, Jesus came to defeat the evil that lay behind the Romans and all other pagan regimes. That is why time and time again Jesus rebukes the demons and drives out evil spirits (Matt. 17:18; Mark 1:23–28; Luke 4:31–37). That is why Jesus sends out the disciples to announce that the kingdom of God is at hand and when they return they exclaim that even the demons submit to them in Jesus' name, prompting Jesus to declare that he saw Satan fall like lightning from the sky (Luke 10:1–18). That is why Jesus announces that he has bound the strong man, meaning that he has attacked and overpowered Satan (Luke 11:14–28).

And in his death and resurrection, Jesus dealt a death-blow to Satan and his army of demons. That is why Paul announces that "having disarmed the powers and authorities, he made a public spectacle of them, triumphing over them by the cross" (Col. 2:15 NIV). That is why Paul pictures the cross as the moment when Christ led the enemy powers in triumphal procession, an image from the Roman world of a victorious general leading his captured foe through the cheering crowds back home (2 Cor. 2:14). The final defeat of the forces of evil will only come when Jesus returns, defeats death, and puts all his enemies under his feet (1 Cor. 15:24–26). Then, all creation will be released from the grip of evil and be set free from its bondage (Rom. 8:21).

The most vivid depiction of this coming eschatological victory comes in Revelation, which brings the imagery of Zechariah's horses into full theological bloom. The horses (the white, red, black, and pale horses in Revelation 6:1–8 closely correspond to the red, black, white, and spotted horses in Zechariah 6:1–8) gallop out to roam the whole earth with judgment. The rider of the white horse goes out as a conqueror (white horses were generally associated with military conquest), the rider of the red horse as a remover of peace, the rider of the black horse as the bearer of famine, and the rider of the pale horse as the bringer of death. All the riders are dispatched by the Lamb as instruments of his judgment upon his enemies.[11] Thus, upon his return, Christ will completely fulfill what Zechariah envisioned: the defeat of all hostile forces and the concrete establishment of the everlasting kingdom.

In the meantime, like the postexilic community, we live with the sure and certain hope that our victorious king is on his way. Despite the apparent temporal success of evil in the world, we are reminded that "the destructive forces that human pride and greed unleash into the world are not unseen by God or out of his control. . . . [He] is still sovereign over human events."[12] We too continue with the kingdom work God has given us to do because we are assured that his victory is certain.

And if that is so, what would it mean for us if we stopped dwelling so much on the difficulties we face and started focusing more on the triumph that he's won, is winning, and will finally win? What would it mean to lift up our eyes from the defeats around us to the victory he has assured for us? What would it mean to look beyond the struggles that weigh us down to the conquest that awaits? We need not be intimidated or dismayed by the apparent victory of evil around us because we know that in Christ we have become more than conquerors (Rom. 8:37), and we are even now being led in triumphal procession (2 Cor. 2:14), always believing with confidence that our God will soon crush Satan under our feet (Rom. 16:20).

FOR FURTHER REFLECTION

1. In what ways did the postexilic community live in the grip of pagan political powers and their military might?

2. In what areas today do you see pagan forces "winning" in the world?
3. In what ways are God's people trampled down through political strength and military might today?
4. How does Jesus signal the victory of God over pagan forces?
5. What will his victory look like when he comes again?
6. As you look at the world around you, where do you need to be reminded that God will ultimately be victorious?

PART THREE

EPILOGUE TO THE
NIGHT VISIONS

CHAPTER TEN

CROWNS, PRIEST, BRANCH, TEMPLE (6:9–15)

The word of the Lord came to me, saying, "Take from the exiles who have come from Babylon—Heldai, Tobijah, and Jedaiah—and go on that same day to the house of Josiah, son of Zephaniah, and take their silver and gold and make crowns. Then, place one on the head of the high priest Joshua, son of Jehozadak, and say to him, 'Thus says the Lord of hosts, "Behold, a man whose name is Branch. From his place he will branch out and build the temple of the Lord. He is the one who will build the temple of the Lord. He will assume majesty. He will sit on his throne and rule. Thus, there will be a priest on his throne and there will be the counsel of peace between the two offices. The crown will serve as a memorial to Helem, Tobijah, Jedaiah, and Hen son of Zephaniah, in the temple of the Lord. Then those from far away will come and will help build the temple of the Lord."' And you will know that the Lord of hosts has sent me to you—if only you will diligently obey the Lord your God." (Zechariah 6:9–15)

For Christ is King, and Priest, and God, and Lord, and angel, and man, and captain, and stone, and a Son

born, and first made subject to suffering, then returning
to heaven, and again with glory, and He is preached as
having the everlasting kingdom.
(Justin Martyr[1])

The oracular epilogue in Zechariah 6:9–15 answers a
question raised in the preceding visions. As encouraging
as the night visions are, there is still the harsh reality of
the present. The monarchy had not yet been restored,
and the glory of a restored kingdom must have seemed
little more than a distant and dim dream. Thus a word
comes from the Lord to Zechariah explaining how things
will unfold—or better, through whom they will unfold—
and encouraging the people to wait expectantly and to
respond faithfully.

A CROWN FOR JOSHUA; A CROWN
FOR THE BRANCH (6:9–15)

The word of the Lord comes to Zechariah and instructs
him to receive silver and gold from a group of envoys who
have brought monetary contributions from the Jewish community still living in Babylon. The arrangement is difficult
to figure out. Either Zechariah is told to go to the house
of Josiah, son of Zephaniah, where he will find three men
who have come from Babylon to bring him silver and gold,
or he is supposed to meet the three men and receive their
gifts and then go to Josiah's house afterward. In either case,
the bringing of gold and silver from a foreign land calls to
mind the Hebrews despoiling the Egyptians on their way
out of Egypt.[2] The bringing of gold and silver will again
precede a new phase of God's redemptive intervention on
behalf of his people (cf. Isa. 60:4–7, 17). Just as he miraculously brought them out of the slavery in Egypt, now he
promises to rescue them from the wreckage of the exile
and its ongoing effects.

126

The three men Zechariah is to meet are Heldai, Tobijah, and Jedaiah. There has been much speculation about who these men were and why they in particular might have been mentioned, but ultimately their identities are uncertain. The Septuagint translates their names as symbolic descriptions, not as proper nouns. All we really know about them is that they have come back from exile as delegates with silver and gold, which Zechariah is told he will need when he arrives at the house of Josiah, son of Zephaniah.

The identity of Josiah is also uncertain, though more clues are given. First, his lineage is recorded, suggesting that he was from an important family. Second, the fact that a ceremony of high symbolic importance is to take place in his house suggests that he occupies a significant role within the postexilic community. Based on these two clues, it is quite possible that Josiah is a priest descended from the Zephaniah mentioned in 2 Kings 25:18 who was the second ranking priest at the time of the exile. Moreover, if Josiah is the second ranking priest within the community as his ancestor was, it would explain why his house was an appropriate place to conduct a symbolic ceremony.[3]

Upon receiving the contributions, Zechariah is instructed to take the silver and the gold and to make crown(s). At this point, a difficulty arises. The word translated "crown" (*'trth*) in most English translations is actually a plural form. Some argue that only one crown is in view. This is typically done either by emending the text to a singular form or by arguing that several ringlets (hence the plural form) are fashioned into one composite crown (as in Job 31:36). Others have argued that the plural form should be respected and that Zechariah does in fact make two crowns, the first for Joshua and the second for the Branch. Those arguing for two crowns in the passage also divide between those who identify the Branch with Joshua's contemporary, Zerubbabel, and those who see it as referring to a future, yet-to-be-identified messianic king.

On the question of whether there was one crown or two crowns, it is important to note that the text-critical evidence is overwhelmingly in favor of the plural form.[4] Furthermore, in the ancient Near East, crowns for both priests and kings were generally made from one metal, not two, meaning that the specification of two different metals being used likely means that more than one crown was being fashioned.[5] Thus, two crowns—one silver and one gold—seem to be prescribed, one for Joshua and one for the unidentified Branch.

The question then becomes whether the second crown, which is designated for the Branch, was intended for Zerubbabel in the present or for an anonymous messianic figure in the future. Those who argue for the former typically do so on the grounds that Zechariah 4:6b–10a explicitly designates Zerubbabel as the one who will build the temple. Since that endeavor is said to be carried out by the Branch in this passage (v. 12b, 13a), then Zerubbabel must be the Branch. The absence of Zerubbabel's name in the current passage is then explained as the result of a later redaction. This argument claims that the second crown was originally intended for Zerubbabel but had to be edited out for political reasons (such as the forceful removal of Zerubbabel by the Persians amid rumblings that he might restore the monarchy). But this hardly makes sense since Zerubbabel is mentioned by name in Zechariah 4. If he needed to be edited out for political reasons, we should expect to see his name absent from the book entirely. On the other hand, those who argue that the Branch is a future messiah typically point to the unfeasibility of restoring the monarchy under Persian rule. But the stifling potential of Persian rule "would hardly have carried much weight with a prophet who relied not on power or might but on the spirit of the Lord."[6]

Perhaps the best way to resolve the problem begins with the recognition that the reference to the Branch was somewhat vague to begin with and probably intentionally so. It would be hard to imagine that there weren't many in the postexilic community who held out hope that Zerubbabel would prove to be the messiah and restore the Davidic line. His Davidic lineage and his work on the temple would have made such a hope at least promising. But history closed the door on this possibility, making clear that the anonymous Branch, though in some ways like Zerubbabel, was still a yet-to-be-identified messianic king who would come in the future. Further confirming this view is the fact that the only other passage in Zechariah that refers to the Branch identifies him as a future being (Zech. 3:8). This temporal designation simply cannot refer to Zerubbabel who, according to Ezra 2–5, had been living in Jerusalem for almost two decades!

Returning to the two crowns we find that they are related. When the first crown is set upon Joshua's head, it is to be a symbolic act that points ahead to the future coronation of the messianic Branch. When Zechariah places the first crown upon Joshua, he is to say, "Thus says the Lord of hosts, 'Behold, a man whose name is Branch. From his place he will branch out and build the temple of the Lord. He is the one who will build the temple of the Lord. He will assume majesty. He will sit on his throne and rule'" (vv. 12–13a). In other words, the coronation of Joshua in the present is a symbolic promise of the coronation of the coming Branch in the future.

As to his identity, two passages from Jeremiah seem to be in the background.

> Behold, the days are coming, declares the Lord, when I will raise up for David a righteous Branch, and he shall reign as king and deal wisely, and shall execute justice and righteousness in the land. (Jer. 23:5 esv)

> In those days and at that time I will cause a righteous Branch to spring up for David, and he shall execute

justice and righteousness in the land. (Jer. 33:15
ESV; cf. Isa. 11:1)

In the light of its larger context, the second passage promises that a descendent of David, described as the Branch,
will sit on the throne. Under his leadership, the Lord will
restore the fortunes of exiled Judah and establish justice,
righteousness, and security in the land.

Building upon this tradition, the oracle in Zechariah 6
indicates that the Branch will emerge from the Davidic line
and will do three things when he comes. First, he will be the
one who will build the temple. Since the construction project
is described as something still in the future, it was likely an
eschatological event of which the present temple construction
was only a shadow.[7] Second, the Branch will assume majesty
that is characteristic of the royal office, either of a human king
(as in Ps. 45:4) or the Divine King (as in Ps. 104:1). Third,
he will sit on his throne and rule in the restored kingdom.

In the future, the prerogative of temple building will
pass back to the royal office. In the postexilic community,
the priests were the leaders of the reconstruction effort.
Hence, Joshua the high priest is the appropriate figure for
the symbolic coronation. But, in the eschatological kingdom, the roles will go back to the way things were before
the exile, when David and his son Solomon spearheaded
the temple building effort.

The postexilic community might have wondered whether
the priests would feel displaced and stripped of power
when the Branch arrives. But the oracle makes clear that
there will be a "counsel of peace" between the offices of
the monarchy and the priesthood. The reason that harmony
will exist is because the Branch will actually "fuse" the
two offices together. As the oracle says, "There will be a
priest on his throne and there will be the counsel of peace
between the two offices."

The idea of a priest sitting on the throne would have
been so peculiar to ancient readers that some have balked at

the possibility that verse 13 could actually be saying such a thing. To make the text less outrageous, a substitute reading of verse 13 is sometimes introduced so that "on his throne" becomes "by his throne" or "on his right hand." Yet, as shocking as it may have appeared, the text says precisely that (cf. Ps. 110). In the person of the Branch, the offices of king and priest will come together harmoniously such that the one on the throne is a king and a priest.

Consequently, until such a figure appears, the second crown is placed in the temple to await his arrival (v. 14).[8] In the meantime, it would serve as a memorial within the temple. Kept in the dwelling place of God, it would remind the people that God was with them and that he would send his Davidic Branch, his messiah, to come and establish the kingdom. It would also have the function of memorializing the generosity of Helem, Tobijah, Jedaiah, and Hen son of Zephaniah (likely the same four individuals in verse 10),[9] reminding the people that those far away will have a part to play in the building of the eschatological temple.

But who are those far away? Are they the still-scattered Jewish exiles or are they people from all the nations? In all likelihood, it is the Gentile nations that are in view. The delegates from the exile represent the geographically dis-persed Jews (vv. 10, 13) and since "those far away" (v. 14) seem to be distinct from them, the host of nations seems the most natural candidate. This is reinforced by verses 12–15, which are concerned with a future, eschatological reality that is frequently associated elsewhere with the influx of Gentiles (e.g., Zech. 2:11; cf. Isa. 11:1–11; Hag. 2:6–9).

Yet, before this is realized, a conditional exhortation to the people is attached. The message of promise will be validated in the events of the future only if the people will diligently obey the Lord. The phrase "if only you will diligently obey the Lord your God" is a partial quotation of Deuteronomy 28:1, which lays out the blessings and curses of the covenant (cf. Deut. 11:13, 27; 15:5).[10] In other words, the promise of the Branch is not intended to lull the people into complacency but to draw them back to the heart of God's covenant relationship with them. If he has promised so much for their future, how are they not to render to him obedience in the present? The promise is sure: if the people will seek the Lord in covenant faithfulness, they can be assured that God will sovereignly bring his promises to pass.[11]

A FUSION OF KING AND PRIEST

The series of night visions have lifted the people's eyes to dreams of peace, justice, God's indwelling presence, righteousness, cleansing, and victory. Perhaps the series of night visions, which painted such a hopeful picture of God's coming kingdom, struck some as entirely too idealistic—too good to be true. Who could actually bring these things to pass, and how would they do it? Should they look to Joshua the high priest? Or to Zerubbabel from the royal line of David? Or was a messiah still yet to come? Zechariah 6:9–15 focuses very specifically on the kind of figure that will be able to bring into fulfillment these lofty promises, namely one who fulfills the prerogatives of both king and priest.

Interestingly, in the later Second Temple period, some strands within Judaism (most notably the Essenes at Qumran) began to expect two messiahs. Born out of dissatisfaction with the Hasmonean corruption of both the political and priestly offices, a belief in the necessity of dual reform emerged. There arose an expectation of two messiahs for Israel, one from the royal line of David and one from the priestly line of Aaron.[12] One was "secular," and the other was "sacred." One was "royal" and the other "religious." One was to perform civic duties and the other to perform cultic duties.

In the New Testament, however, both offices are assigned to the person and ministry of Jesus. For instance, at the beginning of his life as the newborn king, he received expensive gifts—gold, frankincense, and myrrh—from the magi who had come from afar (Matt. 2:1–12) just as the crowns in Zechariah 6 were fashioned from gold and silver that were brought from afar. And at the end of his life as high priest, he offers a profound intercessory prayer for his disciples and those who would believe in him through their ministry (John 17). The writer of Hebrews understands Jesus as after the order of Melchizedek for this very reason. Jesus is the greater Melchizedek since he too is both a king of righteousness and a priest of God Most High (Heb. 7:1–28).

But one event more than any other depicts an actual fusion of the royal and priestly roles in Jesus, namely his ascension. Forty days after his resurrection, Jesus visibly went up into the heavens, an act which the New Testament portrays as both a royal coronation and the consummation of his self-sacrificial priestly offering. The ascension of Jesus both establishes his dominion over all his enemies as the true heir of David (Acts 2:34–36; Eph. 4:8; 1 Peter 3:22) and completes his atoning work as a priest for his people (Heb. 4:14–16; 9:11–14, 24–26). Especially telling is the way the writer of Hebrews describes this work of Christ by mingling the two offices together: "When Christ had offered for all time a single sacrifice for sins, he sat down at the right hand of God, waiting from that time until his enemies should be made a footstool for his feet. For by a single offering he has perfected for all time those who are being sanctified" (Heb. 10:12–14 ESV). In a similar vein, Douglas Farrow writes:

> The central notions of kingship and priesthood are here gathered up. . . . For it was chiefly through these two institutions that Israel guarded within its own corporate life the great quest for the rediscovery of human destiny, and kept its bearings for the

journey. . . . It belonged to the nature of cult and monarchy, especially in their central rituals, to point the people of God towards their goal: not simply ascension *over* the nations but ascension from the chaos and contamination of the nations into the presence and blessings of God, and thus into the promised image-bearing dominion over creation. . . . This goal has finally been reached in the person of Jesus—anointed, ascended, and crowned.[13]

This is precisely how the ascension of Jesus fulfills the hopes and dreams of the night visions of Zechariah. The series of pictures had painted what it would mean for the advent of God's kingdom to overcome the forces of chaos and contamination in the world and to soak the earth with the presence and blessings of God. Those hopes were nowhere foreshadowed more clearly in the life of Israel than in the offices of king and priest. The royal office held out hope that God would establish his dominion over the world, a dominion of peace, justice, and righteousness; the priestly office held out hope that God would restore what had been broken by sin, a restoration characterized by God's renewed presence and his cleansing power. At the end of the night visions, Zechariah 6:9-15 suggests that such dreams can only be realized in one who fulfills and harmonizes the promises of both offices. In other words, it points us ahead to the ministry of Jesus Christ who establishes the Kingdom of God and represents his people to God (see 1 Tim. 6:15; Heb. 8:1; Rev. 19:16).

Now, as the true Branch, Jesus builds the eschatological temple—just as Zechariah forecasted—primarily through the resurrection of his own body (John 2:19), but then derivatively in the life of the church as he gathers people together in union with him, builds them into a holy temple, and fills them with the Spirit (1 Cor. 3:16-17; Eph. 2:19-22; 1 Peter 2:4-5). This began on the heels of the ascension when Christ, the true Priest-King, poured out the Holy Spirit upon the church at Pentecost (John 16:7; Acts 2:1-4).

Nevertheless, Zechariah's night visions may still look audacious today and seem too good to be true. A world of peace, justice, righteousness, and purity seems as distant as ever. Many have taken that as proof that Jesus was not who he said he was, that he was not the long-awaited king or the long-needed priest. But this kind of thinking "misses the point. The early Christians knew the world was still a mess. But they announced, like messengers going off on behalf of a global company, that a new CEO had taken charge. They discovered through their own various callings how his new way of running things was to be worked out."[14]

Consequently, the church today, empowered by the Holy Spirit, is called to live out the mission given to her by her ascended Priest-King. This means that the church must strive to avoid both the Scylla of equating the mission of the church with *merely* socio-political change (i.e., only carrying out Christ's royal dominion) and the Charybdis of *merely* trying to save souls with little regard for the state of the world (i.e., only leading people to Christ's priestly work for them).

Just as Jesus fused together the offices of king and priest, so the church must fuse together the call to tackle social and political problems in kingdom-oriented, Christ-honoring ways and the call to point people to the only one who can cleanse them from their sin and reconcile them to God. Visions of peace (Zech. 1:7-17), justice (Zech. 1:18-21), and victory (Zech. 6:1-8) belong together with visions of cleansing (Zech. 3:1-10), purity (Zech. 5:1-11), and God's indwelling presence (Zech. 2:1-13). They are all part of one glorious tapestry in which God in Christ is overcoming and healing a world broken to pieces by sin, evil, and death. That is what is truly glorious about the fusion of the two offices in Christ. As both priest and king, he is the messiah for every problem plaguing our world, our communities, our lives, and ourselves.

FOR FURTHER REFLECTION

1. What problems in the postexilic community needed to be addressed by a faithful high priest?
2. What problems in the postexilic community needed to be addressed by a godly king?
3. In what ways does Jesus fulfill all the hopes of the postexilic community?
4. As you think about the world today, in what ways do the night visions of Zechariah seem too good to be true?
5. How will the fullness of the night visions be realized in Jesus when he comes again?
6. What practical impact should that make on your life presently? How should it change your view of the world?

CHAPTER ELEVEN

FROM FASTING TO FEASTING (7:1–8:23)

Then, in the fourth year of Darius the king, the word of the Lord came to Zechariah on the fourth day of the ninth month, which is Chislev. Now, those from Bethel had sent Sharezer and Regem-melech along with their men to entreat the favor of the Lord by speaking to the priests who serve in the house of the Lord of hosts and to the prophets, "Should I weep in the fifth month, practicing abstinence as I have done all these years?"

Then the word of the Lord of hosts came to me: "Say to all the people of the land and to the priests, 'When you fasted and lamented in the fifth and seventh months these seventy years, was it really for me that you fasted? And when you were eating and drinking, were you not just eating and drinking for yourselves? Were not these the words that the Lord proclaimed through the earlier prophets, back when Jerusalem was inhabited and tranquil and her towns around her and the Negev and the Shephelah were inhabited.' "

Then, the word of the Lord came to Zechariah: "Thus says the Lord of hosts, 'Administer true justice; show kindness and mercy to each other. Do not oppress the

widow or the orphan, the sojourner or the poor. Do
not plot evil in your hearts against each other. But they
refused to pay attention; instead they turned a stubborn
shoulder and a deaf ear. They hardened their hearts like
flint toward the law and the words that the Lord had
sent by his Spirit through the earlier prophets. Thus,
great wrath came from the Lord of hosts. And even as
he called, they would not listen. So, when they called, I
would not listen,' says the Lord of hosts. 'So I scattered
them among all the nations they had not known and
the land left behind them was desolate, with no one
who came or went. That is how they made a delightful
land into a waste.' "

Then, the word of the Lord of hosts came: "I am
exceedingly jealous for Zion and with great intensity am
I jealous for her." Thus says the Lord: "I have returned
to Zion and I will dwell in Jerusalem. And Jerusalem
will be called the city of faithfulness; and the mountain
of the Lord of hosts, the holy mountain." Thus says
the Lord of hosts: "Old men and old women will again
dwell in the commons of Jerusalem, each one with his
staff in his hand because of his great age. And the commons of the city will be full of boys and girls playing in
its commons." Thus says the Lord of hosts: " 'Though
it may seem too wonderful in the eyes of the remnant
of this people in those days, even so would it be too
wonderful in my eyes?' declares the Lord of hosts."
Thus says the Lord of hosts: "Behold! I will deliver my
people from the eastern lands and from the western
lands. And I will bring them back and settle them in
Jerusalem. Then, they will be my people and I will be
their God, in faithfulness and righteousness."

Thus says the Lord of hosts: " 'May your hands be
strong, you who in these days are listening to the words
from the mouths of the prophets who were there when
the foundations of the house of the Lord were laid,
for the rebuilding of the temple. For before those days

there was no wage for man or beast. And for those going in or out, there was no safety from enemies; I set every man against his neighbor. But now I will not treat the remnant of this people as I did in the former days,' declares the Lord. 'For the seed will prosper—the vine will give its fruit; the land will give its produce; the heavens will give their dew—and I will cause the remnant of this people to inherit all these things. And just as you were a curse among the nations, so in the same way, O house of Judah and house of Israel, when I deliver you, you will become a blessing. Do not fear, but let your hands be strong.' " For thus says the Lord of hosts: " 'Just as I purposed to afflict you when your fathers provoked me to wrath,' says the Lord of hosts, 'and I did not relent, so now I have turned and I have purposed in these days to do good to Jerusalem and to the house of Judah. Do not fear. These are the things you are to do: speak the truth, each one to his neighbor. In your gates, render judgments that are true and make for peace. And none of you should devise evil in your hearts against your neighbor or love a false oath, for all these things I hate,' declares the Lord."

And the word of the Lord of hosts came to me: "Thus says the Lord of hosts, 'The fasts of the fourth, fifth, seventh, and tenth months will become times for rejoicing and gladness, happy occasions for the house of Judah. Therefore love truth and peace.' Thus says the Lord of hosts, 'Peoples and inhabitants of many cities will yet come. And the inhabitants of one city will go to another, saying, "Let us go at once to entreat the favor of the Lord, to seek the Lord of hosts. I myself am going." And so many peoples and numerous nations will come to seek the Lord of hosts in Jerusalem, to entreat the favor of the Lord.' Thus says the Lord of hosts, 'In those days, ten men from nations of every tongue will grab hold—they will grab hold of each Jew by the corner of his robe and say, "Let us go with you for we have heard that God is with you!"' "
(Zechariah 7:1–8:23)

At this our solemn feast
let holy joys abound,
and from the inmost breast
let songs of praise resound;
let ancient rites depart,
and all be new around,
in every act, and voice, and heart.

Remember we that eve,
when, the Last Supper spread,
Christ, as we all believe,
the Lamb, with leavenless bread,
among His brethren shared,
and thus the Law obeyed,
of all unto their sire declared.
(St. Thomas Aquinas[1])

The final passage in the first part of Zechariah is a collection of historical reports and sermonic material that are primarily concerned with a question about fasting. The structure of the passage is concentric:

  A. A Question about Fasting (7:1–3)
    B. A Sermon against Hypocrisy (7:4–14)
      X. The Lord's Promise to Transform Jerusalem (8:1–8)
    B' A Sermon on Sincere Obedience (8:9–17)
  A' The Answer: Fasting Will Turn to Feasting (8:18–23)

A QUESTION ABOUT FASTING (7:1–3)

Almost two years have elapsed since Zechariah received the fantastic revelations in the night visions when he receives another word from the Lord (7:1). The date is the fourth day of the ninth month (Chislev) in the fourth year of Darius' reign (December of 518 B.C.).

140

The resumption of work on the temple began a little more than two years ago, but its completion is still more than two years away.

The question that has prompted the new word regards fasting. A delegation of men have come from Bethel[2] (about twelve miles north of Jerusalem) to inquire of the priests and the prophets as to whether they should continue to observe the fifth month fast just as they have become accustomed to doing during the years of the exile (7:2–3).

The fifth month fast had presumably started in reference to the burning of Jerusalem, the destruction of the city walls, and the exile of the people by the Babylonian army on the seventh day of that month (2 Kings 25:8–11). Since that day marked the "death" of the nation, it was only natural to fast and mourn for it during the long years of the exile ("these seventy years" in verse 5).

Now that the reconstruction of the temple was well underway, the people in Bethel were wondering whether they needed to continue these fasts. More to the point, could they set aside their mourning and with joyful anticipation look for the new age to dawn? Was the nation's restoration, so vividly promised by the prophets, just around the corner? So, the delegation asks with a unified voice, "Should I weep in the fifth month, practicing abstinence as I have done all these years?"

A SERMON AGAINST HYPOCRISY (7:4–14)

Instead of providing an answer to their question (that will come later in chapter 8), the Lord initially criticizes the way in which they observed the fasts (7:4–7). Through a series of rhetorical questions, the Lord exposes the lack of sincerity in the peoples' fasting. In doing so, he addresses not only the fast of the fifth month, but the fast of the seventh month as well.

The fast of the seventh month was tied to the assassination of Gedaliah. In the years before the Babylonian exile, an internal debate had raged within Judah as to whether the people should submit to the Babylonians or resist them. The group that favored submission was also known for advocating social reform along the lines of Deuteronomy. Led by the prophet Jeremiah, this group championed the cause of the foreigner, the orphan, and the widow (Jer. 7:5–6; 22:3; cf. Deut. 10:17–19; 24:17–22; 26:12–13; 27:19). Opposed to the reformers was a nationalistic group that believed the Babylonians should be resisted. King Zedekiah belonged to this group (e.g., 2 Kings 24:20). Thus, when the Babylonian army finally breached the walls of Jerusalem, they dealt with Zedekiah harshly for his resistance and freed Jeremiah from prison (Jer. 39:1–14).

In Zedekiah's place, the Babylonians set Gedaliah on the throne as a loyal vassal (Jer. 40:5), but he was quickly assassinated by one of Zedekiah's officers in the seventh month (2 Kings 25:25; Jer. 41:1–3). Since Gedaliah agreed with Jeremiah and others who wanted to bring about social reform (e.g., Jer. 40:7–12), there was great distress among the reformers over Gedaliah's death. In response, a fast in the seventh month was observed to commemorate the failure of the reform efforts within the nation.[3]

Ironically, the Lord points out that their fasting for the failed reform effort had little to do with hearts that were actually reformed. Instead, their fasting in the fifth and seventh months had not been for the Lord, but only for themselves. They had gone through the religious motions of fasting, all the while revealing unreformed hearts by practicing injustice, oppression, and exploitation (vv. 7–10; cf. Isa. 58:1–14). Earlier reform-minded prophets such as Hosea, Micah, and Amos had also denounced hollow religion that showed no concern for the poor and the oppressed. Yet remarkably, even during the exile, the people did not turn from these practices. Their times of fasting were just as self-indulgent as when they were eating and drinking and had nothing to do with contrite hearts. They were concerned with trying to get back what they had lost by doing the "right things" so that God would reverse their circumstances.

For their fasting to be sincere, the people needed to observe the weightier matters of the law as well (7:8–10). As a long line of prophets had urged, they should administer true justice, show kindness and mercy to each other, not oppress the widow, the orphan, the sojourner, or the poor, and shun evil plots against one another (cf. Mic. 6:8). These prescriptions cover the entire range of relationships, from the legal operations within society to personal relationships with each other and are as broad as the margins of society—widows, orphans, sojourners, and the poor. Since neglecting these matters was among the reasons for the exile (7:11–14), to continue to ignore them while supposedly fasting and lamenting for the exile itself was blatant hypocrisy.

To describe the obstinacy of the people, three vivid metaphors are used. First, they have turned a stubborn shoulder. The image is "that of a stubborn ox that will not allow a yoke on its neck (cf. Hos. 4:16)."[4] Possessing an autonomous spirit, they refuse to submit. Second, the people have turned a deaf ear. Literally, they "made their ears heavy" so that they would not hear (cf. Isa. 6:10). Like a child who plugs his ears and yells "I can't hear you," Israel refused to listen to God. Third, they hardened their hearts like flint. Some translations opt for their hearts being like diamond. The sense is that they are almost unbreakably hard. They have become so calloused that virtually nothing can pierce their hearts or consciences.

Therefore, the Lord justly sent his wrath upon the people. He abandoned them and scattered them into exile. Consequently, the land was left as a waste. What once had been described as delightful, a place flowing with milk and honey, spacious with produce-bearing fields and fruit-yielding vineyards (e.g., Num. 13:27; 16:14) was now desolate.

The land was so ruined that, stated hyperbolically, no one could be spotted walking around (cf. Lam. 1:4). In other words, the land had become such a waste that not even roaming sheepherders found it useful.[5]

THE LORD'S PROMISE TO TRANSFORM JERUSALEM (8:1-8)

Nevertheless, despite the people's failure and the punishment for it, the Lord remains jealous for Zion and promises to return and renew her (8:1-2; cf. Zech. 1:14). In one sense, the Lord has already returned. The initial returnees from exile and the beginnings of temple reconstruction have shown that he has returned to Zion. Yet in another sense, his presence would not be fully felt in the city until a future date when the restoration would be complete. Hence, verse 3 uses both past and future tenses: "I have returned to Zion, and I will dwell in Jerusalem."

When that future date arrives, the city will be characterized by faithfulness and holiness. The picture is an idyllic one. The common areas of Jerusalem will be repopulated and full of old men and women sitting while boys and girls run and play (8:3-5; cf. Jer. 30:18-22). Earlier prophets had condemned these very areas as places of injustice and wickedness (Jer. 5:1; Ezek. 16:23-34) and therefore declared that they would become places of destruction at the hands of foreign armies (Jer. 9:21; Amos 5:16; cf. Lam. 2:11-12; 4:18). But now both the wisdom and blessing of old age as well as the energy and vibrancy of youthfulness would be seen in these very same common areas (cf. Isa. 65:17-21).

No doubt that in the early years of reconstruction such a picture would have seemed too wonderful to imagine (8:6). The people were still trying to pick up the pieces and rebuild what had been destroyed by the Babylonians. Yet, as incredible as it might have seemed, the Lord promised that he would bring it to pass. He would gather in his people dispersed throughout the nations and bring them back home to settle them in Jerusalem (8:7).

The motivation to restore and transform Jerusalem ultimately stems from the Lord's commitment to the covenant. Thus, he declares, "they will be my people and I will be their God" (8:8). Jeremiah and Ezekiel had used the very same formula to describe the covenant relationship that the Lord would (re)establish with his people. Such a relationship would have several notable characteristics. First, it would be established by the Lord cleansing the people of their defilement (Ezek. 11:17–18; 37:23). Second, the Lord would give the people a new heart (Jer. 24:7; 32:37–39; Ezek. 11:19). Third, the Lord would impress the law upon their hearts so that they would walk in his ways and obey his commands (Jer. 31:33; Ezek. 11:20).

A SERMON ON SINCERE OBEDIENCE (8:9–17)

God has already begun blessing the people, as could be seen in the work on the temple (8:9). The prophets who were there when the foundations were laid have been telling the people that they were seeing the new age of God's blessing in its embryonic stage. Besides Zechariah, certainly one of the prophets would have been Haggai whose words to the people were pointed but also encouraging.

> In the seventh month, on the twenty-first day of the month, the word of the LORD came by the hand of Haggai the prophet, "Speak now to Zerubbabel the son of Shealtiel, governor of Judah, and to Joshua the son of Jehozadak, the high priest, and to all the remnant of the people, and say, 'Who is left among you who saw this house in its former glory? How do you see it now? Is it not as nothing in your eyes? Yet now be strong, O Zerubbabel, declares the LORD. Be

strong, O Joshua, son of Jehozadak, the high priest. Be strong, all you people of the land, declares the LORD. Work, for I am with you,' declares the LORD of hosts, 'according to the covenant that I made with you when you came out of Egypt. My Spirit remains in your midst. Fear not.'" (Hag. 2:1–5 ESV)

Similarly, the Lord encourages the people through the prophet Zechariah to take courage in the face of adversity. In a direct allusion to the words of Haggai, the people are told twice to let their hands be strong (8:9, 13) and not to fear (8:13, 15). These words are precisely what the people needed to hear. In the intervening years between the return from exile and the beginning of work on the temple, the economy had been depressed and the people faced harassment from their enemies (8:10; cf. Ezra 4:1–5). Nevertheless, though times were tough, they should go about their work boldly, resting their hopes in what God has promised to do in Jerusalem.

As they continue to strengthen their hands and put aside their fears in order to finish the temple, they would find their faithfulness met with God's abundant goodness. Apparently, when the people had failed to get to work on the temple before 520 B.C., God had withheld the dew from the heavens and the crops from the earth (Hag. 1:10–11). Now that the temple was on its way to completion, God had promised to provide great agricultural bounty (8:11–15; cf. Lev. 26:3–13; Deut. 28:1–14). Fruit would once again come from the vine, produce from the fields, and dew from the heavens. Harvests would be abundant and storehouses full.

In terms of their responsibilities toward one another, they are told to put away the hypocrisy that had characterized their fasting. Instead of dealing falsely with one another, they are to speak the truth and not make deceptive oaths. Instead of allowing injustice within their gates (the place within the city where judicial functions were carried out), they are to render judgments that are true and make for peace (8:16–17).

THE ANSWER: FASTING WILL TURN TO FEASTING (8:18–23)

After the Lord criticizes their hypocrisy and encourages them with his promised transformation of Jerusalem, the question brought by the delegation from Bethel in 7:1–3 is finally addressed (8:18–19). But the people are not explicitly told whether or not they should continue to fast in the present. They are only told that their fasting will become unnecessary when the Lord completes his restorative work. Whether or not they continue to fast in the present is ultimately less important than realizing that a new age is on its way.

In this new age that God will establish, not only will the fifth and seventh month fasts be unnecessary, but the fasts in the fourth and tenth months will be needless too. The fast in the fourth month remembered the initial breach in Jerusalem's wall (see 2 Kings 25:3–7) while the fast in the tenth month remembered the onslaught of the siege (see 2 Kings 25:1). In the new age, all four fasts that had been kept through the years of exile will become superfluous. Mourning will give way to dancing and fasting to feasting. The new work of God will prompt exuberant celebration, and there will be no place for sadness anymore. Festivities and feasting will be the order of the day.

As a result, the greatness of Jerusalem, a city of truth and peace, will become magnetic to the nations (8:20–23; cf. Isa. 2:1–4; 66:18–23; Mic. 4:1–4; Zech. 2:10–11). Just as the passage began with a small delegation from Bethel coming to Jerusalem to entreat the favor of the Lord, so the passage ends with all the nations coming to Jerusalem to entreat the favor of the Lord. A trickle has turned into a flood. Peoples from all over will journey to the Holy

City, encouraging others in nearby towns to join them in their pilgrimage. The image employed is especially vivid. Every Jew will have ten Gentiles (a symbol of universality) clamoring to grab hold of his robe. In fact, the root of the Hebrew word for "grab hold" (khzq) in verse 23 is the same as the root for the word for "be strong" in verses 9 and 13, creating a literary connection.[6] As the people's hands are strong as they continue to work on the temple, so their efforts will translate into the hands of the nations grabbing hold of them in order to come to Jerusalem, the location of the temple and the dwelling place of God.

FASTING FOR THE MESSIAH, FEASTING WITH THE MESSIAH

To summarize, the historical notice places these reports and sermons at a time approximately halfway through the temple's reconstruction. Certainly, many expected that when the temple's walls went up, the Lord himself would come down and the new age would dawn. Now that progress had been made, apparently some were beginning to wonder whether the new age was really coming. Thus, Zechariah 7:1–8:23 addresses the pressing question: should we expect an eschatological change to accompany the temple's construction? On the ground level, this meant, should we continue to mourn and fast or is now the time when our mourning will be turned into dancing?

The answer was a yes and a no. Yes, God is on the move; no, he's not finished yet. Yes, a change has taken place, but it is not the cataclysmic transformation of all things that will ultimately only happen at the end of the age. Thus the question of whether they should continue to fast does not have a simple answer. The more important point is that God is on the move and that the people should join in the work. They are to continue their construction efforts on the temple but add to it a heartfelt reformation of their hearts, observing the weightier matters of the law such as justice and mercy.

Like the delegation from Bethel during the temple's reconstruction, people in Jesus' day were asking similar questions about the role of fasting, though this time the focus was not on the practice within the nation but among the disciples of Jesus. People had noticed that the Pharisees fasted twice a week (cf. Luke 18:12) and that John's disciples engaged in the practice, but that the disciples of Jesus did not. Certainly that must have seemed strange given that Jesus himself was clearly not opposed to fasting (Matt. 4:1–2) and assumed that his disciples would fast too (Matt. 6:16–18). So why weren't the disciples of Jesus fasting?

In response, Jesus told them,

> Can the wedding guests fast while the bridegroom is with them? As long as they have the bridegroom with them, they cannot fast. The days will come when the bridegroom is taken away from them, and then they will fast in that day. No one sews a piece of unshrunk cloth on an old garment. If he does, the patch tears away from it, the new from the old, and a worse tear is made. And no one puts new wine into old wineskins. If he does, the wine will burst the skins—and the wine is destroyed, and so are the skins. But new wine is for fresh wineskins. (Mark 2:19–22 ESV)

In other words, the reason that Jesus' disciples had stopped fasting was because in Jesus something cataclysmic was happening. Just as a new piece of cloth won't fit with an old garment, so what is happening in and through Jesus simply won't fit with the old ways of doing things. And just as putting new wine in old wineskins will simply burst the skins, so what is happening in and through Jesus is so dramatic and pivotal that it will explode the old patterns and practices.

What was happening was that God was on the move; in Jesus, the eschatological kingdom had arrived. The new had moved in on the old. The bridegroom had returned. Just as the appearance of a bridegroom at a wedding sparked celebration for it brought to fulfillment the hopes and longings of the bride, so Jesus' appearance on the stage of history meant that the time of fulfillment was at hand and the only reasonable response from those who recognized it was celebration. The delegation from Bethel had wondered if the eschatological change was about to happen; in Jesus, it really was happening.

The implications for the question of fasting were important. Most fasts, as indicated in Zechariah 7–8, were associated with tragedies within the history of Israel, not least the destruction of Jerusalem and the temple by the Babylonians. In all likelihood, there was an added belief that fasting was "an expression of repentance designed specifically to hasten the coming of the time of redemption."[7] The restoration of the temple was a move toward that time of redemption. But in Jesus, God was finally fulfilling all that the temple had pointed to in the first place. God was coming to dwell among them and to save them. Such a time of restoration should be a cause for celebration, not for mourning. On the great eschatological day of salvation, the only appropriate thing to do is to feast (Matt. 8:11; Luke 13:29; 14:15; 22:30; Rev. 19:9). And since it was arriving in Jesus, it would have been entirely inappropriate for the disciples to fast.

At the same time, and no doubt to the surprise of the disciples, the transition from the old to the new would not be without a wrinkle. Jesus even tells them that there would be a time when he would be taken away from them. At such a time, they will mourn and then fasting would again be appropriate as they wait for his return (Matt. 9:15).

But Jesus does not just leave his disciples to fast when he is taken away from them. Instead, he leaves them with a meal of his ongoing presence. He gives them a feast to sustain them while they wait for his return. At the Passover (a great feast day in the history of Israel), just before his crucifixion, Jesus sat around the table with his disciples, breaking bread and sharing the cup with them. As they feasted, Jesus told them that the meal they were sharing was an emblem of the kingdom of God in their midst and the establishment of the new covenant (Luke 22:14–23; cf. Zech. 8:8). Though he was about to leave them, they would have a feast to nourish them in his absence and to prepare them for the coming feast when he returns (1 Cor. 11:23–26; Rev. 19:9).

So, like the delegation from Bethel, we too may sometimes wonder whether we are really living in the days of an eschatological transition. We may look around at our world and wonder why things don't look more new than old, more transformed than untouched. And likewise, we may then wonder whether we should fast or feast. The answer of course is yes. We should fast and we should feast. We fast because the bridegroom has gone away and we long for his reappearance. We long, just as those in Zechariah's day, for God to intervene in history once again and for the eschatological reality so vividly portrayed in the night visions to become concrete in our world. The only appropriate expression for that is fasting. As we do so, the important point to remember is that God is on the move and that we should join in the kingdom work he has given us to do. In our day, as in Zechariah's, that means that we must give sincere obedience from the heart and attend to the weightier matters of the law such as justice and mercy (James 1:22–27).

Yet in the meantime, there should also be feasting. At the Lord's Supper, we gather around the table and we feast. Looking backwards, we feast because in Jesus the eschatological day has already dawned. It may not be a fully concrete reality, but it is real nonetheless. Looking forward, we feast at the Lord's Table because we long for God and we anxiously anticipate the day when he returns, and we sit around the table with him in the Kingdom.

At present we feast because it nourishes us for the task of joining God in his kingdom-building efforts. As we seek to obey from the heart, work for justice in our world, and show mercy to those in need, feasting at the Lord's Table becomes an indispensable part of kingdom living. As the Russian liturgist Alexander Schmemann beautifully describes,

> [the Eucharist] is the journey of the Church into the dimension of the Kingdom. . . . It is not an escape from the world, rather it is the arrival at a vantage point from which we can see more deeply into the reality of the world . . . [and] become partakers of the world to come. But this is not an "other" world, different from the one God has created and given to us. It is our same world, *already* perfected in Christ, but *not yet* in us. It is our same world, redeemed and restored, in which Christ "fills all things with Himself.". . . Intercession begins here, in the glory of the messianic banquet, and this is the only true beginning for the Church's mission.[8]

In other words, the Lord's Supper is a feast with the Messiah that gives us a taste of what this world will be when his kingdom comes fully on earth as it is in heaven and strengthens us to join in God's kingdom-building efforts toward that end.

We fast for Jesus because he has gone away, and we also fast because we long for him to come again. Yet, at the very same time we feast with him while we wait. We feast because he has come; we feast because he will come again; and we feast because in him God is still on the move, transforming our world from a place of mourning to a place of dancing, from a place of sadness to a place of joy, from a place of temporary fasting to a place of eternal feasting.

FOR FURTHER REFLECTION

1. With the temple being built should the postexilic community have fasted, feasted, or both? Why?
2. What are evidences in the world, in history, and in your own life that in Jesus a cataclysmic change has happened?
3. How might both fasting and feasting be applied in your own life as you seek to join in God's kingdom-building efforts?

PART FOUR

THE APOCALYPTIC VISIONS

CHAPTER TWELVE

THE COMING KING (9:1–11:3)

The burden of the word of the Lord against the land
of Hadrach and Damascus is its resting place—for the
Lord's eyes are on all men as on the tribes of Israel
–and also Hamath which borders on it, and Tyre and
Sidon, though they are very wise. For Tyre has built
siege-works for herself and has amassed silver like dust
and gold like the mud in the streets. But behold, the
Lord will strip away her possessions and strike down
her forces at sea, and she will be devoured by fire.
Ashkelon will see it and fear; Gaza will writhe in great
anguish and Ekron will have its hopes dashed. The king
will perish from Gaza and Ashkelon will be uninhabited. And bastard children will dwell in Ashdod. And
I will cut off the pride of Philistia. And I will clean out
the blood from its mouth and the detestable things from
between its teeth. The ones left over will belong to our
God. They will be like a clan in Judah, and Ekron like
the Jebusites. And I will encamp in my House against
any army who would come or go against them. No
longer will any oppressor overrun them again, for now
I watch over them with my own eyes.

Rejoice greatly, O daughter of Zion! Raise a shout, O
daughter of Jerusalem! For behold, your king is coming to you, righteous and bearing salvation is he, yet

humble and riding on a donkey, on a colt, the foal of a
donkey. And I will cut off the chariot from Ephraim and
the horse from Jerusalem. And the bow of combat will
be cut off for he will speak peace to the nations. His
rule will extend from sea to sea, and from the river to
the ends of the earth.

As for you, because of the blood of your covenant,
I have freed your prisoners from the waterless pit.
Return to your stronghold, O prisoners of hope! Even
today I declare that I will return to you double. For
I have bent Judah to me as a bow and have fitted it
with Ephraim. I will rouse your sons, O Zion, against
your sons, O Greece. And I will use you like a warrior's sword. Then the Lord will appear over them and
his arrow will go forth like lightning. And the Lord
God will blow the battle horn and march out in the
whirlwinds of the south. The Lord of hosts will protect them; they will consume and overcome the sling-
stones. Then they will drink and be boisterous as with
wine; they will be full like a bowl, like the corners
of an altar. On that day, the Lord their God will save
them, as the flock of his people. For they will be like
the crown jewels, sparkling in his land. For how great
is his goodness and his beauty! Grain will make the
young men flourish and new wine the young women.

Ask the Lord for rain in the season of the spring-rain—
the Lord is the one who makes the storm clouds—and
he will give rain showers to them, vegetation in the
field for everyone. For the teraphim speak wickedness;
the diviners see deceptive visions, speak false dreams,
and provide empty comfort. Therefore, the people stray
like a flock, suffering the lack of a shepherd. "My anger
burns against the shepherds and I will punish the male
goats, for the Lord of hosts attends to his flock, the
house of Judah, and he will make them like his majestic
horse in battle. From them will come the cornerstone,
from them the tent peg, from them the bow of combat,

and from them every general will go out together. And
they will be like mighty warriors in battle, trampling
the muddy streets in battle. And they will do battle,
for the Lord is with them, and they will put horsemen
to shame. And I will strengthen the house of Judah
and save the house of Joseph. I will bring them back
because I have compassion on them. Then they will be
as though I had never rejected them, for I am the Lord
their God and I will answer them. Then Ephraim will
be like a mighty warrior, and their hearts will be joyful
as with wine. Their children will see it and be joyful.
Their hearts will rejoice in the Lord. I will whistle to
them and gather them in, for I have redeemed them.
Thus, they will become as numerous as they were
before. Though I scattered them among the peoples,
yet in distant places they will remember me and, with
their children, will survive and return. I will bring them
back from the land of Egypt and I will gather them from
Assyria and I will bring them to the land of Gilead and
to Lebanon until there is no more room for them. And
he will pass through the sea of distress and strike down
the waves of the sea, such that all the depths of the Nile
dry up. Thus, he will bring down the pride of Assyria
and the scepter of Egypt will pass away. And I will
strengthen them in the Lord and in his name they will
walk," declares the Lord. Open your doors, O Lebanon!
Let fire consume your cedars! Howl, O cypress, for the
cedar has fallen; the majestic ones are destroyed! Howl,
O oaks of Bashan, for the impenetrable forest has come
down! Listen to the howling of the shepherds, for their
glory is destroyed; listen to the roaring of the lions, for
the lush banks of the Jordan are destroyed. (Zechariah
9:1–11:3)

With regard to Christ, the law and the prophets and
the evangelists have proclaimed that He was born of a
virgin, that He suffered upon a beam of wood, and that
He appeared from the dead; that He also ascended to
the heavens, and was glorified by the Father, and is the
Eternal King. (St. Irenaeus of Lyons[1])

In the second half of the book of Zechariah, the first major section runs from 9:1 through 11:3. Though the passage contains small, self-contained units, the group is held together by a progression of thought that develops within the section. The dominant theme is the Lord's future royal triumph over the nations for the sake of his people.[2]

THE LORD WILL JUDGE ISRAEL'S ENEMIES (9:1–8)

The initial unit of the oracle begins with a catalog of judgments against Israel's enemies, much like other passages in the prophetic corpus (e.g., Isa. 13–23; Jer. 46–51; Ezek. 25–32; Amos 1:3–2:3; Zeph. 2). In fact, the passage alludes numerous times to Amos' words.

Thus says the LORD:

"For three transgressions of Damascus,
    and for four, I will not revoke the punishment,
because they have threshed Gilead
    with threshing sledges of iron.
So I will send a fire upon the house of Hazael,
    and it shall devour the strongholds of Ben-hadad.
I will break the gate-bar of Damascus,
    and cut off the inhabitants from the Valley of Aven,
and him who holds the scepter from Beth-eden;
    and the people of Syria shall go into exile to Kir,"
                        says the LORD.

Thus says the LORD:

"For three transgressions of Gaza,
    and for four, I will not revoke the punishment,
because they carried into exile a whole people
    to deliver them up to Edom.

160

So I will send a fire upon the wall of Gaza,
 and it shall devour her strongholds.
I will cut off the inhabitants from Ashdod,
 and him who holds the scepter from Ashkelon;
I will turn my hand against Ekron,
 and the remnant of the Philistines shall perish,"
    says the Lord GOD.

Thus says the LORD:

 "For three transgressions of Tyre,
  and for four, I will not revoke the punishment,
 because they delivered up a whole people to Edom,
  and did not remember the covenant of
    brotherhood.
So I will send a fire upon the wall of Tyre,
 and it shall devour her strongholds."
   (Amos 1:3–10 ESV)

Like Amos, Zechariah 9:1–8 begins with a short pronouncement of judgment against cities in Syria—Hadrach,
Damascus, and Hamath—to the north. Then, turning his
attention to the northern coastal region, the prophet first
addresses the Phoenician cities of Tyre and Sidon before
turning to the three Philistine cities to the southwest.

Tyre and Sidon are criticized despite their reputation
for wisdom, and Tyre is singled out for two particular
condemnations (v. 3). First, she has "built siege-works."
In the tenth century B.C., Tyre built defense ramparts that
were 820 yards long and 9 yards thick to fortify the city
(cf. 2 Sam. 24:7).[3] As a result, Tyre had proved especially
resilient to enemy attacks (e.g., Ezek. 29:18). Thus, because
of her great engineering skill, Tyre was proud and self-
confident in her military strength, seeing herself as practically
unassailable (cf. Isa. 23:9; Ezek. 27:3; 28:2, 6). Second, she
has "amassed silver like dust and gold like the mud in
the streets." As a prominent commercial port, Tyre had

accumulated excessive wealth. Consequently, the Lord promises to strike her at the very sources of her pride, her military self-confidence and her shameless materialism. Verse 4 announces the judgment in the reverse order of the accusations in verse 3, suggesting the poetic reversal of Tyre's fortunes. The Lord will strip away her possessions and destroy her naval power. In the end, she will be devoured by fire (cf. Amos 1:9–10).

At the sight of mighty Tyre's destruction, the Philistine cities of Ashkelon, Gaza, and Ekron will tremble (vv. 5–6; cf. Amos 1:6–8). Fear, anguish, and hopelessness will consume them, and with good reason. The monarchy will perish from Gaza, Ashkelon will find itself uninhabited, and Ashdod will only have a population of bastard children. The Hebrew word for "bastard children" (*mamzer*) is used elsewhere only in Deuteronomy 23:2, where it denotes an illegitimate birth from a mixed marriage. The fate of Ashkelon is even worse; she will become depopulated. Gaza will lose its royal house. The loss of kings in Philistia only makes sense in light of the larger emphasis on God's coming universal reign. When God's rule is established over the whole earth, other competing kingships will naturally fall along with their adversarial kingdoms.

Historically, none of the cities mentioned here posed any significant threat to Yehud during the postexilic period. At various times before the Assyrian and Babylonian exiles, Philistia and Syria had troubled Israel, and Tyre had long been notorious for her wealth and pride. But all of them had succumbed to larger powers, whether Babylonian or Assyrian. Thus, their use here is not so much a prophecy of something yet to occur, but a usage of past events to illustrate the supreme conquering power of the Lord in the future when these cities would not just be conquered by men but by the Lord himself. Just as Nebuchadnezzar and his army marched commandingly, conquering cities and nations, so with even greater ease and might will the Lord conquer the world.

When he does, the conquest begun under Joshua's leadership will finally be complete. When Joshua reached old age, there was still much land that had not been taken. Therefore, the Lord promised that he himself would drive out the remaining peoples before Israel. Among those cities still to be conquered were Ashdod, Ashkelon, and Gaza (Josh. 13:1–7). These cities were designated as belonging to Judah even though they were not presently under her control (Josh. 15:45–47). The oracles in Zechariah 9 give assurance that the Lord will finish the conquest and conquer these Philistine cities. But this first unit concludes with a surprise.

Instead of judgment and conquest, cleansing and ingrafting are the last word (v. 7). The promise that the Lord will clean out the blood from Philistia's mouth and the detestable things from between its teeth is a reference to the practices of eating bloody animal flesh and unclean meat, practices considered by the Israelites to be both repulsive and unlawful (Lev. 11:1–24a; 19:26).[4] As a result of the Lord's cleansing of Philistia, he will actually take those who are left over, and they will become his people. The successive allusions to Amos 1 up to this point now produce a powerfully ironic twist. Amos had declared that the remnant of the Philistines would perish under the Lord's judgment, but now there is hope. The Philistine remnant will be saved. They will even be like a clan in Judah.

Hopeless Ekron is promised a similarly bright future. She will become like the Jebusites. When the Israelites first entered the land, the Jebusites were a people living in Jerusalem. The Israelites were unable to dislodge them, and so the Jebusites continued to live alongside the Israelites for generations (see Josh. 15:63; Judg. 1:21). Not until David fully conquered Jerusalem did the Israelites subjugate them and incorporate them into the community (1 Chron. 11:4–7). Therefore, the promise that Ekron will become like the Jebusites not only recalls another example of a former adversary eventually becoming part of the people of God, it also subtly picks up the context: when a king like David arrives on the scene, foreign peoples will not only cease overrunning God's people (v. 8), but will actually be subjugated and grafted into God's family!

A KING WILL COME (9:9–10)

There is cause for great rejoicing because a king is coming (vv. 9–10; cf. Zeph. 3:14–15)![5] First, the king's character is described. More than anything else, he will be known for his righteousness (*tsadiq*). Earlier in Israel's history the ideal king's "righteousness" was typically paired with "justice" (*mishpat*) as a royal idiom for showing special concern for the poor and the oppressed (e.g., Ps. 72:1; Isa. 32:1; Jer. 23:5).[6] In other words, describing a king as righteous meant that he would not only execute justice, govern faithfully, and live with integrity, but also deliver the oppressed and generously support the weak and the poor. In doing so, he would reflect the Lord himself since the Lord shows a special consideration and solidarity with the poor and the marginalized (Ex. 22:21–24; 1 Sam. 2:8; Prov. 14:31; 17:5; Isa. 11:4; Amos 8:1–14). In the postexilic years the concept was deepened such that righteousness was more typically coupled with the notion of covenant faithfulness (*hesed*).[7] The description of the coming king in Zechariah 9:9 as righteous implies that he will be everything Israel and her monarchy were called to be but were not. He will be upright, compassionate, just, merciful, and faithful.

Furthermore, in a number of places the term *righteous* and its cognates occur in salvation contexts, such as Isaiah 40–55, where the restoration promises given to exilic Israel hold out a future in which she will finally be delivered. In such contexts, the term *righteous* is used both to describe the vindication of Israel (Isa. 43:26; 45:25; 50:8) and the faithfulness of God in working salvation (Isa. 41:10; 45:8, 13; 51:5). The two uses climax in the suffering servant, the

Righteous One, who bears the iniquity of the nation only to be vindicated in the end (Isa. 53:11).

With Isaiah 40–55 in the background, it is not surprising that the attribute of righteousness in Zechariah 9:9 is paired with the descriptions that he will bear salvation. The Hebrew word translated as "bearing salvation" (*nosha'*) is passive ("to be saved" or "to be vindicated"), meaning that when he comes bearing salvation, he does not come as one "holding salvation in his hand," but as one who receives salvation. He himself will experience the saving work of God. Like the suffering servant in Isaiah, the coming king of Zechariah 9, though righteous, will undergo an ordeal in which he will experience God's vindication of him. Thus he not only will be characterized by righteousness, but also humility. He is so humble that he will ride "on a donkey, on a colt, the foal of a donkey." Though kings sometimes rode horses and chariots in times of war as a sign of their regal stature and military prowess (Jer. 17:19–25), the custom was to ride donkeys for normal royal functions (cf. Gen. 49:10–11; 2 Sam. 16:2; 17:23; 1 Kings 1:33–38).[8] What sets this king apart is that when he comes riding on a donkey he does so not in worldly power or status, but in meekness and humility.

Second, the king's accomplishments are described. He does not wield the sword but comes as one who, in his humility, is utterly dependent on the Lord to establish worldwide dominion.[9] Through him the Lord will cut off the chariot from Ephraim and the bow of combat from Jerusalem. Both the northern and southern kingdoms will be reunited (cf. Ezek. 36–37) and will no longer need to be at war, neither with each other nor with the surrounding nations. International and intra-national peace will be the order of the day.

But the peace that the king will bring is not merely the absence of conflict. The meaning of peace (*shalom*) is much more robust. It carries with it a sense of harmony, wholeness, and blessedness. Upon the king's advent, he will bring this kind of peace to the nations. And not only will he speak peace to the nations, but his dominion will be worldwide as described in Psalm 72:8: "his rule will extend from sea to sea, and from the river to the ends of the earth." Like Solomon, to whom the psalm is attributed, the coming royal son of David will issue in another golden age of God's rule on the earth in which the boundaries of his dominion will be limitless.

THE LORD WILL FIGHT FOR HIS PEOPLE (9:11-17)

During this process of establishing peace, the Lord will demonstrate his faithfulness to the covenant and rescue Israel (v. 11; cf. Ex. 24:8). The deliverance is described as being freed from the waterless pit, an image that recalls Joseph's deliverance from a well (Gen. 37:23–28) and Jeremiah's rescue from a cistern (Jer. 38:1–13). In the Psalms, the image is expanded to include a restoration from the grave, or Sheol (Pss. 30:3; 40:2; 103:4). In all cases, being delivered from the pit means to have one's life snatched from the jaws of death.

In the nation's history, the "pit" was of course the exile. Israel had undergone a kind of death, and the exiles had become like prisoners of a dungeon (cf. Isa. 42:7). Yet, because of the Lord's promised intervention, they are no longer prisoners of the pit, but prisoners of hope (v. 12a). And their hope is firmly in the Lord's covenant faithfulness, for he would restore them, even returning to them double (v. 12). During the exile, the people had received a double portion of punishment from the Lord's hands (Isa. 40:2), but now the compensation would be proportional. The postexilic community was now promised to receive back double from the Lord's hands (Isa. 61:7).

To accomplish this, the Lord declares that he will fight for his people and that he will use them to do it. The southern kingdom (Judah) and the northern kingdom (Ephraim) will become "weapons" in the Lord's hands as he goes to war. Judah will be like an archer's bow in the hand of the Lord and Ephraim like the arrows notched in the bow and pulled back in preparation to shoot.[10] The sons of Zion will be like a warrior's sword against the sons of Greece.[11] With them in hand, the Lord will march out to battle with frightening power and strength against the powers of the world. His appearance on the battlefield is marked by visions of lightning, sounds of a battle horn, and the feel of storm clouds (v. 14; cf. Ex. 19:16–17; 2 Sam. 22:14–15).

At the battle's end, the people will have cause to rejoice over the goodness and beauty, the power and might, of their Divine Warrior. In celebration of his victory on their behalf, the people will consume the sling stones used against them in battle and become boisterous as those drunk with wine and as full of alcohol as the corners of the altar are of blood (v. 15). As they flock under his care, the people will be like crown jewels, flourishing with the prosperity of grain and new wine (vv. 16–17; cf. Isa. 62:1–3).

THE LORD WILL TURN THE WORLD
UPSIDE DOWN (10:1–11:3)

For that coming prosperity to be realized rain was needed. Recently there had been a drought (Hag. 1:10–11), and perhaps the temptation to turn to other gods was strong within the community. Such a temptation would not have been new. Throughout Israel's history, she had a propensity to defect to the gods of the other nations, particularly when rain was needed. Prophets like Elijah had sharply rebuked the people and leaders like King Ahab for turning to the Canaanite god Baal, who was thought to control the storm clouds (e.g., 1 Kings 16:30–32). To justify their apostasy, they had surrounded themselves with false prophets who would tell them what they wanted to hear and confirm them in their unfaithfulness (e.g., 1 Kings 18:19; 22:1–12). More recently, Jeremiah had complained that lying prophets had lured the people into false worship. Only the Lord, Jeremiah insisted, could open the heavens and bring rain (Jer. 14:13–22).

But, lest the people fall away into apostasy in the present day as they had been prone to do in years past, they are told to ask the Lord for rain (10:1). After all, he is the one who makes the storm clouds, provides rain, and then produces good harvests. They are not to listen to the false prophets and the diviners who seek to lead them astray (10:2; cf. Isa. 44:25; Jer. 14:14; 27:9). Nor are they to worship the teraphim, or household gods, which were a regular temptation in preexilic Israel as well as an object of Babylonian devotion (1 Sam. 15:23; 2 Kings 23:24; Ezek. 21:21; Hos. 3:4). Such faithlessness will incur the Lord's wrath in due time, and by punishing the false leaders, the Lord will reveal his deep care for the house of Judah (10:3; cf. Ezek. 13).

Moreover, he will turn the world upside down by lifting up his people who have suffered not only at the hands of foreign nations, but also under their own corrupt leadership. Two significant themes are interwoven to make the point. First, military imagery is used once again. The house of Judah will be like a majestic warhorse (10:3). From them will come the strength and stability of a cornerstone, the endurance of a tent peg, the courage and power of the combat bow, and the leadership of a unified class of generals (10:4).[12] Like mighty warriors, they will see decisive victories as though trampling through the muddy streets and putting horsemen to shame (10:5). Similarly, Ephraim will be like a mighty warrior, whose victory will make the hearts of adults and children rejoice (10:7). In other words, the Lord will go to battle and his people will participate in the victory.

Second, the theme of the people returning from exile is employed, recast as a second exodus. The Lord will bring back the house of Judah (the southern kingdom) and the house of Joseph (the northern kingdom) such that they will no longer be rejected (10:6). The Lord will whistle to the ten northern tribes (represented by Ephraim) who had been lost to the Assyrian exile in the eighth century B.C., gathering them back and redeeming them, replenishing their population (10:8). Even though he scattered them to distant places, they will again remember the Lord and return to the land (10:9). Within the biblical tradition, remembering is more than just a cognitive awareness of facts; it is a reappropriation of the history and significance of an event or relationship. It makes the past present.[13] Thus, just as he long ago led their ancestors in Egypt out of bondage, through the sea, and into freedom, so that redemptive stream of God's work will flow through their present day, retrieving those once scattered in Egypt and Assyria, gathering them in, and renewing their strength (10:10–12).

Turning the world upside down certainly means that the Lord will lift up his people, but he will also simultaneously bring low their powerful oppressors through judgment (11:1–3). Just as the Lord whistled to his people, calling on them to return from exile, so he also calls out to Lebanon proclaiming that their destruction is imminent (11:1–2). The very things that were sources of glory and pride are demolished. In Lebanon, the cedars were a special source of pride and frequently symbolized health and strength (e.g., Ps. 92:12; Hos. 14:5–6). That is why Solomon used them in constructing the temple (1 Kings 7:2), and why they were imported again in the postexilic period for the rebuilding of the temple (Ezra 3:7). Thus, the Lord declares that the cedars of Lebanon will be consumed; the majestic forest of Bashan will fall. In Jordan, the lush banks will be ruined (11:3). The text literally reads, "the pride of Jordan is destroyed." Elsewhere it is clear that "the pride of Jordan" is a way of referring to the lush banks since they were a special source of pride (cf. Jer. 12:5; 49:19; 50:44).[14] By ruining these lush banks the Lord would bring low the pride of Jordan. Fittingly, the whole section comes full circle with the judgment on foreign enemies opening (9:1–6) and closing (11:1–3) the section.

THE HUMBLE BUT CONQUERING KING

The most puzzling aspect of Zechariah 9:1–11:3 is the jolting contrast between the predominant war imagery used to describe the Lord's coming judgment of Israel's enemies and the peaceful advent of the coming king characterized by humility and righteousness briefly mentioned in Zechariah 9:9–10. The natural question is, why does a passage so overwhelmingly concerned with describing the Lord's conquest of the nations also include a description of a coming king characterized by humility and peace? Perhaps the strangeness of Zechariah 9:9–10 explains why the passage is not cited at all in the messianic descriptions of the Dead Sea Scrolls, and why the qualities of peace and gentleness are very rarely ascribed to the messiah in other Jewish writings before Christ.[15]

However, as Jesus approaches Jerusalem in what will become his Passion Week, he very deliberately acts out the coming of the humble and righteous king described in Zechariah (Matt. 21:1–11; John 12:12–16). When Jesus and his disciples arrive at Bethphage on the Mount of Olives, Jesus sends two of his disciples ahead of the group into the next village. He tells them that there they will find a donkey with her colt. They are to untie them and bring them back to Jesus so that he can use the colt to ride into Jerusalem.

Matthew and John clearly recognize that Jesus is acting out the prophecy in Zechariah because both quote Zechariah 9:9 in their description, though each with a different emphasis. John does not cite the verse alone but couples it with a partial citation of Zephaniah 3:16, a verse that in context describes the Lord returning to Zion as king and subduing the nations. John also shortens Zechariah 9:9 to include only the part about a king sitting on a donkey, while omitting the characterizations of him being righteous, saved (i.e., vindicated), and humble. Moreover, in John the episode follows the seven signs of Jesus' messianic power and precedes the declaration of the Pharisees that the whole world seems to be following him. All together, John seems to use Zechariah 9:9 to focus rather singularly on Jesus as the rightful king of the whole world.

Similar to John, Matthew also blends two Old Testament passages in his description of Jesus' triumphal entry. He cites Isaiah 62:11 along with Zechariah 9:9, both of which are part of eschatological passages describing Israel's salvation through a messianic individual. Significantly, Matthew (unlike John) also includes Zechariah's characterization of the king as humble. Whereas John uses Zechariah 9:9 to emphasize Jesus' universal kingship, Matthew is more concerned with showing what kind of king Jesus is as he enters Jerusalem, namely one who is gentle, peaceful, and humble.

Fittingly, the Passion Week not only begins with Jesus acting out Zechariah's humble king coming to Jerusalem, it ends with him resolving the tension of the text itself. In his crucifixion and resurrection, he profoundly embodies both the humility of the king and the success of the Lord's conquest. On the cross, Jesus wore a crown, but it was a crown of thorns, and he hung below the humiliating mockery of a sign inscribed with the words, "The King of the Jews." But in the resurrection, he was vindicated ("saved") and exalted as the righteous victor over all the earth. He dethroned all principalities and powers and is lifted up as the King of Kings and Lord of Lords (Eph. 1:16–23; Rev. 19:16).

The tension ingrained in Zechariah 9:1–11:3 is finally resolved in Jesus. He is peaceful, yet he conquers the world. He is gentle, yet he overcomes. He is meek, yet he is vindicated. He is humble, yet he turns the world upside down. This has a profound implication for the church. At the end of the first century, Clement of Rome wrote, "The coming of our Lord Jesus Christ, the Sceptre of God's Majesty, was in no pomp of pride and haughtiness—as it could so well have been—but in self-abasement. . . . You see, dear friends, what an example we have been given. If the Lord humbled Himself in this way, what ought we to do, who through Him have come under the yoke of His grace?"[16]

As those whose hearts have been conquered by the humble grace of Christ, the church in her mission is entirely "upside down" from the way the world works. In his letter to the Philippians, Paul argued that the pattern of Christ's incarnation and atonement provides the mold for those who have come "under the yoke of his grace."

> Do nothing from rivalry or conceit, but in humility count others more significant than yourselves. Let each of you look not only to his own interests, but also to the interests of others. Have this mind among yourselves, which is yours in Christ Jesus, who, though he was in the form of God, did not count equality with God a thing to be grasped, but made himself nothing, taking the form of a servant, being born in the likeness of men. And being found in human form, he humbled himself by becoming obedient to the point of death, even death on a cross. (Phil. 2:3–8 ESV)

And that incarnational and sacrificial humility is the means through which Christ became exalted as King and Lord over all the earth.

> Therefore God has highly exalted him and bestowed on him the name that is above every name, so that at the name of Jesus every knee should bow, in heaven and on earth and under the earth, and every tongue

confess that Jesus Christ is Lord, to the glory of God
the Father. (Phil. 2:9–11 ESV)

Therefore, the church does not seek to change the world
through pomp, pride, or power, but through Christlike
meekness, humility, and weakness. As we are shaped in
our hearts and minds by our king who is gentle and humble
of heart (Matt. 11:29), we become living transcripts of his
grace and humble instruments that he uses to change the
world around us.

Practically speaking, the twelfth-century monk Bernard
of Clairvaux described humility as an outworking of certain dispositions of the heart and mind.[17] For instance, he
taught that it means releasing your desire to exercise your
own will and to protect your rights within the community.
It is often so tempting to assert ourselves, to think that we
are owed something, and to believe that we are entitled
to certain things. It is easy for us to believe that we have
rights and that we should stand up and fight for them. But
that is not the way of our humble king. Instead, he went
to the cross, humble and humiliated for us. As we are
shaped by his grace, we release our own desires to exert
our own wills and to protect our rights. When we do, the
kingdom comes.

And the kingdom comes when we decide to submit
willingly to our authorities. We often believe that we should
not have to submit to anyone. We are self-assured and
independent. We think we know best, for ourselves and
for others. How often do we refuse to submit to those in
authority over us, if not with our bodies then at least with
our hearts? But that is not the way of our humble king.
He submitted himself to his Father's will even to death,
the death on a cross. As we are shaped by his grace, we
decide to submit willingly to our authorities too. When we
do, the kingdom comes.

And the kingdom comes when we exercise quiet and
restrained speech. We are often quick to speak and slow

to listen. We want to be heard more than we want to hear. We want to assert ourselves and have our point of view recognized. But that is not the way of our humble king. When the Sadducees questioned him, he spoke sparingly and then only to acknowledge the truth. As we are shaped by his grace, we decide to exercise quiet and restrained speech too. When we do, the kingdom comes.

And the kingdom comes when we have patience in the face of accusations. Nothing can be personally harder than facing accusations, especially when they are unfair or unjust. We want to set the record straight and jump to our own defense. We cannot stand to be misrepresented. But that is not the way of our humble king. He was falsely accused and misrepresented. As we are shaped by his grace, we decide to have patience in the face of accusations too. When we do, the kingdom comes.

And the kingdom comes when we renounce all senses in which we believe that we are holier than others. We have such a tendency to look at others and think they are much worse than we are. Their guilt is greater. We have the specks, but they have the planks. We see someone else do something and we think to ourselves, "I would never do that." We see someone else struggling and we think that we are incapable of the same. We look at their sins and they always seem to weigh more than ours. But we must remember our humble king who, though righteous and holy, took upon himself the sin of the world. As we are shaped by his grace, we decide to view others with grace and not to think too highly of ourselves, but to live in a place of brokenness, humility, and meekness. Because when we do, the kingdom comes.

Our world does not work this way. But the way of the humble yet conquering king is entirely upside down from the way of the world. It may be counterintuitive, but the gospel always is. It is humility that will conquer the world for Christ. It is gentleness that will overcome the forces of evil. It is meekness that will triumph over the powers, authorities, and principalities of this dark world. It is even weakness that will emerge as the possessor of true strength. And in the end, the eyes of this world will be opened to a humble king sitting not just on a donkey, but on the throne. On that day, the chariot and the combat bow will be no more because he will speak peace to the nations, and his reign will extend from sea to sea and from the river to the ends of the earth.

FOR FURTHER REFLECTION

1. What about the portrait of the coming king in Zechariah 9:1–11:3 would have been most surprising to the postexilic community?
2. What about the portrait would have been perhaps confusing? Why?
3. How does Jesus embody the fullness of the message of Zechariah 9:1–11:3?
4. What does Jesus teach us about how Christians should try to impact the world?
5. What about such a calling is most challenging to you?
6. Where can you embody Christlike humility in your life right now? How might such humility bring God's kingdom to bear in your world?

CHAPTER THIRTEEN

THE REJECTED SHEPHERD (11:4–17)

Thus says the Lord my God, "Shepherd the flock meant for slaughter, whose buyers will slaughter them and escape punishment, whose sellers will say, 'Blessed be the Lord, for I'll get rich!' and whose shepherds will have no pity on them. For I will no longer show pity on the inhabitants of the land," declares the Lord. "Behold, I will cause each man to fall into the hand of his neighbor and into the hand of his king, and they will break the land into pieces and I will not rescue them from their hand." So I pastured the flock meant for slaughter, that is the afflicted flock. And I took two staffs, one I called "favor" and the other I called "union" and I pastured the flock. I did away with three shepherds in one month. So I became impatient with them and they also began to loathe me. So I said, "I will not be your shepherd. The one who is to die, let him die; the one who is to be lost, let him be lost; and those who remain, let them devour each other's flesh." Then I took my staff called "favor" and I cut it in two in order to annul my covenant, which I had made with all the peoples. So it was annulled on that day. Thus the afflicted flock, which was watching me knew that it was the word of the Lord. Then I said to them, "If it is good in your eyes, give me my wages; if not, then don't." So they weighed out my wages—thirty pieces of silver. Then the Lord said to me, "Throw it to the assayer—that magnificent price which I was worth to them." So I took the thirty pieces of silver and threw them into the house of the Lord, to the assayer. Then I took the second staff, the one called "union," and broke it in two in order to annul the brotherhood between Judah and the house of Israel.

Then the Lord said to me, "Once again, take for yourself the equipment of a foolish shepherd. For, behold, I am raising up a shepherd in the land who does not tend to the lost, seek the young, heal the broken, or support the frail, but instead devours the flesh of the fat one and tears off their hoofs. Woe to the worthless shepherd who abandons the flock! May the sword descend upon his arm and upon his right eye! May his arm be completely withered and may his right eye be completely blind!" (Zechariah 11:4–17)

What wondrous punishment is this to render!
For erring sheep is slain the Shepherd tender;
The Lord, the just one, for the servant payeth,
Who Him betrayeth.
(Johann Sebastian Bach[1])

The transition from Zechariah 9:1–11:3 to Zechariah 11:4–17 may seem abrupt and disjointed at first. The former section paints a glorious picture of a reunified, restored, and victorious people in the land, while the latter is filled with biting irony and an overall outlook of doom. In reality, the shepherd narrative of Zechariah 11:4–17 is critical. Lest the people become too starry-eyed over the promised future, here they are abruptly warned that something needs to be done about their present leadership, which had become disastrously corrupt.

THE REJECTION OF THE PROPHETIC
SHEPHERD (11:4–14)

The shepherds (leaders) of Israel were introduced briefly in Zechariah 9:1–11:3 (specifically 10:2–3 and 11:3). Now the theme comes into full bloom with an extended prophetic symbolic action that is overwhelmingly judgmental in tone because the present situation is a wreck. The leadership in Israel had become predatory and self-serving, exploiting others for their own benefit. They were like self-absorbed shepherds who callously raised and slaughtered their sheep for monetary gain and then praised the Lord for his generosity! Such behavior was deeply hypocritical. Leaders in the ancient Near East, especially kings, were given the title shepherd because of their obligation to care for the needs of their people and to protect them from external threats (e.g., Num. 27:17; 2 Sam. 5:2; Ps. 78:70–72). But the flock of Israel living under these shepherds became like sheep "meant" for slaughter.

Significantly, the only other prophet to use such terminology was Jeremiah (the form of the Hebrew word for "slaughter" [*haregah*] is found only in Jeremiah and Zechariah 11). He had complained that the people gave lip service to the Lord but that their hearts were hardened toward him. Having become frustrated with their wickedness, Jeremiah pleads with the Lord to "drag them off like sheep to be butchered! Set them apart for the day of slaughter!" (Jer. 12:3 NIV) Listening to Jeremiah, it appears (and will become confirmed as the passage unfolds) that the people were just as recalcitrant as the leaders and deserved to be slaughtered (cf. Zech.11:6, 8b–14).

Though the Lord's patience is almost spent, he dispatches the prophet to make one last appeal (v. 4–5), all the while knowing that the end result will still be widespread oppression throughout the land (v. 6). He is told to shepherd the flock as a symbolic enactment of the coming Davidic shepherd of the people. He intends to pasture the flock, paying special attention to the oppressed (v. 7a). He seeks to unify the people and in a single month gets rid of three particularly bad leaders, though from our historical distance we have no idea who they were (vv. 7b–8a).

To portray the ministry of this good shepherd, the prophet takes two staffs, calling one Favor and one Union. Such a symbolic action recalls Ezekiel's two staffs (Ezek. 37:15–28). Ezekiel's two staffs had represented Judah and Ephraim (i.e., the southern and northern kingdoms). When he joined them, it was symbolic of the Lord's promise to gather his people back from exile and to reunify them into one undefiled nation. Central to such a redemptive work would be the advent of a singular Davidic shepherd as their king, through whom the Lord would renew the people, establish an everlasting covenant, and mediate his presence in a permanent sanctuary. Brought into a postexilic context, such an action reminded the people that the Lord's promise to bring a Davidic shepherd to rule them was still in force.

But the symbolic enactment suggests that, instead of welcoming such a good shepherd with open arms, the people inexplicably detest him and reject him (v. 8b), causing the shepherd to become weary of dealing with them. Exasperated, the shepherd throws up his hands, leaves them to their own devices, and effectively says, "Fine! I'm not going to be your shepherd any longer. The dying can die and the perishing can perish. Devour one another if you want, but I'm through with you!" (v. 9). To show his disgust, he takes the staff called Favor and breaks it. In doing so, he nullifies the covenant that he had previously made with the various tribes of the northern and southern kingdoms (vv. 10–11). God will no longer show his covenant favor upon them since they have rejected the good shepherd.

The people, who are apparently not all that moved by the prophet's words, pay him for his time with thirty pieces of silver and send him on his way (v. 12). Though sometimes equated with the value of a slave's life (Ex. 21:32), the denomination of thirty pieces of silver is more likely an idiomatic expression for a paltry sum of money.[2] Such a devaluation of the shepherd's ministry is insulting (the reader senses the bitter sarcasm in the ironic description of the money as "magnificent").

Infuriated, the Lord tells the prophet/shepherd to throw the money to the assayer (v. 13). The Hebrew word for "throw" (*hashlikehu*) is one of intensity, "indicating the hurling of a vile and rejected thing."[3] But why throw it to the assayer (*yotser*) in the temple? Apparently such an act had a deliberate symbolic quality to it. In the Persian period, the *yotser* was a relatively high-ranking official in the temple administration. The highest official was the royal commissioner, a position originally introduced into temples by the Babylonians and charged with controlling the intake and allocation of the temple tax, frequently paid in precious metals among other things. The Persians then added a subordinate official called the *yotser* who directed the temple foundry (and later the temple mint when Persian coins began to be minted) and assayed the precious metals received. The *yotser* was instrumental in providing taxes to the Persian authorities, and the Persian authorities in kind took care of the *yotser* and the rest of the temple hierarchy.[4]

Returning to Zechariah 11, when the people paid the shepherd such a paltry price, the Lord took it as a personal insult and proof that he was not worth very much to them ("that magnificent price which *I* was worth to them"). This being true, nothing could be more fitting than for the shepherd to hurl the thirty pieces of silver into the very place that should have been the Lord's dwelling among his people but instead had become a place of economic collusion with the Persian authorities.

Continuing in his disgust, the prophet breaks the second staff called Union, announcing that the brotherhood between Judah and Israel is now severed. The hope of reunification promised by Ezekiel was conditioned upon the installment of the coming Davidic king. If the people were going to reject the Davidic shepherd in whom all the hopes of unity rested, then they were essentially foreclosing the possibility that there might be a reunification of all the tribes too. They would essentially be turning their backs on the glorious promise of reunification pictured in Ezekiel 37 (and in Zech. 9:1–11:3).

THE INSTALLMENT OF THE WORTHLESS SHEPHERD (11:15–17)

Since the people want nothing to do with the good shepherd, the Lord gives them what they deserve: a worthless shepherd. The prophet is to dress up like a shepherd, taking up the equipment necessary to carry out a brutal "ministry" among the flock. His actions demonstrate that the worthless shepherd will care nothing for the well-being of the flock, but will ravage them for his own benefit. He will not care for the lost, seek the young, heal the injured, or support the frail. Instead, he will be like a beast that tears their limbs off and feeds on their meat. In other words, the worthless shepherd is just like those Ezekiel denounced for trampling the flock (Ezek. 34:1–10). Such is the fate of a flock that reject the good shepherd in favor of doing whatever they please; they get what they deserve. But even though the Lord has raised up this worthless shepherd to punish his people, he will also bring just judgment on the shepherd for his cruelty (v. 17). He will cut off the shepherd's arm and blind him, rendering him incompetent to rule any longer.

THE REJECTION OF THE GOOD SHEPHERD

Though the original historical references of the good shepherd and the worthless shepherd are probably lost, the New Testament leaves little doubt as to who fills these roles. In John 10, Jesus provides a cutting contrast between himself and the other leaders of the day. Describing them as thieves and robbers, Jesus rebukes them for coming only to steal, kill, and destroy. Some of them wanted revolution against the imperial powers. Others wanted the people to submit to Rome in order to protect their own positions of power. Both kinds of self-serving leaders, like the predatory shepherds in Zechariah, were happy to exploit the people in order to serve their own ambitions.

On the other hand, Jesus came that people might have the abundant life. "I am the Good Shepherd," he says. Unlike the leaders of his day, Jesus has a true shepherd's heart; he cares deeply for the sheep and is even willing to lay down his life for his people (John 10:10–11). As the good shepherd, Jesus' heart broke when he looked out over Jerusalem because the people were like sheep without a shepherd (Matt. 9:36; Mark 6:34). As the good shepherd, Jesus sensed a special calling to the lost sheep of the house of Israel (Matt. 15:24). As the good shepherd, he was will-ing to leave ninety-nine sheep to chase after one lost sheep that had gone astray (Matt 18:12; Luke 15:4–6).

Finally, as the good shepherd, Jesus' heart beat for the recovery of all the tribes of Israel, including the lost ones. Perhaps that is why Jesus spent so much time ministering in the northern regions, formerly the territory of the ten lost tribes. It certainly was why he selected exactly twelve disciples. As if taking the severed stick named Union and putting it back together, Jesus made the powerfully escha-tological statement that he was reconstituting the twelve tribes of Israel. As Gerhard Lohfink points out,

> Reference to the twelve tribes evoked a central point of Israel's eschatological hope. Although the system of twelve tribes had long since ceased to exist . . . the complete restoration of the twelve-tribe people was expected for the eschatological time of salvation. . . .

Against the background of this very lively hope Jesus' constitution of twelve disciples could only be grasped as a *symbolic prophetic action*: The Twelve exemplified the awakening of Israel and its gathering in the eschatological salvific community, something beginning then through Jesus.[5]

But like the good shepherd of Zechariah 11, Jesus would ultimately regather and restore Israel not through a great demonstration of charisma, but through his own betrayal and rejection. Even at the outset of his gospel, John makes clear that Jesus came to his own, but his own received him not (John 1:11). As his ministry wore on, Jesus was not even welcome in his own hometown (Matt. 13:57; Mark 6:4; Luke 4:24).

The contrast between Jesus as the good but rejected shepherd over against the wicked shepherds of Israel reaches a fever pitch in the parable of the tenants (Matt. 21:33–46; Mark 12:1–12; Luke 20:9–19). Jesus tells the story of a vineyard owner who entrusted his vineyard to some farmers. At harvest time, he sent servant after servant to collect his portion of the harvest, but they were all beaten or killed. Finally, he sent his son, but they killed him too and threw him out of the vineyard. Jesus clearly means to implicate the chief priests, the teachers of the law and the elders as the farmers who are the worthless leaders of Israel. He labels them as murderers for killing the prophets and reveals that he sees where his conflict with them is heading. It will end with blood on their hands because they will reject and kill the Son who was sent to them. The parable concludes with a quotation of Psalm 118: "The stone that the builders rejected has become the cornerstone; this was the Lord's doing, and it is marvelous in our eyes" (Matt. 21:42 ESV). In other words, Jesus' death would be the very means through which he would build the new eschatological temple. His rejection would be the means of God's work of restoration.

In the final hours of his life, this divine plan was worked out when Jesus was rejected not only by the leaders, but by the masses themselves, including his own disciples. The accompanying pilgrims who had one week earlier shouted "Hosanna" were in short time drowned out by the Jerusalem crowds shouting "Crucify him!" When the dispatch from the chief priests, the teachers of the law, and the elders came to arrest Jesus, the whole company of disciples deserted him (Matt. 26:56; Mark 14:50). Even Peter, one of Jesus' closest friends, disowned him to save his own skin (Matt. 26:69–75; Mark 14:66–72; Luke 22:54–62).

But the most consequential betrayal came from Judas Iscariot (Matt. 26:14–16; 27:1–10). Seeing an opportunity to make some extra money, he went to the chief priests asking what they would give him if he handed Jesus over to them. They paid him thirty silver coins and when he found opportunity, Judas led an armed crowd to Gethsemane where they arrested Jesus. Early the next morning the chief priests and the elders decided to put Jesus to death. When Judas saw it, he was seized with regret and tried to return the money. When the leaders refused to accept it, he threw it into the temple and committed suicide. Gathering up the silver coins, the chief priests used it to purchase a potter's field.

Matthew concludes the episode by stating,

> Then was fulfilled what had been spoken by the prophet Jeremiah, saying, "And they took the thirty pieces of silver, the price of him on whom a price had been set by some of the sons of Israel, and they gave them for the potter's field, as the Lord directed me." (Matt. 27:9–10 ESV)

As is well-documented, the citation is from Zechariah 11:12, 13 but with significant modifications to fit Matthew's narrative. In Zechariah, the silver is thrown to the assayer (*yotser*) with no mention of a potter's field. Likely, the notion of a potter's field is picked up from passages such as Jeremiah 19:1–13 and 32:6–9 (which may explain Matthew's ascription of the text to Jeremiah since he is the more prominent prophet and one especially associated with rejection[6]). But Matthew is doing more than just taking two unrelated texts and stitching them together. Though the yotser was originally an assayer in the temple (and that is the reference in Zechariah), later interpreters tended to read it as a craftsman or a potter. Therefore, for Matthew's contemporaries the concept of a potter was already embedded in both the text from Zechariah and the text from Jeremiah, making them natural to bring together. The end result is that Matthew interprets Judas' betrayal of Jesus for a paltry sum of money as the historical climax of God's good shepherd undergoing devaluation and rejection for a greater redemptive purpose.

However, the greater purpose does not just embrace the restoration of Israel; it also includes the whole world in God's redemptive design, just as Jesus had already hinted (John 10:16). Perhaps that is why Matthew emphasizes that the thirty pieces of silver was "blood money," and that it was specifically used to purchase a field for the burial of foreigners. As Craig Blomberg perceptively proposes,

> Because money is paid to secure Jesus' death, Matthew may also be suggesting what Matt. 20:28 states more clearly: Jesus' death is a ransom, the price paid to secure a slave's freedom. That this "blood money" was subsequently used to buy a burial ground for foreigners may hint at what Matthew will explicitly highlight in his closing verses: Jesus' death makes salvation possible for all the peoples of the world.[7]

Such a worldwide hope was carried by the apostles as they fanned out across the Mediterranean world preaching the gospel of God's reconciling redemption. Yet not surprisingly, as they went about as heralds of the good news, they encountered rejection just as their Shepherd had. In some instances, it was precisely through their rejections that God continued to move in people's hearts to restore them back to himself. For instance, when Peter and John were preaching to the people, they were seized and thrown in jail (Acts 4:3). But Luke immediately notes that "many of those who had heard the word believed, and the number of the men came to about five thousand" (Acts 4:4 ESV). In other cases, the rejections produced a scattering that was providentially used by God to reach others with the good news.

> Now those who were scattered because of the persecution that arose over Stephen traveled as far as Phoenicia and Cyprus and Antioch, speaking the word to no one except Jews. But there were some of them, men of Cyprus and Cyrene, who on coming to Antioch spoke to the Hellenists also, preaching the Lord Jesus. And the hand of the Lord was with them, and a great number who believed turned to the Lord. (Acts 11:19–21 ESV)

The same continues to be true. All those whose hearts have been reconciled back to God through the Good Shepherd's rejection are called to be shaped by what he has done for them. He was rejected by men that we might be accepted by God. He was betrayed that we might be reconciled. He was hated that we might know his love.

It should not be surprising when God calls us to submit to rejection and betrayal so that his grace might touch the hearts and lives of others as well. Alexander Schmemann once noted that at some point everyone who believes in Christ must go through Matthew 26:56 too, that is, everyone must go through times when he or she is rejected and left all alone.[8] It is part of following the rejected Shepherd. Instead of becoming hardened toward those who reject us, and more importantly, the Good Shepherd we represent, our hearts should break for them. The consequences of rejecting the Good Shepherd are always disastrous. In

Zechariah, God proclaimed that he would turn the people over to a cruel shepherd who would brutally give them what they deserve. What then will become of the person who rejects Jesus, the true Good Shepherd? Will they not receive the tragic penalty of their rejection when God gives them over to their own evil devices (cf. Rom. 1:18–32; 2:8)? As we look at our own hearts, might we never turn away from our Good Shepherd, but always be willing to follow where he leads, even when that means into the crucible of rejection for his sake.

Yet even in rejection, followers of Christ are reassured that it is part of God's larger redemptive purposes. Perhaps it will be used by him to give others a picture of what our Redeemer went through on our behalf. Perhaps it will be used providentially to position us for further redemptive work by God in the lives of others. Perhaps it will be used by the Father to draw us closer to the heart of him who was rejected on our behalf. But whatever the greater purposes of God in those times, even if we never come to know his designs for them, we are nevertheless reassured that as we follow Jesus into places of rejection and betrayal, we will also be renewed once again in his acceptance, reconciliation, and love.

FOR FURTHER REFLECTION

1. In the postexilic community, how were both the leaders and the people culpable of sin?
2. How did their sins lead them to reject the prophetic shepherd?
3. How was the implementation of a worthless shepherd a just action by God for their sins? How did the punishment "fit" the crime?
4. How was Jesus' rejection something redemptive?
5. In what ways have you experienced betrayal and rejection? Are there ways God has used those experiences redemptively in either your life or in the life of others?

CHAPTER FOURTEEN

THE PIERCED ONE (12:1–13:9)

The burden of the word of the Lord concerning Israel.
The Lord who stretched out the heavens, established
the earth, and formed the spirit of man within him,
declares: "Behold, I am making Jerusalem a cup of staggering to all the surrounding peoples. And the siege
against Jerusalem will also be against Judah. In that
day, I will make Jerusalem a heavy stone; all who lift it
will surely injure themselves. And all the nations of the
earth will gather against her. In that day," declares the
Lord, "I will strike every horse with panic and its rider
with madness. But, I will keep my eyes upon the house
of Judah while I will strike every horse of the peoples
with blindness. Then the chiefs of Judah will say in
their hearts, 'The inhabitants of Jerusalem are strong
because the Lord of hosts is their God.' In that day, I
will make the chiefs of Judah like a flaming pot among
pieces of wood, like a flaming torch among sheaves of
grain. They will devour all the surrounding peoples to
the right and to the left, while Jerusalem will still be
inhabited in her own place, in Jerusalem. And the Lord
will deliver the tents of Judah first, so that the glory
of the house of David and the glory of the inhabitants
of Jerusalem may not be greater than that of Judah. In
that day, the Lord will defend the inhabitants of Jerusalem so that even the feeblest among them will be like

189

David, the house of David like a divine being, like the angel of the Lord before them. And it will be such that in that day I will seek to destroy all the nations that come against Jerusalem.

"And I will pour out on the house of David and on the inhabitants of Jerusalem a spirit of grace and supplication. Then they will look on me, on the one whom they have pierced and they will mourn for him as one mourns over an only son and will grieve bitterly as one grieves bitterly over a first-born. In that day, the mourning in Jerusalem will be as great as the mourning in Hadad-rimmon in the plain of Megiddo. The land will mourn, each family by itself—the family of the house of David by itself and their wives by themselves; the family of the house of Nathan by itself and their wives by themselves; the family of the house of Levi by itself and their wives by themselves; the family of the house of Shimeites by itself and their wives by themselves; all the families that are left, each family by itself, and their wives by themselves.

"In that day, a fountain will be opened for the house of David and for the inhabitants of Jerusalem, to cleanse them from sin and impurity. And it will be such that in that day," declares the Lord of hosts, "I will cut off the names of the idols in the land and they will not remember them anymore. Also, I will remove the prophets and the spirit of uncleanness from the land. And it will be such that if anyone prophesies again, his father and mother who bore him will say to him, 'You shall not live for you have spoken deceitfully in the name of the Lord.' And his father and mother who bore him will pierce him through when he prophesies. And it will be such that in that day every prophet will be ashamed of his vision when he prophesies. They will not put on a hairy cloak in order to deceive. And he will say, 'I am not a prophet; I am a man who works the ground, for a man sold me in my youth.' And if he is asked, 'What

are these wounds on your back?' he will say, 'Those are
from being beaten in the house of my friends.'

"Awake, O sword, against my shepherd, against the
one who is close to me," declares the Lord of hosts.
"Strike the shepherd and the flock will be scattered
and I will turn my hand against the little ones. And
throughout the land," declares the Lord, "two-thirds
will be cut off and perish and one-third will be spared.
Then, I will bring that one-third into the fire and I will
refine them as one refines silver and I will test them as
one tests gold. Then they will call upon my name and
I will answer them. I will say, 'They are my people'
and they will say, 'The Lord is our God.' "
(Zechariah 12:1–13:9)

Survey my compressed and sightless eyes,
and my afflicted cheeks;
see my parched tongue poisoned with gall,
and my countenance pale with death.
Behold my hands pierced with nails,
and my arms drawn out,
and the great wound in my side;
see the blood streaming from it,
and my perforated feet,
and blood-stained limbs.
Bend your knee,
and with lamentation adore the venerable wood of
    the cross,
and with lowly countenance stooping to the earth,
which is wet with blood,
sprinkle it with rising tears,
and at times bear me and my admonitions in your
    devoted heart.
(Lactantius[1])

Zechariah 12–14 hangs together as a large unit, headed
by the phrase "the burden (i.e., oracle) of the word of the
Lord" (cf. Zech. 9:1; Mal. 1:1) and structured according

to the refrain of "in that day." The first major subsection, which runs from Zechariah 12:1–13:9, focuses on the Lord's defense of Jerusalem and his work of transformation among the people, resulting in their contrition and cleansing.

GOD'S DEFENSE OF JERUSALEM (12:1–9)

At the outset, the Lord is described as the one who stretched out the heavens, established the earth, and formed the spirit of man within him in order to ground the ensuing oracle in God's creative work. Ultimately what will follow is a work of new creation. Just as God once exercised his might and strength to form the world and to give life to mankind at the beginning of history, so he will work in the latter days to re-form the world and to give life once again to his people at the end of history. The coming restorative work will be a new creation.

The Lord's work of restoration will begin with a resounding defense of Jerusalem. When attacked, Jerusalem will be like a "cup of staggering" to the surrounding peoples. Within the prophetic tradition, drinking from the Lord's cup meant enduring his wrath. For instance, when the Babylonian army razed Jerusalem and exiled the people, the Lord declared, "Wake yourself, wake yourself, stand up, O Jerusalem, you who have drunk from the hand of the LORD the cup of his wrath, who have drunk to the dregs the bowl, the cup of staggering" (Isa. 51:17 ESV; cf. Jer. 51:7). Now however, Jerusalem is not the drinker of the cup, but the cup itself that will be the instrument of the Lord's wrathful judgment upon the nations who attack her.

The nations will gather themselves together and lay siege to the city. Judah too will undergo attack, presumably as the armies march toward Jerusalem. Nevertheless, the Lord will make the city impenetrable like a "heavy rock" or an "immovable stone."[2] The result will be that any attempt to cause her harm will only result in the assailant's injury.

Interestingly, the only other place the Hebrew word for "injure" (*srt*) is used refers to a bloody laceration that one might get by trying to lift a rugged rock with bare hands (Lev. 21:5).[3]

The scene is reminiscent of Sennacherib's invasion in the eighth century. The Assyrian army marched toward Jerusalem, overtaking the northern kingdom and destroying much of Judah before the Lord miraculously put to death a huge number within the Assyrian camp (2 Kings 19:1–37; 2 Chron. 32:1–23). Sennacherib returned to his own country where he was killed. By attempting to attack Jerusalem, he put himself under the judgment of God and invited his own injury. This miraculous intervention must have confirmed a long-standing belief that the Lord gave special protection to Jerusalem (Zion) when enemies attacked her. The theme, as clearly seen in a number of Psalms (e.g., Pss. 46; 48; 76), probably stretches back to the days of the united monarchy. David withstood attacks from the Philistines immediately after conquering and securing Jerusalem (2 Sam. 5:17–25) and Solomon endured at least three revolts with two coming from vassal states (1 Kings 11:14–25).[4] Yet even in those early days, the royal city had been preserved.

Similarly, the Lord declared to the postexilic community that one day he would again defend Jerusalem against the nations and keep watch over Judah. He would strike the attacking armies with a plague that would devastate the horses and their riders. This language is similar to the covenant curses in Deuteronomy (e.g. Deut. 28:28), implying that the punishment for covenant disobedience is now extended to include the nations who assault Jerusalem. This is to be expected within the larger vision of the book, since the promises of salvation are also extended to the nations as well.[5] On such a day, the Lord declared that he would make Judah's leaders like a flaming pot among pieces of wood, like a flaming torch among sheaves of grain. Flaming torches were commonly used in warfare (e.g., Judg. 7:16; 15:4–5), producing the image of the conquered Judeans partnering with the assailants against Jerusalem in laying siege to the city. They become part of the Lord's battle strategy to consume and destroy Jerusalem's enemies.

In order to protect Judah from being overshadowed by Jerusalem, the Lord declares that he will save the dwelling places in Judah first. Nevertheless, Jerusalem's deliverance will be remarkable. So remarkable that the lowliest in the city will be like King David, and the house of David will be almost divine, like the angel of the Lord.

A SPIRIT OF GRACE; A TIME FOR MOURNING (12:10-14)

The Lord's great work on behalf of his people is now matched by a great work within his people. External deliverance will be accompanied by internal renewal. The Lord declares that he will pour out on the Davidic house and the inhabitants of Jerusalem a spirit of grace and supplication (cf. Ezek. 39:29; Joel 2:28–29). In fact, the Hebrew word for "grace" (khen) is the same word used in Zechariah 4:7 when Zerubbabel brings forth the top stone of the temple and the people shout "Grace! Grace!" because they recognize that God was working among them.

Then the Lord declares, "they will look on me, on the one whom they have pierced and they will mourn for him as one mourns over an only son and will grieve bitterly as one grieves bitterly over a first-born" (Zech. 12:10). One of the most enigmatic statements of the book, it is difficult to understand in what way the people could be said to have "pierced" the Lord, especially since the dominant use of "pierce" (dqr) in the rest of the Old Testament is a physical stabbing caused by a sword or spear (e.g., Num. 25:8; Judg. 9:54; 1 Sam. 31:4). This has led some to suggest various emendations to avoid what seems nonsensical. However, what is probably in view is the execution of someone representing the Lord within the city, perhaps by mob force during the panic produced by the approaching armies, and the community's subsequent recognition that they had wrongly executed someone who truly did speak for God (cf. Zech. 13:2–6 below).

When the people realize what they have done, their grief will be like the mourning in Hadad-rimmon in the plain of Megiddo. The allusion is to the mourning in Israel following the death of King Josiah, one of the most righteous kings in Israel's history. In the waning years before the Babylonian exile, Josiah went out to battle Neco, the king of Egypt, on the plain of Megiddo. During the battle, Egyptian armies shot Josiah and shortly after he died from the piercing. Upon his burial, all of Judah and Jerusalem mourned for him, a mourning that became a tradition in Israel (2 Chron. 35:20–25).

Similarly, the mourning for the one who was pierced encompasses the whole community. Every family group enters the lamentation, including the families of royal lineage (the house of David and his son Nathan) and priestly lineage (the house of Levi and his son Shimei). And the mourning itself will be as bitter as the grieving over the loss of a first-born son. Perhaps there is an allusion here to the kind of wailing that rose within Egypt when the Lord went through the land at midnight striking all the first-born sons of the Egyptians, a wailing that was described as something worse than ever has been or ever will be (Ex. 11:4–6).

THE PURIFYING FOUNTAIN (13:1–9)

Yet mourning will give way to cleansing. A purifying fountain will be opened up to the house of David and the inhabitants of Jerusalem in order to cleanse them from their sin and impurity. Ezekiel had envisioned the restored temple as the locus of God's cleansing work in the future, symbolized by streams of water pouring out of it (Ezek. 47). The symbolism is developed here to show that God working through the rebuilt Temple will purify the land from its uncleanness. The form of the cleansing will be the eradication of idolatry, the false prophets, and the spirit of impurity that exists in the land. The renewal will be so thoroughgoing that mothers and fathers will have no tolerance for false prophecy, even if it comes from their son. They will give him up to the death penalty, the designated punishment for false prophecy according to Deuteronomy (13:5–10), even stabbing him themselves when he begins to prophesy. The Hebrew word for "stabbing" is the same as used earlier in 12:10, indicating that the people, convicted and remorseful for piercing the true representative of God, now turn their swords to pierce those false prophets who truly deserve it. Even self-designated prophets will give up their pretensions and return to working the land. They will claim to have been farmers all their lives. If asked about the wounds on their bodies, presumably received from self-flagellation during pagan religious rituals (cf. 1 Kings 18:28), they will attempt to hide their involvement with the bogus claim that they are wounds incurred at their friends' houses.

Immediately following is a declaration of judgment against a shepherd, leaving the reader perhaps with the impression that Zechariah 13:7–9 is not connected to the preceding passage.[6] But this section actually is connected and continues the theme of purging the impurities from the postexilic community. In 13:1, the promise to purify the house of David and the inhabitants of the land had been made. In 13:2–6, the purification of the land had been described in detail. Now, in 13:7–9, the purification of the house of David, that is the Jerusalem leadership, is described. The description begins with a sword, which undoubtedly is the Lord's instrument of judgment (cf. Jer. 12:12; 47:6; Ezek. 21:1–32; 29:8), being aroused in order to attack a shepherd. Opinions differ as to whether this shepherd is the same as the good shepherd of Zechariah 11:4–14, the worthless shepherd of Zechariah 11:15–17, the pierced one of Zechariah 12:10, or some other historical figure entirely.

Though it is difficult to be certain, the literary placement of the passage seems to tip the scales in favor of understanding the stricken shepherd of 13:7 as a good shepherd whose violent end affects a purification of the Davidic line.[7] This reading also makes the most sense of the immediately following verses which emphasize the purifying effect of suffering on the populace, as well as the fact that the Lord refers to this shepherd as "my" shepherd and as "one who is close to me." Just as the stabbed prophet of Zechariah 12:10 serves a greater redemptive purpose for the people, so too does the violent death of the good but stricken shepherd of Zechariah 13:7. Both are pierced for the sake of the people. Nevertheless, the immediate consequences are disastrous. When the shepherd is stricken, the people scatter, chaos ensues, and many perish. The populace suffers, especially the "little ones" (i.e., the flock) who find that God's hand is against them. But in the end, one-third of the people will be preserved. Like silver and gold that are refined in the fire, they will be purified and restored. As the Lord's renewed people, they will call upon his name and will live in covenant with him (cf. Hos. 2:23).

Without question, the details of 13:7–9 clearly allude to the end of the Judean monarchy and the subsequent judgment of exile. The only other place in the prophets in which the idiom of putting a king (shepherd) to the sword is found is in Jeremiah's description of Nebuchadnezzar's capture of King Zedekiah, the final king to reign in Judah (Jer. 21:7).[8] The result of Zedekiah's fall is a scattering of his subjects and a plunge into national exile. Elsewhere the exile is described as a furnace of affliction, a time of testing and refining (Isa. 48:10), which afterwards would be marked with covenant renewal (Jer. 31:31–33).

Historically then, the end of the Judean monarchy is a fitting adumbration of the eschatological outlook envisioned by the prophet. Just as in the final days of Judah before the

Babylonian exile, the purification of the royal line in the future will be accomplished by the striking of a particular leader. His death will produce a scattering of the flock, but with the eventual result of purifying a remnant who will call upon the name of the Lord.

THE PIERCED MESSIAH

The overall flow of 12:1–13:9 is that God will defend Jerusalem, and in the aftermath the people will mourn for the one whom they pierced, which will lead to purification of the people, the land, and the leadership. The eschatological purification is catalyzed by the two enigmatic figures, the prophet of 12:10 and the shepherd of 13:7, who are both pierced for the redemptive benefit of the people.

The New Testament writers see the fulfillment of both pierced figures in the final events of Jesus' life. The night before his death Jesus was with his disciples celebrating the Passover. Afterward, they went out to the Mount of Olives where Jesus predicted that they all would fall away. The basis for such a prediction, Jesus maintains, is that it was already foretold: "I will strike the shepherd and the sheep will be scattered" (Matt. 26:31; Mark 14:27; cf. Zech. 13:7). Just like the shepherd in Zechariah, Jesus will be struck down and his followers will disperse. Peter confidently asserts that he will never leave Jesus and the others follow suit. Of course, they almost immediately go back on their promise. Interestingly, in both accounts the citation of Zechariah 13:7 follows immediately on the heels of Jesus' declaration over the cup at the Passover: "This is the blood of the covenant" (Matt. 26:27–29; Mark 14:24–25). The timing of this statement is startling because Jesus prophesies the disciples' unfaithfulness immediately after celebrating a covenant renewal meal that ideally would cement their covenant loyalty to him![9]

Undoubtedly, there are larger designs at work. While the juxtaposition of the two statements highlights the grievousness of the disciples' disloyalty in one sense, it also reveals something about the larger redemptive purposes involved in the shedding of Jesus' blood. By making the two statements back-to-back, Jesus seems to be interpreting "the blood of God's covenant in the light of the words that speak of striking the shepherd. Jesus' blood will restore Israel's covenant relationship with God and will make possible the nation's renewal."[10] The striking of Jesus would serve as the blood-shedding basis of the new covenant. He would be struck down so that we might be lifted up; he would be wounded that we might be healed (1 Peter 2:24); he would undergo the tribulation of the cross that we might be purified and renewed (cf. Zech. 13:8–9).

The next day when the soldiers at Calvary pierce Jesus' side with a spear, John sees another connection to Zechariah and states that such an action was the fulfillment of Zechariah 12:10 (John 19:31–37). However, the connection is much more sophisticated than a haphazard connection to the cross using a prophetic passage about piercing. Within John's Gospel, the cross becomes the climactic moment in which Jesus' glory is revealed, the revelation of his true identity. As Christopher Tuckett concludes,

> By emphasizing the fact that it is the pierced, crucified one whom others will "see" in the future, the evangelist may then be seeking to shift attention away from the resurrection as some kind of happy ending that puts right the cross, and to emphasize the centrality of the cross as the supreme moment of revelation. . . . John presents his readers with a stark "gospel" of a Jesus—and a God—who shows his truest colours as the crucified one. . . . For John there is no other 'seeing' of the risen Lord which is on offer to believers here on earth.[11]

Actually, the connection may be even more pregnant than that. In the original context of Zechariah, not only do the people look upon the one whom they have pierced, but they do so as a response to the Lord's pouring out a spirit of grace (Zech. 12:9). The result is a life-restoring fountain of water that cleanses the people, the leadership, and the land from their sin (Zech. 13:1). John seems to capitalize on the conjunction of these three themes—seeing the pierced one, the pouring out of the Spirit, and the fountain of water—and the groundwork had already been laid earlier in his Gospel. During the Feast of Tabernacles, Jesus had stood in the temple and declared: "If anyone thirsts, let him come to me and drink. Whoever believes in me, as the Scripture has said, 'Out of his heart will flow rivers of living water' " (John 7:37b–38 ESV). Significantly, John adds the explanatory comment, "Now this he said about the Spirit, whom those who believed in him were to receive, for as yet the Spirit had not been given, because Jesus was not yet glorified" (John 7:39 ESV). John connects for the reader the two themes of living water and the outpouring of the Spirit, and he indicates that they will be brought together in Jesus.

When the soldiers pierce the side of Jesus and water flows out as well as blood, John gains the third of these themes, that of the piercing. John quotes Zechariah 12:10 and by doing so brings in the wider context of Zechariah 12–13. The crucifixion is a "sign" to those looking on, not of defeat, but of the inauguration of God's glorious eschatological work. Through the death of Christ, God is purifying his people. Those who look with faith on the one who was pierced will have their sins forgiven and will receive the outpouring of the Holy Spirit upon Jesus' subsequent glorification. In contrast, those who do not now recognize the true identity of the crucified one will one day mourn when they see the pierced one returning in unveiled glory to judge the world (Rev. 1:7).

But even those of faith should mourn in the present because in the final events of Jesus' life we are not just shown God's "truest colors," we are shown ours as well. Whether in the desertion of the disciples the night before or in the angry faces of those gathered around the cross as Jesus was pierced through, we see a reflection of our own hearts. We are deicidal at our core.[12] If we examine ourselves carefully, we will be shocked at how often our natural impulse is either to run away from God or to exterminate him. We too are the sheep that so easily scatter because, like the disciples, we often care much more about ourselves than we do about God. And we too regularly pierce our Lord's heart when we, like the soldiers, think little of trampling upon the Father's love.

Yet it is precisely the moment of the crucifixion that we also see how amazing God's grace is. At the cross, we are shown our God-killing hearts and at the same time God's humanity-loving heart. We see our desire to flee from God, and we see God's desire to pursue us. We see our desire to pick up the piercing spear against God, and we see God's desire to pick up the piercing nails for us. The only proper response is mourning and thankful joy. We mourn because of what we have done, and what we continue to do. We mourn because we keep running away. We mourn because we keep trying to remove God from our lives. And yet, we must also rejoice with thanksgiving. We rejoice because we have a God who shows mercy to deicidal people. We rejoice because we are pursued by a God who loves a flock in flight. We rejoice because we have a God who reveals his indescribable glory and his inexhaustible grace even through the piercing of his one and only Son.

FOR FURTHER REFLECTION

1. What is the connection between mourning for sin and cleansing from it?

2. In what ways do the two enigmatic figures of Zechariah 12:10 and 13:7 teach us about God's ways of redemption?

3. In your own life, how do you run away from God or try to remove him from your life?

4. What does heartfelt mourning look like in someone's life?

5. How does the appropriation of Zechariah 12:1–13:9 by the Gospel writers show us both the depth of our sin and the greatness of God's saving grace?

CHAPTER FIFTEEN

THE FINAL RENEWAL (14:1–21)

Behold, a day is coming for the Lord when your spoil will be divided up in your midst. And I will gather all the nations against Jerusalem for battle. Then the city will be captured, the houses plundered, and the women raped. Half the city will go out into exile, but the rest of the people will not be cut off from the city. Then the Lord will go out and fight against those nations as when he fights on a day of battle.

On that day, his feet will stand on the Mount of Olives, which lies east of Jerusalem, and the Mount of Olives will be split in two from east to west, leaving a very large valley. Then, half of the mountain will be moved to the north and half to the south. You will flee through the valley of my mountains, for the valley of the mountains will stretch to Azal. Thus, you will flee just as you fled during the earthquake in the days of Uzziah, king of Judah. Then the Lord my God will come, and all the holy ones with him.

And in that day, there will be no daytime light or nighttime frost. And it will be continuously daytime (it is known only to the Lord)—no day and no night; even in the evening time there will be light. In that day, living waters will go out from Jerusalem, half of them toward the eastern sea and half of them toward the western sea, in both summer and winter. And the Lord will be king over all the earth. In that day, the Lord will be the only one and his name the only one.

Then all the land, from Geba to Rimmon, south of Jerusalem, will become like a plain. But Jersualem will remain perched where it is, from the Gate of Benjamin to the place of the First Gate, down to the Corner Gate, and from the Tower of Hananel to the king's wine-presses. And they will dwell in it. The city will never again be devoted to destruction, but Jerusalem will dwell in security.

And this will be the plague with which the Lord will strike all the peoples who have waged war against Jeru-salem: their flesh will rot while they are standing on their feet; their eyes will rot in their sockets; their tongues will rot in their mouths. In that day, there will be a great panic caused by the Lord so that each man will seize the hand of his neighbor and raise his hand against his neighbor's hand. And Judah will also fight in Jerusalem. The wealth of all the surrounding nations will be gath-ered in—vast amounts of gold, silver, and garments. The same kind of plague will strike the horses, mules, cam-els, and donkeys and all the animals in those camps.

And all those who remain from all the nations that came against Jerusalem will go up year after year to bow down to the King, the Lord of hosts, and to keep the Feast of Booths. And if any of the families of the earth do not go up to bow down to the King, the Lord of hosts, then they will receive no rain. And if the fam-ily of Egypt will not go up and come in, then they will receive no rain; instead they will receive the plague with which the Lord will strike the nations that will not go up and keep the Feast of Booths. Such will be the punishment on Egypt and on all the nations that will not go up to keep the Feast of Booths.

In that day, there will be inscribed on the bells of the horses, "Holy to the Lord." And the pots in the house of the Lord will be like the basins before the altar. And every pot in Jerusalem and Judah will be holy to the Lord of hosts. And all who sacrifice will come in and take from them and boil the meat in them. And there will never again be a trader in the house of the Lord of hosts in that day. (Zechariah 14:1–21)

[Christ said,] 'You Lord have made me a second beginning for all on the earth. . . . In me you see the nature of man made clean, its faults corrected, made holy and pure. Now give me the good things of your kindness, undo the abandonment, rebuke corruption and set a limit on your anger. [For] I have conquered Satan himself.' (St. Cyril of Alexandria[1])

The final chapter in the book of Zechariah picks up numerous themes from the preceding chapters and works them together for a powerful symphonic description of a day when everything will be renewed and set right again. Themes such as the Day of the Lord, the Davidic king, the Divine Warrior, the judgment on the nations leading to their salvation, streaming waters of renewal, the restoration of Jerusalem's fortunes, and God's defense of his royal city all reach their climactic presentation in Zechariah 14. The chapter itself contains numerous small units, the first one being a description of the eschatological battle of the last day.

THE LAST BATTLE (14:1–5)

Announcement is made that a day of the Lord is coming, revealing that the focus of the chapter is eschatological in nature. As a concept, the "day of the Lord" is rooted in the ancient concept of holy war in the past, which the prophets have transfigured into the cosmic victory of the Lord in the future. "The Day of Yahweh encompasses a pure event of war, the rise of Yahweh against his enemies, his battle and his victory. . . . It derives from the tradition of the holy wars of Yahweh, in which Yahweh appeared personally, to annihilate his enemies."[2] On that day, the prophets proclaimed, the Lord would intervene with a jolt into history in order to fight for his people and to judge the nations. This cataclysmic intervention is precisely what is in view in the final chapter of Zechariah. Verses 1–3 are loaded with war terminology: spoil, divided, war, capture, plunder, exile, cut off, battle, combat.

The battle commences when the Lord gathers all the nations to Jerusalem to fight against the city. In Zechariah 12, the nations were gathering against Jerusalem, and God defended her. But in this climactic oracle a shift of emphasis occurs. Now it is not the nations who are gathering against the city on their own initiative, it is God who is bringing the nations against Jerusalem and the results are much graver.[3] The city will be captured, the houses plundered, and the women raped, with half the city going into exile. The situation is similar to Jeremiah's oracle against Jerusalem and Zedekiah (Jer. 21:3–7). There the Lord declared his intention to use the Babylonian army as his weapon of attack against a sinful Jerusalem (cf. also Ezek. 38:19–23; 39:10). Similarly, when the day of the Lord arrives, the Lord brings judgment on the city for its sin—a judgment described in graphic terms. Nevertheless, the ultimate intent is not to annihilate Jerusalem but to purge it and to refine a remnant, just as in Zechariah 12:1–13:9.

Afterward, the Lord will turn his attention to the attacking nations, fighting against them (and for his people) as in the day of battle. When the Lord appears, he will stand on the Mount of Olives to the east of Jerusalem. This is not an incidental point. When the Lord departed from the temple at the beginning of the exile, he left the city and stood on the Mount of Olives (Ezek. 11:23). And his return was to be from the same eastern direction (Ezek. 43:1–3). Thus, the expectation of the Lord's return led the people to look in the same direction: east toward the Mount of Olives.

When the Lord plants his feet on the mountain, it will split in two from east to west, forming a large valley in the middle. Then half of the mountain will move northward and the other half will move southward, providing an easy pathway of movement. First, the people can use the valley as an escape route out of Jerusalem to flee just as they did when the earthquake hit during the eighth century reign of King Uzziah (cf. Amos 1:1).[4] Second, the valley will provide an open alley for the Lord to come, flanked by his heavenly entourage of holy ones, in royal procession to Zion.

PARADISE REVISITED; JERUSALEM RESTORED (14:6–11)

Suddenly the battle scene is interrupted to portray briefly the transformation that will ultimately result from the Lord's return to Zion. The change in mood from verses 1–5 to verses 6–11 is dramatic. The day of battle will be like a day of darkness and doom before giving way to a new day of ceaseless light (cf. Isa. 60:1–6, 19–20). On that day, there will be no daytime light or nighttime frost. The daytime will be continuous such that even in the evening there will be light. The disruption to the normal cycles of day and night is significant. In God's promise to Noah, he had promised that the normal rhythms of seasons and days would not cease for as long as the earth endures (Gen. 8:22). To claim that the eschatological battle would produce a time of continuous daytime without frost was to declare that this vision is the long-awaited goal of history. And when it arrives, the promise to Noah will no longer need to be in effect since all things will purified and renewed. "Floodwaters will be replaced by living waters."[5]

This vision of living waters streaming out to the nations is the continuation of a theme within the book of Zechariah (13:1) but also outside it. In Ezekiel's powerful vision of the renewed temple (Ezek. 47:1–12), he saw water coming out from under the threshold. The streams continued to build until such an enormous volume of refreshing, life-giving water was flowing out of the temple that it turned the Dead Sea into a fresh water lake teeming with marine life. Zechariah 14 develops this theme, but intensifies it by envisioning the living water flowing out not just from the Temple but from the whole city of Jerusalem and not just to the east but to the west as well. Half of the water flows east to the Dead Sea; half flows west to the Mediterranean Sea. And it never stops. In both summer and winter, living water continues to gush out of the city.

So it will be with the advent of the Lord. His defeat of evil will bring about his unchallenged supremacy as King over all the earth. He will be recognized universally as the only true God, and his name will be revered as the only name (cf. Deut. 4:33–35; 6:4). Just as copious streams will engulf a place of death, like the Dead Sea, and transform it into a wellspring of life, so the advent of the Great King will overwhelm all his enemies and turn a world held in the deadly grip of evil into a place of new life.

On that day, the whole land, from Geba to Rimmon, will become like a plain. Before the exile, Geba and Rimmon denoted the northern and southern boundaries of Judah during the days of Josiah's reform.[6] In other words, the land will be restored to her preexilic, pre-disaster state, and being "leveled out," will provide a geological setting for the crown jewel of the new creation, the city of Jerusalem. Raised up and set in its place, Jerusalem will thus become the central starting point of God's final work of renewal in the whole created order. It will be "the central point of reference with respect to the two most elemental aspects of earthly existence, water and land. Just as the streams of life-giving water flow out from the city along the east-west axis, the land drops off along the axis extending northward toward Geba and southward toward Rimmon."[7]

The city itself will then be defined by distinct boundaries, stretching from the Gate of Benjamin (on the city's northern side) to the place of the First Gate (the location of which is now lost but possibly denotes an old gate on the east side of the city), down to the Corner Gate (on the western side), and from the Tower of Hananel (probably near the northwest corner) down to the king's winepresses in the south.[8] The boundaries are not only a way of tracing the city's limits but are more importantly an allusion to Jeremiah 31 where the Lord had promised that the city would be rebuilt from the Tower of Hananel to the Corner Gate (Jer. 31:38). Part of the promise to Jeremiah was that the whole city would once again become holy, never again to be uprooted or demolished (Jer. 31:39–40; cf. Zech. 14:20–21). In other words, the boundaries paint a picture of Jerusalem as a city entirely safe from the threat of violence.

This implies a completely different relationship between Israel and the other nations. Previously, the struggle against pagan nations and their idols meant a need for holy war (*herem*). But on the day of the Lord, the city will never again be devoted to destruction (*herem*), meaning that Jerusalem will never have to fight again; she will dwell in security from now on (cf. Zech. 2:1–13). Neither will she have to worry about internal corruption from idolatry (cf. Zech. 13:2–6) since the places previously popular for idol worship will have been destroyed (vv. 4–5, 10). The nations will have been converted from corrupting attackers to fellow worshippers.

THE BATTLE FINALE (14:12–15)

Before the nations can be transformed they must be judged. After a brief interlude to offer a glimpse of the final renewal, the eschatological battle resumes with a particularly ghastly scene. The Lord will strike those encamped around Jerusalem with a gruesome plague such that the soldiers will begin to disintegrate, with their flesh, eyes, and tongues rotting. The result will be chaos and panic among the troops, with soldiers turning to attack one another, and an opportunity to plunder any gold, silver, and clothing available.

The scene calls to mind two previous episodes in Israel's history. First, when the Assyrian army under Sennacherib was advancing upon Jerusalem, the Lord miraculously delivered the city by striking the army with a terrible plague (2 Kings 19:8–37). Second, the plundering of gold, silver, and garments from the nations echoes the plundering of the Egyptians during the exodus (Ex. 3:22). On the last day, there will be an immediate reversal of Jerusalem's judgment. In verse 2, Jerusalem was plundered by the marauders, but now the roles are quickly reversed. The nations that plundered Jerusalem are now plundered themselves, having their vast amounts of gold, silver, and garments looted.

THE HARVEST OF NATIONS (14:16–19)

Nevertheless, just as judgment on Jerusalem will preserve a remnant among its inhabitants, so the judgment against the nations will also preserve a band of survivors. Having been spared, these survivors become worshippers of the Lord, the Great King, streaming to Jerusalem to fall down before him (cf. Isa. 2:1–4; 56:6–8; 60:3–5; 66:18–23; Mic. 4:1–4). This mass flocking into the city will happen at the Feast of Booths.

Why? There are at least two reasons. First, the Feast of Booths was a celebration of the Lord's great work of redemption in the events of the exodus. As such it became synonymous with the Lord's deliverance of the people, by fighting against their enemies and liberating them to worship him. It is little wonder that the expected work of redemption from the bonds of exile began to be expressed in terms of a new exodus (e.g., Isa. 43:14–21; 63:11–13; 64:1–3; Jer. 23:7–8). In this final vision, this motif is expanded into eschatological dimensions, looking ahead to when God's final battle will destroy evil and transform all the nations into worshippers who will march into the Promised Land to serve him as King. Naturally, there will be no more appropriate feast during which this should happen than the Feast of Booths.

Second, the Feast of Booths was celebrated at harvest time (Deut. 16:13), giving it the alternate name of the Feast of Ingathering (Ex. 23:16; 34:22). Therefore, in the imagery of verse 8, the streams of water will flow out to all the lands, and the irrigation will then naturally produce a harvest of nations that can then be ingathered back into Jerusalem.

EVERYTHING MADE HOLY (14:20–21)

The result would be a thoroughgoing holiness. The bells of the horses would be inscribed with the words "Holy to the Lord," which were previously engraved on the high priest's turban (Ex. 28:36–37). Even something as ordinary as horses' bells would be as sacred as the high priestly garb and the horses themselves, previously used for battle, are now under the Lord's domain and become ornamented with holy objects. Similarly, the cooking pots in the temple would be as holy as the basins in front of the altar. Even the most common pot would become holy, so holy that anyone wishing to sacrifice could readily use them.

On that day, there would no longer even be a trader in the house of the Lord. The Hebrew word for "trader" (khna'ani) is sometimes translated "Canaanite," leading some to conclude that this is intended to bar unclean peoples from the temple precincts. But given that the previous verses just celebrated the ingathering of all the nations for worship in Jerusalem, such an ethnic exclusion seems at the very least strange.[9] Stronger is the case for reading the word as referring "not to a particular nationality, but to those who make extortionate profits out of the worshippers. Once the King comes, money-making will no longer mar the Temple courts, nor merchants' greed take the joy out of sacrificial giving."[10] Instead, everything in the city will be so sanctified that merchants will no longer be able to profit by peddling their ritually pure objects and animals to worshippers.

THE RENEWAL OF ALL THINGS

Zechariah 14 paints a dramatic picture of the Divine Warrior defending Jerusalem against attacking enemies, triumphantly proceeding with his holy ones to Jerusalem from the Mount of Olives, and inaugurating a new order of creation in which the Lord's enemies are conquered and converted and all things profane become sacred. In the New Testament, Jesus' entry into the Holy City is deliberately modeled on the triumphal procession of the Divine Warrior of Zechariah 14 as well as certain characteristics of Greco-Roman entrance processions.[11] The connection to Zechariah 14 is three-fold. First, Jesus begins his journey into Jerusalem at the Mount of Olives (Mark 11:1; cf. Zech. 12:4). Second, Jesus proceeds into Jerusalem with his disciples in tow (Mark 11:1; cf. Zech 12:5). Third, Jesus cleanses the temple by driving out the money changers (Mark 11:15–17; cf. Zech. 14:20–21). Mark seems to have the general pattern of Zechariah 14 in mind as he narrates Jesus' entry into Jerusalem. The point is that Jesus is the Divine Warrior who, in coming to the Holy City, is inaugurating the new eschatological age in which the Lord's enemies are defeated and all things profane are sanctified.

But there is more. If Zechariah 14 is the Old Testament base for Mark's shaping of Jesus' entry into Jerusalem, the contemporary pattern of Greco-Roman entrance processions fills out the portrait. In these processions, the victorious warrior-king is accompanied by citizens or soldiers into the city with celebratory acclamations and symbolic depictions of his authority. Once the warrior-king has come into the city, he symbolically appropriates the city through some sort of ritual such as a sacrifice. Similarly, Jesus enters the city with his disciples amid shouts of "Hosanna! Blessed is he who comes in the name of the Lord! Blessed is the coming kingdom of our father David! Hosanna in the highest!" (Mark 11:9b–10 ESV) as the crowds acknowledge his authority by laying down cloaks and palm branches on the road (Mark 11:8), which is unmistakably an acclamation of military triumph (cf. 1 Macc. 13:51; 2 Macc. 10:7; Rev. 7:9).

Jesus plays out the pattern of the Divine Warrior's procession in Zechariah 14 and the Greco-Roman warrior-king's entrance parade. He begins at the Mount of Olives and enters Jerusalem with his disciples amid shouts of acclamation and symbolic recognitions of his authority. At this point, the reader would expect the last element of the pattern to take place, namely that Jesus would appropriate the city through a ritual such as a sacrifice in the temple and establish his ongoing reign.

But just when the reader expects Jesus to complete his triumphal procession, something unexpected happens. Jesus simply looks around and walks out (Mark 11:11)! The next day he returns to Jerusalem, and it appears that he is finally about to appropriate the city and temple when he zealously drives out the money changers in the temple. Instead, Jesus rejects the temple, a point Mark subtly emphasizes by framing the temple cleansing with the cursing of the fig tree (Mark 11:12–14, 20–21). A little later Jesus himself makes the rejection explicit to his disciples when they are together back on the Mount of Olives, in language again alluding to Zechariah's final chapter (Mark 13:1–37).

What is most surprising is the way that Jesus as the Divine Warrior completes his triumphal procession. He walks not into the city, but out of it. On his way, he is not borne up by the praises of the people, but weighed down by the beams of a cross. When he arrives at his destination, he sacrifices not an animal on an altar but himself on Golgotha. There the procession finishes not with the exaltation of his glory, but the humiliation of his defeat.

Or did it? Three days later, the slain Divine Warrior made another procession, this time back up from the grave. Resurrected and ascended, he conquered all his enemies. Suddenly the final steps in the earthly procession look altogether different. In Jesus' combat with the forces of evil, it turns out that his defeat was actually his victory, and their victory actually their defeat. Through the cross, the slain Warrior has triumphed over them (Col. 2:15).

And it was precisely through the surprising ending to the procession that the era of blessedness has begun in our world. Just as the Divine Warrior's procession from the Mount of Olives to Jerusalem inaugurated the new order of creation in Zechariah 14, so also through Christ's procession along the same route that culminated in his death and resurrection, the new creation has dawned (2 Cor. 5:17; Gal. 6:15). Through his resurrection and ascension, the Holy Spirit has been poured out on the church at Pentecost, like living water flowing out of Jerusalem for the harvesting of the nations (John 7:37–39; 16:7; Acts 2). On that day in Jerusalem the nations gathered, though not for battle but for blessing.

It was an inauguration and anticipation of the end of the story when Jesus, the Divine Warrior, will appear to defeat evil once and for all and to renew all of creation. On that day, there will be a great and final battle. The kings of the earth (symbolized by the "kings of the East") will gather once again to attack the people of God (Rev. 16:12–16; cf. Zech. 12:3; 14:2–3). Confident that they will prevail, the kings end up being crushed by the satanic forces that have deceived them. The event is punctuated by a devastating earthquake reminiscent of the earthquake that split the

Mount of Olives in Zechariah (Rev. 16:17–21; cf. Zech. 14:3–5). The beast, the false prophet, the dragon, and their followers are resoundingly defeated by the Divine Warrior, Jesus Christ, the King of Kings and Lord of Lords who is mounted on the white horse and flanked by the armies of heaven (Rev. 19:11–21; 20:7–10; cf. Zech. 14:5). Upon his final and conclusive defeat of evil, every knee will bow and every tongue will confess that Jesus Christ is Lord. He will be acknowledged as the only Lord and his name will be the only one worshipped (1 Cor. 15:25–28; Phil. 2:10–11; cf. Rom. 14:11; Zech. 14:9).

Furthermore, his defeat of the evil powers, and his exaltation as Lord over the whole world will usher in the fullness of the new creation that already began with Jesus' resurrection. The present created order will be fully and concretely soaked with the presence of God that redeems, sanctifies, transforms, and transfigures it into something altogether glorious and resplendent (Rev. 21:1–22:5). In John's description of this new creation—this new heaven and new earth—he overtly connects it to the early chapters of Genesis (and implicitly to numerous themes in Zechariah 14). Genesis 1:1 begins with the words, "In the beginning God created the heavens and the earth." Revelation ends with a picture of the new heaven and the new earth. In Genesis, God calls into being the luminaries—the sun, moon, and stars; in John's final vision "there will be no more night. They will not need the light of a lamp or the light of the sun, for the Lord God will give them light" (cf. Zech. 14:6–7). In Genesis, Paradise is created as a garden, watered by a river and stocked with the tree of life. In John's final vision, Paradise is recreated, complete with the river of the water of life and on each side of the river there is the tree of life (cf. Zech. 14:8). In Genesis, the human beings that God created disobeyed, which brought upon the human race and this earth a curse of pain and suffering. In John's final vision, there is no longer any curse and God himself wipes away every tear from our eyes. There is no more death or mourning or crying or pain.

In other words, from Genesis 1–3 through Zechariah 14 to Revelation 21–22 the point is that our world's destiny is a thoroughly redemptive transformation. One day it will no longer bear the scars and wounds from its brokenness but will become so utterly soaked by the presence of God himself that it will be transfigured into something glorious, radiant, and holy (Rev. 21:16–18; cf. Zech. 14:20–21). Until then, all those who are in Christ—Jew as well as Gentile— become a community of the new creation (2 Cor. 5:17). *"The church embodies the power of the resurrection in the midst of a not-yet-redeemed world. . . .* The church is, in Paul's remarkable phrase, the community of those 'upon whom the ends of the ages have met' (1 Cor. 10:11). In Christ, we know that the powers of the old age are doomed, and the new creation is already appearing."[12]

The church as the community of the new creation strains against the old order, calling it into question and always pointing ahead toward the day when there is a new heaven and a new earth. "Those who hope in Christ can no longer put up with reality as it is, but begin to suffer under it, to contradict it."[13] We are to embody a new way of being, giving flesh and blood expression to the Spirit- directed new order of things and providing this world with a sneak peek of its glorious destiny. We are to show this world that redemption is coming to sweep it up, sanctify, transform, and transfigure it into something altogether glo- rious and resplendent.

And we are to point it to Jesus Christ, the Divine War- rior who will come again to conquer evil once and for all. For he is "Faithful and True, and in righteousness he judges and makes war. His eyes are like a flame of fire, and on his head are many diadems, and he has a name written that no one knows but himself. He is clothed in a robe dipped in blood, and the name by which he is called is The Word of God. And the armies of heaven, arrayed in fine linen, white and pure, were following him on white horses. From his mouth comes a sharp sword with which to strike down the nations, and he will rule them with a rod of iron. He will tread the winepress of the fury of the wrath of God the Almighty. On his robe and on his thigh he has a name written, King of kings and Lord of lords" (Rev. 19:11–16 ESV). In the meantime, as we wait for the advent of our Divine Warrior to put evil underfoot and to redeem this world broken by sin and death, we lift up our eyes, we long for God, and we cry out, "Maranatha! Come Lord Jesus, come! And even so, come quickly!"

FOR FURTHER REFLECTION

1. How would the promise of the Divine Warrior have provided hope and encouragement to the postexilic community?
2. How might the promise of the Divine Warrior in Revelation provide hope and encouragement to those today?
3. How does Jesus embody the Divine Warrior and how does he inaugurate the new creation promised in Zechariah?
4. What does it mean for the church corporately and you personally to live in light of the new creation?

NOTES

ACKNOWLEDGMENTS

1   Maximus the Confessor, "The Four Hundred Chapters on Love" in *Maximus Confessor: Selected Writings,* trans. George C. Berthold (New York: Paulist Press, 1985), 86.

CHAPTER ONE: READING ZECHARIAH

1   Chaim Potok, *In the Beginning* (New York: Alfred A. Knopf, 1976), 3.

2   Fuller treatments of the history of this period can be accessed from any number of histories of Israel. The two most helpful works in terms of clearly laying out the relevant data are J. Maxwell Miller and John H. Hayes, *A History of Ancient Israel and Judah,* 2nd ed. (Louisville: Westminster John Knox, 2006) and Iain Provan, V. Philips Long, and Tremper Longman III, *A Biblical History of Israel* (Louisville: Westminster John Knox, 2003). Miller and Hayes are moderate-critical in their approach; Provan, Long, and Longman are conservative and evangelical.

3   Scholars have long noted the differences in language, form, and content between the two versions of Cyrus' edict in Ezra 1:2–4 and 6:2–5. In language 1:2–4 is given in Hebrew, while 6:2–5 is in Aramaic. In form, 1:2–4 is given as an oral report, while 6:2–5 is given as a written decree. In content, 1:2–4 emphasizes the repatriation of exiled Judeans but lacks any details about the reconstruction of the temple, while 6:2–5 omits the repatriation but details the physical aspects of the temple. Moreover, 1:2–4 states that "all [the Lord's] people" were to spearhead the reconstruction all the while receiving financial assistance "by the men of his place," while 6:2–5 fails to mention who is responsible for the actual construction, but does state that "the cost be paid from the royal treasury." Bedford notes

and discusses the three main positions: (1) the majority position is that 6:2–5 is original, while 1:2–4 is either derived from 6:2–5 or an entirely free creation; (2) both are original, the differences being explained by their respective purposes and genres; (3) neither are original. See Peter Ross Bedford, *Temple Restoration in Early Achaemenid Judah,* JSJSup 65 (Leiden: Brill, 2001), 111–32. Position three seems unlikely since one would expect two fabrications to exhibit more harmony than these two texts do. Advocates of position two generally argue that Ezra 1:2–4 derives from oral proclamations made by heralds and was only later written down, while 6:2–5 reflects the official written document stored in the royal archives (see H. G. M. Williamson, *Ezra, Nehemiah* [WBC 16; Waco: Word, 1985], 6–7). Advocates of position one argue that "these are differences in substance, not style, and cannot be resolved by harmonization." (Sara Japhet, "The Temple in the Restoration Period: Reality and Ideology," *USQR* 44.3 [1991]): 195–251. Japhet goes on to argue that Ezra 1:2–4 was theologically constructed in order to highlight the true redemptive significance of the edict.)

4   The translation is from Bill T. Arnold and Bryan E. Beyer, ed., *Readings from the Ancient Near East* (Grand Rapids: Baker, 2002), 148–49.

5   The boundaries are those given in the map of Yehud in Anson Rainey and R. Steven Notley, *The Sacred Bridge: Carta's Atlas of the Biblical World* (Jerusalem: Carta, 2006), 296.

6   John Bright, *A History of Israel,* 3rd ed. (Philadelphia: Westminster, 1981), 365 n. 57. Population estimates range from close to 50,000 down to, for example, Carter's estimate of 13, 350. Charles E. Carter, *The Emergence of Yehud in the Persian Period: A Social and Demographic Study* (JSOTSS 294; Sheffield: Sheffield Academic, 1999), 199–201.

7   When the foundations were laid has been a matter of debate. Ezra 3:10 seems to suggest that the foundations were laid in 537 B.C., while Haggai and Zechariah seem to indicate that it took place under the leadership of Zerubbabel in 520 B.C. Both Andersen and Kessler argue that '*ysd*' can have, and in this case does have, a broad meaning such that the event of 537 was the initial activity of a religious rite, and the event in 520 was a more formal act of

inauguration and construction. See Francis I. Andersen. "Who Built the Second Temple?" *ABR* 6 (1958): 1–35; John Kessler, *The Book of Haggai: Prophecy and Society in Early Persian Yehud* (VTSup 91; Leiden: Brill, 2002), 59–90. If this is true, however, another difficulty surfaces. Ezra 5:16 claims that the work has been underway "from that time until now," while it is clear from Haggai and Zechariah that there was a delay of almost two decades in which no work was done until Zerubbabel restarted the effort. Why the seemingly disparate accounts? Williamson's explanation is helpful: "We have argued . . . that the altar was rededicated soon after the return in Cyrus' reign, when we may surmise that Sheshbazzar was still governor. We also argued that the account of the foundation-laying . . . should be referred to the time of Darius. What mattered to the Jews was that enough had been done at the first to show that Cyrus' edict was not simply ignored; they therefore felt able to justify their present activity as being its continuation, which may have been true in spirit, though clearly not in letter." Williamson, *Ezra, Nehemiah*, 79.

8 Much ink has been spilled over the differences between Ezra (who assigns the blame for the stalled reconstruction efforts to external problems) and Haggai and Zechariah (who assign the blame to the internal conflicts between Jewish parties). The issues are complex but it is ultimately unnecessary to view them as irreconcilable. Haggai and Zechariah likely focus on the internal conflicts because their overriding concern is to make way for the Lord's return to Zion. Ezra, on the other hand, views the situation from the removed perspective of a century after the events. By that point, with Persia still in power, the more pressing issue is how Judah negotiates its life with Samaria and Persia. For a balanced discussion of the historical issues involved, see Sara Japhet, "'History' and 'Literature' in the Persian Period: The Restoration of the Temple" in *Ah, Assyria . . . Studies in Assyrian History and Ancient Near Eastern Historiography Presented to Hayim Tadmor*, Mordechai Cogan and Israel Ehp'al eds. (Jerusalem: Magnes Press, 1991), 174–88.

9 I think the sometimes supposed internal dichotomy in the Jewish community between an "eschatological" party and a "theocratic" party (as argued in Paul Hanson, *The Dawn of Apocalyptic*

[Minneapolis: Fortress, 1975] and Otto Plöger, *Theocracy and Eschatology,* trans. S. Rudman [Richmond: John Knox, 1968]) is exaggerated. More sober is Williamson's contention that "shifting historical circumstances caused general opinion to tilt now this way and now that, though with representatives of either extreme balancing such shifts at all times." Williamson, *Ezra, Nehemiah,* li.

10 Rainer Albertz, *A History of Israelite Religion in the Old Testament Period,* vol. 2, *From the Exile to the Maccabees,* trans. John Bowden (OTL; Louisville: Westminster John Knox, 1994), 451.

11 Jon L. Berquist, *Judaism in Persia's Shadow: A Social and Historical Approach* (Minneapolis: Fortress, 1995), 27. For the view that the level of Persian involvement in the reconstruction efforts was fairly limited, see also Kessler, *The Book of Haggai,* 86–88. The limited involvement would also explain why the delay in construction went seemingly unaddressed by the Persian authorities.

12 Barry G. Webb, *The Message of Zechariah: Your Kingdom Come* (BST; Downers Grove: InterVarsity, 2003), 26.

13 Gerhard von Rad, *Old Testament Theology,* vol. 2, *The Theology of Israel's Prophetic Traditions,* trans. D. M. G. Stalker (New York: Harper and Row, 1965), 288.

14 Proposals for the date of composition of Zechariah 9–14 typically fall within the range from as early as the late 6th or early 5th century (see Byron Curtis, *Up the Steep and Stony Road: The Book of Zechariah in Social Location Trajectory Analysis* [Leiden: Brill, 2006]; Andrew E. Hill, "Dating Second Zechariah: A Linguistic Reexamination," *HAR* 6 [1982]: 105–34) to as late as the early 3rd century B.C. (see Georg Fohrer, *Introduction to the Old Testament,* trans. David E. Green [Nashville: Abingdon, 1968], 468.)

15 Raymond B. Dillard and Tremper Longman III, *An Introduction to the Old Testament* (Grand Rapids: Zondervan, 1994), 431.

16 For the data, see Mark C. Black, "The Rejected and Slain Messiah Who Is Coming with His Angels: The Messianic Exegesis of Zechariah 9–14" (PhD diss., Emory University, 1990), 6, 9.

17 George Barna, *Growing True Disciples: New Strategies for Producing Genuine Followers of Christ* (Colorado Springs: Waterbrook, 2001), 42–43.

18 David Kinnaman and Gabe Lyons, *unChristian: What a New Generation Really Thinks about Christianity . . . And Why It Matters* (Grand Rapids: Baker, 2007), 11, 42.

CHAPTER TWO: THE CALL OF ZECHARIAH

1 Augustine, *The Works of Saint Augustine: A Translation for the 21st Century Series,* part 3, vol. 2, *Sermons on the Old Testament (20–50),* trans. Edmund Hill, O.P. (Hyde Park: New City Press, 1990), 46.

2 The dates are given in Carol L. Meyers and Eric M. Meyers, *Haggai, Zechariah 1–8* (AB 25B; New York: Doubleday, 1987), xlvi. The final two sections, Zech. 9–11 and Zech. 12–14, are not dated but presuppose a time after the completion of the temple (see Zech. 11:13; 14:20–21).

3 Zechariah's genealogy has received attention due to the apparent discrepancy with Ezra 5:1 and 6:14, which refer to Zechariah as the son, not the grandson of Iddo (the NIV alleviates the discrepancy by translating the verses in Ezra as "descendent of Iddo"). Several possibilities exist but the most probable, it seems to me, is that Ezra's concern for the priesthood has led to the "direct" connection between the priest Iddo and his grandson Zechariah (cf. Neh. 12:16 if these are the same people).

4 Two months earlier, Haggai had issued a similar call to repentance (Hag. 1:1–11), which the people had obeyed (Hag. 1:12), leaving open the question of why Zechariah would need to repeat the call. Proposed solutions vary, but Tollington argues: "Clearly the motivation for repentance in Zechariah is quite different from that in Haggai, because whereas Haggai focused on the traditional concept of agricultural blessings and curses, in Zechariah an appeal to history and the remembrance of the exile as evidence of Yahweh's righteous justice is used to prompt the change of heart." Janet E. Tollington, *Tradition and Innovation in Haggai and Zechariah 1–8* (JSOTSS 150; Sheffield: JSOT Press, 1993), 204.

5 Carroll Stuhlmueller, *Rebuilding with Hope: A Commentary on the Books of Haggai and Zechariah* (ITC; Grand Rapids: Eerdmans, 1988), 56.

6 For more reasons, see Mark J. Boda, *Haggai, Zechariah* (NIVAC; Grand Rapids: Zondervan, 2004), 176–77 and Peter R. Ackroyd, *Exile*

and Restoration: A Study of Hebrew Thought in the Sixth Century B.C. (OTL; Philadelphia: Westminster, 1968), 202.

7   Peter C. Craigie, *Twelve Prophets,* vol. 2 (DSB; Philadelphia: Westminster, 1985), 161–62.

8   N. T. Wright, *Jesus and the Victory of God* (Minneapolis: Fortress, 1996), 246–58.

9   Quoted in Philip Schaff, *History of the Christian Church,* vol. 7, *The German Reformation, The Beginning of the Protestant Reformation up to the Diet of Augsburg, 1517–1530,* 2nd ed. (Peabody: Hendrickson, 2006), 160 n. 2 (emphases in the original). The translation of the first thesis is Schaff's; see ibid., 158–59. Schaff notes that Luther used the Vulgate rendering, which favored the Roman Catholic view that Jesus was talking about outward acts of penance. His view was sharpened a year later when Melanchthon introduced him to the correct meaning of the Greek word.

10 Richard F. Lovelace, *Dynamics of Spiritual Life: An Evangelical Theology of Renewal* (Downers Grove: InterVarsity Press, 1979), 383.

11 Augustine, *Confessions,* trans. F. J. Sheed (Indianapolis: Hackett, 1993), 138–39.

12 Ephraim Radner, *The End of the Church: A Pneumatology of Christian Division in the West* (Grand Rapids: Eerdmans, 1998), 277, 278.

13 John Chrysostom, *Homilies on the Acts of the Apostles and the Epistle to the Romans,* NPNF First Series, vol. 11 (Peabody: Hendrickson, 2004), Homily XXXVI:227 (translation modernized).

14 Ambrose, *Concerning Repentance,* NPNF Second Series, vol. 10 (Peabody: Hendrickson, 2004), Book II.X:357. The version given here reflects the paraphrased version in St. Francis de Sales, *Introduction to the Devout Life* (New York: Random House, 2002), 136.

CHAPTER THREE: LONGING FOR THE PEACE OF GOD: THE VISION OF THE HORSEMAN

1   John Chrysostom, *Homilies on Colossians,* NPNF First Series, vol. 13 (Peabody: Hendrickson, 2004), Homily III:273.

2   Ralph L. Smith, *Micah–Malachi* (WBC 32; Waco: Word, 1984), 189.

3   Joyce G. Baldwin, *Haggai, Zechariah, Malachi* (TOTC 24; Downers Grove: InterVarsity, 1972), 93–94.

4   Throughout the Old Testament, the angel of the Lord is a somewhat enigmatic "character." A common popular interpretation is that he is the pre-incarnate Christ, though it seems unlikely. It is worth noting that in some places the angel of the Lord seems to be identified with the Lord himself (Gen. 16:7–14; Ex. 3:1–8; Judg. 2:1–5; 6:11–18; 13:21–23), while in other places the angel of the Lord seems to be distinct (2 Sam. 24:15–16; 1 Chron. 21:15–30). The safest interpretation is that he has a unique closeness to YHWH with a special mediating role between the Lord and people.

5   John J. Collins, *Introduction to the Hebrew Bible* (Minneapolis: Fortress, 2004), 405–6. Collins also believes that the myrtle trees at night contribute to this allusion: "The trademarks of this system were speed and secrecy. In this vision the element of secrecy is conveyed by the shadows of the myrtle trees and the fact that the vision is at night."

6   For the data, see David L. Petersen, *Haggai and Zechariah 1–8* (OTL; Philadelphia: Westminster: 1984), 149–50.

7   Babylon and Assyria are presumably left unnamed in the oracle since by Zechariah's day both have already gotten their just desserts. The generic designation of "nations" widens the condemnation to any and every nation characterized by arrogance and brutality.

8   Of course, "peace be with you" is a standard greeting. Yet, it is clear from the context that it functions as more than just merely a greeting in John's account. See Andrew Purves, *Reconstructing Pastoral Theology: A Christological Foundation* (Louisville: Westminster John Knox, 2004), 42.

9   Will and Ariel Durant, *The Lessons of History*, (New York: Simon and Schuster, 1968), 81.

10 Béla Vassady, *Limping Along . . . Confessions of a Pilgrim Theologian* (Grand Rapids: Eerdmans, 1985), 223. Vassady goes on to describe in moving detail how he and his family experienced the peace of Christ while bombs were exploding around them in Budapest during World War II. See pages 228–29.

11 Augustine, *City of God*, trans. Henry Bettenson (New York: Penguin Books, 2003), 878.

12 David Augsburger, *Dissident Discipleship: A Spirituality of Self-Surrender, Love of God, and Love of Neighbor* (Grand Rapids: Brazos, 2006), 125–26.

CHAPTER FOUR: LONGING FOR THE JUSTICE OF GOD:
THE VISION OF THE HORNS AND THE BLACKSMITHS

1 Leo the Great, *Sermons*, NPNF Second Series, vol. 12 (Peabody: Hendrickson, 2004), Sermon LXXXII.VI:196 (translation modernized).

2 Peter R. Ackroyd, *Exile and Restoration: A Study of Hebrew Thought of the Sixth Century B.C.* (OTL; Philadelphia: Westminster, 1968), 178.

3 This suggestion is offered by Ralph L. Smith, *Micah-Malachi* (WBC 32; Waco: Word, 1984), 193.

4 Mark Boda, *Haggai, Zechariah* (NIVAC; Grand Rapids: Zondervan, 2004), 215. Michael H. Floyd, *Minor Prophets: Part 2* (FOTL XXII; Grand Rapids: Eerdmans, 2000), 361–62.

5 For instance, Barry Webb has seen a more narrow reference here to the temple builders (as in Ezra 3:7), thus providing an expansion on 1:16, which promised that the temple would be rebuilt. On this reading, the vision asserts that through the humble work of rebuilding the temple, the unjust nations would be laid low. See Barry G. Webb, *The Message of Zechariah: Your Kingdom Come* (BST; Downers Grove: InterVarsity, 2003), 76–77. While I think this reads more into the word than is warranted, the final theological point shows little difference: "The revolutionary message of this vision is that the judgment of the world is already being put into effect wherever God deploys his workmen" (ibid., 78).

6 Carol L. Meyers and Eric M. Meyers, *Haggai, Zechariah 1–8* (AB 25B; New York: Doubleday, 1987), 139.

7 Peter C. Craigie, *Twelve Prophets, vol. 2* (DSB; Philadelphia: Westminster, 1985), 168.

8 Philip Graham Ryken, ed. *The Communion of Saints: Living in Fellowship with the People of God* (Phillipsburg: P&R, 2001), 160–61.

9 Lesslie Newbigin, *The Gospel in a Pluralist Society* (Grand Rapids: Eerdmans, 1989), 137–38.

10 Of the many excellent books by John Perkins, see particularly the account of his own life in John Perkins, *Let Justice Roll Down* (Ven-

tura: Regal, 1976) and his explanation of how Christians can work for biblical justice where they are in John Perkins, *With Justice for All* (Ventura: Regal, 1982).

11 Perkins, *With Justice for All*, 14.

12 This threefold strategy is outlined in Perkins, *With Justice for All*. Also, see John M. Perkins, *Beyond Charity: The Call to Christian Community Development* (Grand Rapids: Baker, 1993) and Robert D. Lupton, *Compassion, Justice, and the Christian Life: Rethinking Ministry to the Poor* (Ventura: Regal, 2007).

13 Helmut Thielicke, *Notes from a Wayfarer: The Autobiography of Helmut Thielicke,* trans. David R. Law (New York: Paragon House, 1995), 58 (emphasis in the original).

CHAPTER FIVE: LONGING FOR THE PRESENCE OF GOD: THE VISION OF THE MAN WITH A MEASURING LINE

1 Hilary of Poitiers, *On the Trinity*, NPNF Second Series, vol. 9 (Peabody: Hendrickson, 2004), II.XXV:59.

2 The Hebrew word for "measuring line" in 1:16 (*qv*) is different from the words used in 2:1 (*khvl*), though they are synonyms.

3 The angel who issues the command is the "angel who was speaking to me," not the angel he encounters. The closest antecedent is the 3ms suffix of *liqra'tho*.

4 On rapidly succeeding verbs functioning as a literary device to convey intense purposefulness, see Robert Alter, *The Art of Biblical Narrative*, (Basic Books, 1981), 8.

5 Barry G. Webb, *The Message of Zechariah: Your Kingdom Come* (BST; Downers Grove: InterVarsity, 2003), 81.

6 David Stronach, *Pasargadae: A Report on the Excavations Conducted by the British Institute of Persian Studies from 1961 to 1963* (Oxford: Oxford University Press, 1978), 141–42, fig. 3, plates 107a, 107b.

7 Zechariah 2:8 is notoriously difficult. There are two textual problems. The first is the phrase "after his glory sent me" that may be taken in one of three ways: (1) Zechariah is motivated by God's glory (as I take it; as does McComiskey: Thomas E. McComiskey, "Zechariah," in *The Minor Prophets*, vol. 3, ed. Thomas McComiskey [Grand Rapids: Baker, 1998], 1059. He nicely translates it as "in pursuit of glory has he sent me."); or (2) Zechariah is sent after he

beholds the glory of the vision; or (3) Zechariah is sent at God's insistence (whereupon "glory" is taken in its sense of "heaviness"). The second problem is the phrase "touches the apple of my eye." The difficulty is whether it should be "his eye" (i.e., the Babylonians' eye) or "my eye" (i.e., the Lord's eye). The latter makes more sense and is typically explained as a scribal emendation to avoid any irreverence. See Emanuel Tov, *Textual Criticism of the Hebrew Bible*, 2nd ed. (Minneapolis: Fortress, 2001), 65–66.

8   N. T. Wright believes that Jesus is intentionally echoing this night vision in his Olivet Discourse, specifically Mark 13:24–31. See N. T. Wright, *Jesus and the Victory of God* (Minneapolis: Fortress, 1996), 363.

9   Richard Bauckham, *The Theology of the Book of Revelation* (Cambridge: Cambridge University Press, 1993), 140.

10   N. T. Wright, *For All God's Worth: True Worship and the Calling of the Church* (Grand Rapids: Eerdmans, 1997), 101.

CHAPTER SIX: LONGING FOR THE RIGHTEOUSNESS OF GOD: THE VISION OF THE HIGH PRIEST AND THE PURE VESTMENTS

1   John Calvin, *Institutes of the Christian Religion*, ed. John T. McNeill, trans. Ford Lewis Battles (Louisville: Westminster John Knox, 1960), 1:726–27.

2   Adapted from Carol L. Meyers and Eric M. Meyers, *Haggai, Zechariah 1–8* (AB 25B; New York: Doubleday, 1987), lvi.

3   I have kept the more generic "Accuser" as opposed to transliterating the word as "Satan" to avoid anachronistically imposing the later devilish attributes to this individual that became common in the New Testament and which are often taken for granted by the modern reader. In the Old Testament, the satan is "an ambiguous figure, a member of the divine council, whose role appears to be that of testing and probing the character of human beings." Leland Ryken, James C. Wilhoit, Tremper Longman III, *Dictionary of Biblical Imagery* (Downers Grove: InterVarsity, 1998), 760.

4   Verse 2 begins with "and he said." Most English translations supply the words *the Lord*, indicating the Lord steps in to rebuke the Accuser. However, the antecedent in verse 1 is clearly the angel of

the Lord. Also, the closest referent for the burning stick is Jerusalem, though the context makes clear that it must refer to Joshua.

5   See the well-argued case of Tiemeyer who bases her judgment on the contrast between the first and second person pronouns as well as the evidence from textual versions. Lena-Sofia Tiemeyer, "The Guilty Priesthood (Zech 3)" in *The Book of Zechariah and Its Influence,* ed. Christopher Tuckett (Burlington: Ashgate, 2003), 12. VanderKam makes the same judgment because only the first two clauses are introduced with a conditional word and because they have a different syntactical structure than the others. See James C. VanderKam, "Joshua the High Priest and the Interpretation of Zechariah 3," *CBQ* 53 (1991): 558–59.

6   Meyers and Meyers, *Haggai, Zechariah 1–8,* 196.

7   This reading is suggested by VanderKam, "Joshua the High Priest and the Interpretation of Zechariah 3," 567–70.

8   Louis Wilken, *The Spirit of Early Christian Thought* (New Haven: Yale University Press, 2003), 36–42. Also, in a rich study of the theme of garments in Scripture, Gary Anderson notes that this baptismal ritual not only points to the cleansing one presently has in Christ, but also to the future clothing in glorious immortality that those in Christ will enjoy at the resurrection on the last day (1 Cor. 15:53). See Gary A. Anderson, *The Genesis of Perfection: Adam and Eve in Jewish and Christian Imagination* (Louisville: Westminster John Knox, 2001), 117–34.

CHAPTER SEVEN: LONGING FOR THE PURPOSES OF GOD: THE VISION OF THE GOLDEN LAMPSTAND AND THE TWO OLIVE TREES

1   Helmut Thielicke, *The Silence of God,* trans. G. W. Bromiley (Grand Rapids: Eerdmans, 1962), 63.

2   For the difficulties involved in the historical reconstruction of the early Persian period, see the introductory chapter.

3   Carol L. Meyers and Eric M. Meyers, *Haggai, Zechariah 1–8* (AB 25B; New York: Doubleday, 1987), 252.

4   Both the word for bowl and the word for lampstand are feminine, making it ultimately inconclusive which is the referent. Strictly speaking, however, the lampstand is the more likely referent. See

the discussion in David Petersen, *Haggai and Zechariah 1–8* (OTL; Philadelphia: Westminster, 1984), 220–21.

5 Vern Poythress, *The Shadow of Christ in the Law of Moses* (Phillipsburg: P&R, 1991), 19.

6 Bruce K. Waltke, *An Old Testament Theology* (Grand Rapids: Zondervan, 2007), 460.

7 While it is true that Joshua would have received a priestly anointing, it is unlikely that Zerubbabel would have been anointed. The Persians would not have done so when they appointed him and the Judeans would probably not have done so since it may have been perceived as a threat to Persian sovereignty. Moreover, this explains Zechariah's hesitancy, in contrast to Haggai, of attaching the designation "governor" to Zerubbabel. Most English translations, however, opt for "anointed," presumably out of deference to the theme of messianism present in the final form of the Book of the Twelve.

8 Jon D. Levenson, *Sinai and Zion: An Entry into the Jewish Bible* (San Francisco: Harper & Row, 1985), 140.

9 The standard work is Richard S. Ellis, *Foundation Deposits in Ancient Mesopotamia* (New Haven: Yale University Press, 1968). Also see Antti Laato, "Zachariah 4,6b–10a and the Akkadian Royal Building Inscriptions," *ZAW* 106 (1994): 53–69.

10 Syntactically, the shouts may be attributed to either Zechariah or the people. Given the parallel with verse 10, in which the people rejoice when the stone of distinction is brought forth, it is probably more likely that the shouts come from the people when the top stone is brought forward as well.

11 For a detailed discussion of the options, see Meyers and Meyers, *Haggai, Zechariah 1–8*, 253.

12 Frank Moore Cross, *Canaanite Myth and Hebrew Epic* (Cambridge: Harvard University Press, 1997), 194.

13 Ulrich Luz, *Matthew 8–20*, trans. James E. Crouch (Hermeneia; Minneapolis: Fortress, 2001), 261.

14 Data given in Craig A. Evans, "The Shout of Death" in *Jesus, The Final Days: What Really Happened*, ed. Troy A. Miller (Louisville: Westminster John Knox, 2009), 3–4.

15   Quoted in Rodney Stark, *The Rise of Christianity* (New York: Harper
     Collins, 1997), 82, 83.

CHAPTER EIGHT: LONGING FOR THE AUTHORITY OF GOD: THE VISIONS OF THE FLYING SCROLL AND THE WOMAN IN THE BASKET

1   Karl Barth, *Church Dogmatics*, trans. G. W. Bromiley and T. F.
    Torrance (Edinburgh: T&T Clark, 1936–1977), I.2: 866.

2   Joyce G. Baldwin, *Haggai, Zechariah, Malachi* (TOTC 24; Downers
    Grove: InterVarsity, 1972), 127.

3   Strictly speaking, monetization was a later development, so "infla-
    tion" at this point is in terms of commodities not currency (as we
    tend to think of it).

4   Peterson takes the indictment for swearing falsely by the Lord's
    name as actually a conflation of two commandments, the third
    commandment against taking the Lord's name in vain (Ex. 20:7)
    and the ninth commandment against bearing false witness (Ex.
    20:16). Thus, the two evils explicitly named in Zechariah 5:1–4 draw
    from the language of three of the Ten Commandments (including
    the eighth commandment against stealing, Ex. 20:15) in order "to
    create the notion of serious infractions that remain unpunished."
    David L. Petersen, *Haggai and Zechariah 1–8* (OTL; Philadelphia:
    Westminster, 1984), 250.

5   Baruch Halpern, "The Ritual Background of Zechariah's Temple
    Song," *CBQ* 40 (1978): 179.

6   Michael H. Floyd, *Minor Prophets: Part 2* (FOTL XXII; Grand Rapids:
    Eerdmans, 2000), 387.

7   Dominic Rudman, "Zechariah 5 and the Priestly Law," *SJOT* 14
    (2000): 194–206.

8   Baldwin, *Haggai, Zechariah, Malachi*, 128.

9   For the archaeological and epigraphical data, see Amihai Mazar,
    Archaeology of the Land of the Bible: 10,000—586 B.C.E. (ABRL; New
    York: Doubleday, 1992), 497, 502. Philip J. King and Lawrence E.
    Stager, *Life in Biblical Israel* (Louisville: Westminster John Knox,
    2001), 348–51. William G. Dever, *Did God Have a Wife? Archaeol-
    ogy and Folk Religion in Ancient Israel* (Grand Rapids: Eerdmans,
    2005), 176–251. Mark S. Smith, *The Early History of God: Yahweh*

and the Other Deities in Ancient Israel (Grand Rapids: Eerdmans, 2002), 108–37. That the woman is to be associated with idolatry may also be strengthened by the description of her sitting (*yshv*), a term often used to describe the Lord's enthronement (e.g., 1 Sam. 4:4; 2 Sam. 6:2; 2 Kings 19:15; 1 Chron. 13:6; Pss. 80:1; 99:1; Isa. 37:16). See Michael H. Floyd, "The Evil in the Ephah: Reading Zechariah 5:5–11 in Its Literary Context," *CBQ* 58 (1996): 61.

10 The following data is taken from Ronald J. Sider, *The Scandal of the Evangelical Conscience: Why Are Christians Living Just Like the Rest of the World?* (Grand Rapids: Baker, 2005), 17–29.

11 Friedrich Wilhelm Nietzsche, *Thus Spoke Zarathustra: A Book for All and None*, trans. Adrian Del Caro (Cambridge: Cambridge University Press, 2006), 71.

12 Robert K. McIver, "The Parable of the Weeds Among the Wheat (Matt 13:24–30, 36–43) and the Relationship Between the Kingdom and the Church as Portrayed in the Gospel of Matthew," *JBL* 114 (1995): 648. There has always been debate over whether the parable is addressing the mixture of the righteous and the wicked in the world or in the church. McIver surveys and evaluates the two options and favors the "ecclesiological" interpretation over the "universalist" interpretation. However, even if the universalist interpretation is correct, the ecclesiological interpretation as secondary is still derivatively true and is even reinforced in principle by the parable of the net (Matt. 13:47–50).

13 St. John of the Cross, "The Living Flame of Love" in *The Collected Works of St. John of the Cross*, trans. Kieran Kavanaugh and Otilio Rodriguez (Washington: ICS Publications, 1991), 648–51.

14 Arland J. Hultgren, *The Parables of Jesus: A Commentary* (Grand Rapids: Eerdmans, 2000), 302.

CHAPTER NINE: LONGING FOR THE VICTORY OF GOD: THE VISION OF THE FOUR CHARIOTS

1 Melito of Sardis, "A Homily on the Passover," in *The Christological Controversy*, trans. and ed. Richard A. Norris, Jr. (Philadelphia: Fortress, 1980), 46–47.

2 Gerhard von Rad, *Old Testament Theology*, vol. 2, *The Theology of Israel's Prophetic Traditions*, trans. D. M. G. Stalker (New York:

Harper and Row, 1965), 287. Though von Rad does not spell out his reasons, the suggestion that this vision takes place at daybreak is presumably based on two considerations: (1) as the last in a series of visions occurring over the span of a night, it would make sense for it to occur at dawn; (2) the colors of the horses in the first vision are generally those of sunset, while the colors of the horses in this final vision are generally those of sunrise.

3 Othmar Keel, *The Symbolism of the Biblical World: Ancient Near Eastern Iconography and the Book of Psalms,* trans. Timothy J. Hallett (New York: Seabury, 1978), 22.

4 Volkmar Fritz, *1 & 2 Kings* (CC; Minneapolis: Fortress, 2003), 408.

5 Carol L. Meyers and Eric M. Meyers, *Haggai, Zechariah 1–8* (AB 25B; New York: Doubleday, 1984), 319.

6 See the detailed discussion in David L. Petersen, *Haggai and Zechariah 1–8* (OTL; Philadelphia: Westminster, 1984), 263–64.

7 Joyce G. Baldwin, *Haggai, Zechariah, Malachi* (TOTC 24; Downers Grove: InterVarsity, 1972), 131–32. See also Petersen, *Haggai and Zechariah 1–8*, 263–64; Meyers and Meyers, *Haggai, Zechariah 1–8*, 326.

8 Rex Mason, *The Books of Haggai, Zechariah, and Malachi* (CBC; Cambridge: Cambridge University Press, 1977), 61.

9 Everett Ferguson, *Backgrounds of Early Christianity* (Grand Rapids: Eerdmans, 1993), 497–98.

10 See N. T. Wright, *What Saint Paul Really Said: Was Paul of Tarsus the Real Founder of Christianity?* (Grand Rapids: Eerdmans, 1997), 41–44.

11 Dennis E. Johnson, *The Triumph of the Lamb: A Commentary on Revelation* (Phillipsburg: P&R, 2001), 117–24.

12 Thomas E. McComiskey, "Zechariah," in *The Minor Prophets*, vol. 3, ed. Thomas E. McComiskey (Grand Rapids: Baker, 1998), 1110.

CHAPTER TEN: CROWNS, PRIEST, BRANCH, TEMPLE

1 Justin Martyr, *Dialogue with Trypho*, ANF, vol. 1 (Peabody: Hendrickson, 2004), XXXIV: 211.

2 Peter R. Ackroyd, *Exile and Restoration: A Study of Hebrew Thought in the Sixth Century B.C.* (OTL; Philadelphia: Westminster, 1968), 195.

3   These suggestions are made by Carol L. Meyers and Eric M. Meyers, *Haggai, Zechariah 1–8* (AB 25B; New York: Doubleday, 1987), 344–45.

4   This is true both from the available manuscripts as well as from the fact that the plural reading is the more difficult one. See James C. VanderKam, *From Joshua to Caiaphas: High Priests after the Exile* (Minneapolis: Fortress, 2004), 39 n. 145.

5   Meyers and Meyers, *Haggai, Zechariah 1–8*, 350.

6   John J. Collins, "The Eschatology of Zechariah" in *Knowing the End from the Beginning: The Prophetic, the Apocalyptic and their Relationships,* ed. Lester L. Grabbe and Robert D. Haak (JSPSup 46; New York: T&T Clark, 2003), 79.

7   This is not an anomalous distinction. For instance, Tobit (written in the late 3rd or early 2nd century B.C.) distinguishes between the temple already built and the eschatological temple (Tobit 14:5). Tobit also connects the eschatological age with an ingathering and the bringing of gold and other precious metals/stones (cf. Tobit 13:16–17).

8   The word for "crown" is ambiguous; it could be singular or plural and the textual evidence is largely divided. However, the verb is clearly singular, meaning that the singular "crown" is probably the right reading. Moreover, the singular reading fits well with the flow of the argument. The passage begins with two crowns. One of them is placed on the head of the high priest Joshua. The other crown is ultimately for the messianic Davidic branch and is to be placed within the temple (once it is finished), until such a time when the future Davidic ruler arises to wear it.

9   Thomas E. McComiskey, "Zechariah," in *The Minor Prophets*, vol. 3, ed. Thomas E. McComiskey (Grand Rapids: Baker, 1998), 1118–19.

10 Ralph L. Smith, *Micah-Malachi* (WBC 32; Waco: Word, 1984), 219. The difference between the two texts is that Zechariah 6:15 is in the plural, while Deuteronomy 28:1 is in the singular.

11 On the nature of historical contingencies, see Richard L. Pratt Jr., "Hyper-Preterism and Unfolding Biblical Eschatology," in *When Shall These Things Be: A Reformed Response to Hyper-Preterism,* ed. Keith A. Mathison (Phillipsburg: P&R, 2004), 121–54, especially 146–48.

12 John J. Collins, *The Scepter and the Star: The Messiahs of the Dead Sea Scrolls and Other Ancient Literature* (ABRL; New York: Doubleday, 1995), 74–101.

13 Douglas Farrow, *Ascension and Ecclesia: On the Significance of the Doctrine of the Ascension for Ecclesiology and Christian Cosmology* (Grand Rapids: Eerdmans, 1999), 26 (emphasis in the original).

14 N. T. Wright, *Surprised by Hope: Rethinking Heaven, the Resurrection, and the Mission of the Church* (New York: HarperCollins, 2008), 111–12.

CHAPTER ELEVEN: FROM FASTING TO FEASTING

1 Thomas Aquinas, "Sacris Solemniis" in *Hymns of the Breviary and Missal,* trans. J. D. Chambers, ed. Matthew Britt (New York: Benzinger Brothers, 1922), 185–86.

2 Beginning with Wellhausen, a popular suggestion has been that "Bethel" should be understood as part of a compound name, Bethel-sharezer. On this reading, the men would not have come from Bethel, but from Babylon. However, the case for Bethel as the origin of the delegation is well made by McComiskey based on the syntax of the verse as well as the implication of verse 5 that the delegation came from within the land. Thomas E. McComiskey, "Zechariah," in *The Minor Prophets*, vol. 3, ed. Thomas E. McComiskey (Grand Rapids: Baker, 1998), 1124.

3 Rainer Albertz, *A History of Israelite Religion in the Old Testament Period,* vol. 1, *From the Beginnings to the End of the Monarchy,* trans. John Bowden (OTL; Louisville: Westminster John Knox, 1994), 242.

4 Ralph L. Smith, *Micah-Malachi* (WBC 32; Waco: Word, 1984), 227.

5 David L. Peterson, *Haggai and Zechariah 1–8* (OTL; Philadelphia: Westminster, 1984), 295.

6 Carol L. Meyers and Eric M. Meyers, *Haggai, Zechariah 1–8* (AB 25B; New York: Doubleday, 1987), 443.

7 William L. Lane, *The Gospel of Mark* (NICNT; Grand Rapids: Eerdmans, 1974), 109.

8 Alexander Schmemann, *For the Life of the World: Sacraments and Orthodoxy,* rev. ed. (Crestwood: St. Vladimir's Seminary Press, 1973), 26, 27, 42, 44–45 (emphasis in the original).

CHAPTER TWELVE: THE COMING KING

1 Irenaeus, *Fragments from the Lost Writings of Irenaeus*, ANF, vol. 1 (Peabody: Hendrickson, 2004), fragment LIII:577.

2 The logical progression in this chapter roughly follows Butterworth's suggestion. Mike Butterworth, *Structure and the Book of Zechariah* (JSOTSS 130; Sheffield: Sheffield Academic Press, 1992), 195, 237.

3 Joyce G. Baldwin, *Haggai, Zechariah, Malachi* (TOTC 24; Downers Grove: InterVarsity, 1972), 160.

4 Rex Mason, *The Books of Haggai, Zechariah, and Malachi* (CBC; Cambridge: Cambridge University Press, 1977), 86.

5 Just as debate rages over whether the suffering servant in Isaiah 53 is an individual or corporate Israel, so a similar but less well-known debate exists over Zechariah 9:9. The view that Zechariah 9:9 refers to a single individual is the majority view, while a few interpreters have opted for the view that the king is a personification of a collected remnant. See the discussion in Adrian M. Leske, "Context and Meaning of Zechariah 9:9," *CBQ* 62 (2000): 663–78 and Rex Mason, "The Use of Earlier Biblical Material in Zechariah 9–14: A Study in Inner Biblical Exegesis" in *Bringing Out the Treasure: Inner Biblical Allusion in Zechariah 9–14,* ed. Mark J. Boda and Michael H. Floyd (New York: T&T Clark, 2003), 28–45. Ultimately, for the Christian who identifies Jesus as the coming king of Zechariah 9:9, the end result is essentially the same since Jesus is not only the Messiah of Israel but also the true embodiment of corporate Israel in a single person. See N. T. Wright, *The Climax of the Covenant: Christ and the Law in Pauline Theology* (Minneapolis: Fortress, 1992), 18–40.

6 Moshe Weinfeld, *Social Justice in Ancient Israel and the Ancient Near East* (Publications of the Perry Foundation for Biblical Research in the Hebrew University of Jerusalem; Minneapolis: Fortress Press, 1995), 7–12.

7 Ibid., 19.

8 Philip J. King and Lawrence E. Stager, *Life in Biblical Israel* (Louisville: Westminster John Knox, 2001), 115.

9 Iain Duguid, "Messianic Themes in Zechariah 9–14," in *The Lord's Anointed: Interpretation of Old Testament Messianic Texts,* ed. Philip Satterthwaite (Carlisle: Paternoster, 1995), 268.

10 Shalom Paul, "A Technical Expression from Archery in Zechariah IX 13a," *VT* 39 (1989): 495–97.

11 Many scholars assume that the reference to Greece must either be a later gloss or else evidence of a composition date after Alexander the Great. But, there is no reason that a reference to Greece could not be made in the early Persian period. See Mark Boda, *Haggai, Zechariah* (NIVAC; Grand Rapids: Zondervan, 2004), 421; David L. Petersen, *Zechariah 9–14 and Malachi* (OTL; Louisville: Westminster John Knox, 1995), 62–63.

12 The symbolic meanings are given in Baldwin, *Haggai, Zechariah, Malachi*, 174.

13 See Brevard Childs, *Memory and Tradition in Israel* (London: SCM Press Ltd., 1962), 53–54.

14 Petersen, *Zechariah 9–14 and Malachi*, 79.

15 Clay Alan Ham, *The Coming King and the Rejected Shepherd: Matthew's Reading of Zechariah's Messianic Hope* (NTM 4; Sheffield: Sheffield Phoenix Press, 2005), 30–34, 44–45. However, the text does take on messianic implications in later rabbinic literature.

16 Clement of Rome, "The First Epistle of Clement to the Corinthians" in *Early Christian Writings,* trans. Maxwell Staniforth (New York: Penguin, 1968), 29–30.

17 The following lanes of application are drawn from Bernard of Clairvaux, "On the Steps of Humility and Pride" in *Bernard of Clairvaux: Selected Works,* trans. G. R. Evans (New York: Paulist Press, 1987), 99–143.

CHAPTER THIRTEEN: THE REJECTED SHEPHERD

1 Johann Sebastian Bach, *The Passion of Our Lord According to St. Matthew,* trans. John Sullivan Dwight (Boston: Oliver Ditson, 1907), ix.

2 Erica Reiner, "Thirty Pieces of Silver," *JAOS* 88 (1968):186–90.

3 Elizabeth Achtemeier, *Nahum-Malachi* (IBC; Louisville: Westminster John Knox, 1986), 157.

4   Joachim Schaper, "The Jerusalem Temple as an Instrument of the Achaemenid Fiscal Administration," *VT* 45 (1995): 528–39.

5   Gerhard Lohfink, *Jesus and Community: The Social Dimensions of Christian Faith,* trans. John P. Galvin (Philadelphia: Fortress; New York: Paulist Press, 1984), 10 (emphases in the original).

6   Clay Alan Ham, *The Coming King and the Rejected Shepherd: Matthew's Reading of Zechariah's Messianic Hope* (NTM 4; Sheffield: Sheffield Phoenix Press, 2005), 62.

7   Craig L. Blomberg, "Matthew" in *Commentary on the New Testament Use of the Old Testament,* ed. G. K. Beale and D. A. Carson (Grand Rapids: Baker, 2007), 97.

8   Alexander Schmemann, *The Journals of Father Alexander Schmemann 1973–1983* (Crestwood: St. Vladimir's Seminary Press, 2002), 149.

CHAPTER FOURTEEN: THE PIERCED ONE

1   Lactantius, *A Poem on the Passion of the Lord*, ANF, vol. 7 (Peabody: Hendrickson, 2004), 327.

2   Two natural questions arise. First, after the Babylonian destruction of Jerusalem in the face of many who believed that the city was inviolable, how would anyone in the postexilic community regain confidence that Jerusalem would be inviolable in the future? Second, given that Jerusalem is small and largely insignificant in the postexilic world, what would make the whole world turn its attention to it? Stuhlmueller persuasively argues that "Zechariah is writing theologically about the history of Jerusalem and is centering all peoples and nations around Yahweh, enthroned in the Jerusalem temple as king (cf. Pss. 96–99)." Carroll Stuhlmueller, *Rebuilding with Hope: A Commentary on the Books of Haggai and Zechariah* (ITC; Grand Rapids: Eerdmans, 1988), 146.

3   Hinckley G. Mitchell, "Zechariah" in *A Critical and Exegetical Commentary on Haggai, Zechariah, Malachi, and Jonah,* H. G. Mitchell, J. M. P. Smith, and J. A. Bewer (ICC; New York: Charles Scribner's Sons, 1912), 322.

4   J. J. M. Roberts, "The Davidic Origin of the Zion Tradition," *JBL* 92 (1973): 329–44.

5 Rex Mason, *The Books of Haggai, Zechariah, and Malachi* (CBC; Cambridge: Cambridge University Press, 1977), 116.

6 Due to their shared subject matter of shepherds and sheep, Zechariah 11:4–17 and 13:7–9 are sometimes believed to have been connected to one another originally, with the latter becoming displaced at a later time. For a survey of the issue and a balanced approach, see James D. Nogalski, "Zechariah 13:7–9 as a Transitional Text: An Appreciation and Re-evaluation of the Work of Rex Mason" in *Bringing Out the Treasure: Inner Biblical Allusion in Zechariah 9–14*, ed. Mark J. Boda and Michael H. Floyd (New York: T&T Clark, 2003), 292–304.

7 Stephen L. Cook, "The Metamorphosis of a Shepherd: The Tradition History of Zechariah 11:17 + 13:7–9," *CBQ* 55 (1993):453–66.

8 Carol L. Meyers and Eric M. Meyers, *Zechariah 9–14* (AB 25C; New York: Doubleday, 1993), 387.

9 Rikk E. Watts, "Mark" in *Commentary on the New Testament Use of the Old Testament*, ed. G. K. Beale and D. A. Carson (Grand Rapids: Baker, 2007), 233.

10 Craig A. Evans, "Jesus and Zechariah's Messianic Hope" in *Authenticating the Activities of Jesus*, ed. Bruce Chilton and Craig A. Evans (Leiden: Brill, 1999), 386.

11 Christopher M. Tuckett, "Zechariah 12:10 and the New Testament" in *The Book of Zechariah and Its Influence*, ed. Christopher Tuckett (Burlington: Ashgate, 2003), 119.

12 Elizabeth Achtemeier, *Nahum-Malachi* (IBC; Louisville: Westminster John Knox, 1986), 163.

CHAPTER FIFTEEN: THE FINAL RENEWAL

1 Cyril of Alexandria, *On the Unity of Christ*, trans. John A. McGuckin (Crestwood: St. Vladimir's Seminary Press, 1995), 106.

2 Gerhard von Rad, "The Origin of the Concept of the Day of Yahweh," *JSS* 4 (1959): 103, 104.

3 Readers have regularly noticed inconsistencies between Zechariah 12 and 14, this being only one of them. But as Peter Craigie notes, "To complain that chapters 12 and 14 seem at points to contradict each other is to miss the main issue. . . . Each chapter is, as it were, a snapshot of the coming Day of the Lord; each is taken from a

different angle, with different foreground and background, but each one ultimately points to God's final victory and peace." Peter C. Craigie, *Twelve Prophets*, vol. 2 (DSB; Philadelphia: Westminster, 1985), 220.

4   The text is sometimes emended from "and you shall flee" to "and it will be stopped up," producing the reading that the valley between the mountains will be filled in. But the Masoretic reading makes sense as it stands, and as Meyers and Meyers note, there is no evidence that during the 8th century earthquake any valley was filled in or blocked. Carol L. Meyers and Eric M. Meyers, *Zechariah 9–14* (AB 25C; New York: Doubleday, 1993), 427.

5   Konrad Schaefer, "The Ending of the Book of Zechariah: A Commentary," *RB* 100 (1993): 190.

6   Ibid., 206.

7   Michael H. Floyd, *Minor Prophets, Part 2* (FOTL XXII; Grand Rapids: Eerdmans, 2000), 554.

8   Though somewhat conjectural, the locations of these landmarks generally follows the suggestions made by Meyers and Meyers, *Zechariah 9–14*, 444–47.

9   Henk Jan de Jonge, "The Cleansing of the Temple in Mark 11:15 and Zechariah 14:21" in *The Book of Zechariah and Its Influence,* ed. Christopher Tuckett (Burlington: Ashgate, 2003), 90.

10   Joyce G. Baldwin, *Haggai, Zechariah, Malachi* (TOTC 24; Downers Grove: InterVarsity, 1972), 208.

11   The following details are dependent upon Paul Brooks Duff, "The March of the Divine Warrior and the Advent of the Greco-Roman King: Mark's Account of Jesus' Entry into Jerusalem," *JBL* 111 (1992): 55–71 and Tremper Longman III and Daniel G. Reid, *God is a Warrior* (Grand Rapids: Zondervan, 1995), 121–24.

12   Richard B. Hays, *The Moral Vision of the New Testament: A Contemporary Introduction to New Testament Ethics* (San Francisco: HarperCollins, 1996), 198 (emphasis in the original).

13   Jürgen Moltmann, *Theology of Hope: On the Ground and Implications of a Christian Eschatology,* trans. James W. Leitch (New York: Harper & Row, 1967), 21.

FOR FURTHER READING

The following works were referred to or cited in the text.

Commentaries on Zechariah

Achtemeier, Elizabeth. *Nahum-Malachi*. Interpretation. Louisville: John Knox, 1986.

Baldwin, Joyce G. *Haggai, Zechariah, Malachi*. Tyndale Old Testament Commentary 24. Downers Grove: InterVarsity, 1972.

Boda, Mark J. *Haggai, Zechariah*. NIV Application Commentary. Grand Rapids: Zondervan, 2004.

Craigie, Peter C. *Twelve Prophets*. Vol. 2. Daily Study Bible. Philadelphia: Westminster, 1985.

Floyd, Michael H. *Minor Prophets, Part 2*. Vol. 22. Forms of the Old Testament Literature. Grand Rapids: Eerdmans, 2000.

Mason, Rex. *The Books of Haggai, Zechariah, and Malachi*. Cambridge Bible Commentary. Cambridge: Cambridge University Press, 1977.

McComiskey, Thomas E. "Zechariah." In *The Minor Prophets*. Vol. 3. Edited by Thomas E. McComiskey, 1003–1244. Grand Rapids: Baker, 1998.

Meyers, Carol L. and Eric M. Meyers. *Haggai, Zechariah 1–8*. Vol. 25B. Anchor Bible. New York: Doubleday, 1987.

_____. *Zechariah 9–14*. Vol. 25C. Anchor Bible. New York: Doubleday, 1993.

Mitchell, Hinckley G. "Zechariah." *A Critical and Exegetical Commentary on Haggai, Zechariah, Malachi, and Jonah*. H. G. Mitchell, J. M. P. Smith, and J. A. Bewer. International

Critical Commentary, 107–217. New York: Charles Scribner's Sons, 1912.

Petersen, David L. *Haggai and Zechariah 1–8*. Old Testament Library. Philadelphia: Westminster, 1984.

_____. *Zechariah 9–14 and Malachi*. Old Testament Library. Louisville: Westminster John Knox, 1995.

Smith, Ralph L. *Micah-Malachi*. Vol. 32. Word Biblical Commentary. Waco: Word, 1984.

Stuhlmueller, Carroll. *Rebuilding with Hope: A Commentary on the Books of Haggai and Zechariah*. International Theological Commentary. Grand Rapids: Eerdmans, 1988.

Webb, Barry G. *The Message of Zechariah: Your Kingdom Come*. Bible Speaks Today. Downers Grove: InterVarsity, 2003.

Other Works

Ackroyd, Peter R. *Exile and Restoration: A Study of Hebrew Thought in the Sixth Century B.C.* Old Testament Library. Philadelphia: Westminster, 1968.

Albertz, Rainer. *A History of Israelite Religion in the Old Testament Period*. Vol. 1, *From the Beginnings to the End of the Monarchy*. Translated by John Bowden. Old Testament Library. Louisville: Westminster John Knox, 1994.

_____. *A History of Israelite Religion in the Old Testament Period*. Vol. 2, *From the Exile to the Maccabees*. Translated by John Bowden. Old Testament Library. Louisville: Westminster John Knox, 1994.

Alter, Robert. *The Art of Biblical Narrative*. New York: Basic Books, 1981.

Ambrose. *Concerning Repentance*. Vol. 10. Nicene and Post-Nicene Fathers, Second Series. Peabody: Hendrickson, 2004.

Andersen, Francis I. "Who Built the Second Temple?" *ABR* 6 (1958): 1–35.

Anderson, Gary A. *The Genesis of Perfection: Adam and Eve in Jewish and Christian Imagination*. Louisville: Westminster John Knox, 2001.

Aquinas, Thomas. "Sacris Solemniis." In *Hymns of the Breviary and Missal*. Translated by J. D. Chambers. Edited by Matthew Britt, 185–87. New York: Benzinger Brothers, 1922.

Arnold, Bill T. *Readings from the Ancient Near East*. Edited by Bryan E. Beyer. Grand Rapids: Baker, 2002.

Augsburger, David. *Dissident Discipleship: A Spirituality of Self-Surrender, Love of God, and Love of Neighbor*. Grand Rapids: Brazos, 2006.

Augustine. *City of God*. Translated by Henry Bettenson. New York: Penguin Books, 2003.

_____. *Confessions*. Translated by F. J. Sheed. Indianapolis: Hackett, 1993.

_____. *The Works of Saint Augustine: A Translation for the 21st Century*. Part 3, vol. 2, *Sermons on the Old Testament (20–50)*. Translated by Edmund Hill, O.P. Hyde Park: New City Press, 1990.

Bach, Johann Sebastian. *The Passion of Our Lord According to St. Matthew*. Translated by John Sullivan Dwight. Boston: Oliver Ditson, 1907.

Barna, George. *Growing True Disciples: New Strategies for Producing Genuine Followers of Christ*. Colorado Springs: Waterbrook, 2001.

Barth, Karl. *Church Dogmatics*. Translated by G. W. Bromiley and T. F. Torrance. Edinburgh: T&T Clark, 1936–77.

Bauckham, Richard. *The Theology of the Book of Revelation*. Cambridge: Cambridge University Press, 1993.

Bedford, Peter Ross. *Temple Restoration in Early Achaemenid Judah*. Vol. 65. Supplements to the Journal for the Study of Judaism. Leiden: Brill, 2001.

Berquist, Jon L. *Judaism in Persia's Shadow: A Social and Historical Approach*. Minneapolis: Fortress, 1995.

Black, Mark C. "The Rejected and Slain Messiah Who Is Coming with His Angels: The Messianic Exegesis of Zechariah 9–14." PhD diss., Emory University, 1990.

Blomberg, Craig L. "Matthew." In *Commentary on the New Testament Use of the Old Testament*. Edited by G. K. Beale and D. A. Carson, 1–109. Grand Rapids: Baker, 2007.

Bright, John. *A History of Israel, 3rd edition*. Philadelphia: West-minster, 1981.

Butterworth, Mike. *Structure and the Book of Zechariah*. Vol. 130. Supplements to the Journal for the Study of the Old Testament. Sheffield: Sheffield Academic Press, 1992.

Calvin, John. *Institutes of the Christian Religion*. Translated by Ford Lewis Battles. Edited by John T. McNeill. Louisville: Westminster John Knox, 1960.

Carter, Charles E. *The Emergence of Yehud in the Persian Period: A Social and Demographic Study*. Vol. 294. Supplements to the Journal for the Study of the Old Testament. Sheffield: Sheffield Academic, 1999.

Childs, Brevard S. *Memory and Tradition in Israel*. London: SCM Press Ltd., 1962.

Chrysostom, John. *Homilies on the Acts of the Apostles and the Epistle to the Romans*. Vol. 11. Nicene and Post-Nicene Fathers, First Series. Peabody: Hendrickson, 2004.

_____. *Homilies on Colossians*. Vol. 13. Nicene and Post-Nicene Fathers, First Series. Peabody: Hendrickson, 2004.

Clement of Rome. "The First Epistle of Clement to the Corinthi-ans." In *Early Christian Writings*. Translated by Maxwell Staniforth, 23–51. New York: Penguin, 1968.

Collins, John J. "The Eschatology of Zechariah." In *Knowing the End from the Beginning: The Prophetic, the Apocalyptic and their Relationships*. Vol. 46. Supplements to the Journal for the Study of the Pseudepigrapha. Edited by Lester L. Grabbe and Robert D. Haak, 74–84. New York: T&T Clark, 2003.

_____. *Introduction to the Hebrew Bible*. Minneapolis: For-tress, 2004.

_____. *The Scepter and the Star: The Messiahs of the Dead Sea Scrolls and Other Ancient Literature*. Anchor Bible Reference Library. New York: Doubleday, 1995.

Cook, Stephen L. "The Metamorphosis of a Shepherd: The Tradition History of Zechariah 11:17 + 13:7–9," *CBQ* 55 (1993):453–66.

Cross, Frank Moore. *Canaanite Myth and Hebrew Epic*. Cambridge: Harvard University Press, 1997.

Curtis, Byron. *Up the Steep and Stony Road: The Book of Zechariah in Social Location Trajectory Analysis.* Leiden: Brill, 2006.

Cyril of Alexandria. *On the Unity of Christ.* Translated by John A. McGuckin. Crestwood: St. Vladimir's Seminary Press, 1995.

Dever, William G. *Did God Have a Wife? Archaeology and Folk Religion in Ancient Israel.* Grand Rapids: Eerdmans, 2005.

Dillard, Raymond B. and Tremper Longman III. *An Introduction to the Old Testament.* Grand Rapids: Zondervan, 1994.

Duff, Paul Brooks. "The March of the Divine Warrior and the Advent of the Greco-Roman King: Mark's Account of Jesus' Entry into Jerusalem," *JBL* 111 (1992): 55–71.

Duguid, Iain. "Messianic Themes in Zechariah 9–14." In *The Lord's Anointed: Interpretation of Old Testament Messianic Texts.* Edited by Philip Satterthwaite, 265–80. Carlisle: Paternoster, 1995.

Durant, Will and Ariel. *The Lessons of History.* New York: Simon and Schuster, 1968.

Ellis, Richard S. *Foundation Deposits in Ancient Mesopotamia.* New Haven: Yale University Press, 1968.

Evans, Craig A. "Jesus and Zechariah's Messianic Hope." In *Authenticating the Activities of Jesus.* Edited by Bruce Chilton and Craig A. Evans, 373–88. Leiden: Brill, 1999.

————. "The Shout of Death." In *Jesus, The Final Days: What Really Happened.* Edited by Troy A. Miller, 1–38. Louisville: Westminster John Knox, 2009.

Farrow, Douglas. *Ascension and Ecclesia: On the Significance of the Doctrine of the Ascension for Ecclesiology and Christian Cosmology.* Grand Rapids: Eerdmans, 1999.

Ferguson, Everett. *Backgrounds of Early Christianity.* Grand Rapids: Eerdmans, 1993.

Floyd, Michael H. "The Evil in the Ephah: Reading Zechariah 5:5–11 in Its Literary Context," *CBQ* 58 (1996): 51–68.

Fohrer, Georg. *Introduction to the Old Testament.* Translated by David E. Green. Nashville: Abingdon, 1968.

Fritz, Volkmar. *1 & 2 Kings*. Continental Commentary. Minneapolis: Fortress, 2003.

Halpern, Baruch. "The Ritual Background of Zechariah's Temple Song," *CBQ* 40 (1978): 167–90.

Ham, Clay Alan. *The Coming King and the Rejected Shepherd: Matthew's Reading of Zechariah's Messianic Hope*. Vol. 4. New Testament Monographs. Sheffield: Sheffield Phoenix Press, 2005.

Hanson, Paul. *The Dawn of Apocalyptic*. Minneapolis: Fortress, 1975.

Hays, Richard B. *The Moral Vision of the New Testament: A Contemporary Introduction to New Testament Ethics*. San Francisco: HarperCollins, 1996.

Hilary of Poitiers. *On the Trinity*. Vol 9. Nicene and Post-Nicene Fathers, Second Series. Peabody: Hendrickson, 2004.

Hill, Andrew E. "Dating Second Zechariah: A Linguistic Reexamination," *HAR* 6 (1982): 105–34.

Hultgren, Arland J. *The Parables of Jesus: A Commentary*. Grand Rapids: Eerdmans, 2000.

Irenaeus. *Fragments from the Lost Writings of Irenaeus*. Vol. 1. Ante-Nicene Fathers. Peabody: Hendrickson, 2004.

Japhet, Sara. " 'History' and 'Literature' in the Persian Period: The Restoration of the Temple." In *Ah, Assyria . . . Studies in Assyrian History and Ancient Near Eastern Historiography Presented to Hayim Tadmor*. Edited by Mordechai Cogan and Israel Ehp'al, 174–88. Jerusalem: Magnes Press, 1991.

_____. "The Temple in the Restoration Period: Reality and Ideology," *USQR* 44.3 (1991): 195–251.

John of the Cross. "The Living Flame of Love." In *The Collected Works of St. John of the Cross*. Translated by Kieran Kavanaugh and Otilio Rodriguez, 638–715. Washington: ICS Publications, 1991.

Johnson, Dennis E. *The Triumph of the Lamb: A Commentary on Revelation*. Phillipsburg: P&R, 2001.

de Jonge, Henk Jan. "The Cleansing of the Temple in Mark 11:15 and Zechariah 14:21." In *The Book of Zechariah and Its*

Influence. Edited by Christopher Tuckett, 87–100. Burlington: Ashgate, 2003.

Keel, Othmar. *The Symbolism of the Biblical World: Ancient Near Eastern Iconography and the Book of Psalms.* Translated by Timothy J. Hallett. New York: Seabury, 1978.

Kessler, John. *The Book of Haggai: Prophecy and Society in Early Persian Yehud.* Vol. 91. Supplements to Vetus Testamentum. Leiden: Brill, 2002.

King, Philip J. and Lawrence E. Stager. *Life in Biblical Israel.* Louisville: Westminster John Knox, 2001.

Kinnaman, David and Gabe Lyons. *unChristian: What a New Generation Really Thinks about Christianity . . . And Why It Matters.* Grand Rapids: Baker, 2007.

Laato, Antti. "Zachariah 4,6b–10a and the Akkadian Royal Building Inscriptions," *ZAW* 106 (1994): 53–69.

Lactantius. *A Poem on the Passion of the Lord.* Vol. 7. Ante-Nicene Fathers. Peabody: Hendrickson, 2004.

Lane, William L. *The Gospel of Mark.* New International Commentary on the New Testament. Grand Rapids: Eerdmans, 1974.

Leo the Great. *Sermons.* Vol. 12. Nicene and Post-Nicene Fathers, Second Series. Peabody: Hendrickson, 2004.

Leske, Adrian M. "Context and Meaning of Zechariah 9:9," *CBQ* 62 (2000): 663–78.

Levenson, Jon D. *Sinai and Zion: An Entry into the Jewish Bible.* San Francisco: Harper & Row, 1985.

Lohfink, Gerhard. *Jesus and Community: The Social Dimensions of Christian Faith.* Translated by John P. Galvin. Philadelphia: Fortress; New York: Paulist Press, 1984.

Longman III, Tremper and Daniel G. Reid. *God is a Warrior.* Grand Rapids: Zondervan, 1995.

Lovelace, Richard F. *Dynamics of Spiritual Life: An Evangelical Theology of Renewal.* Downers Grove: InterVarsity Press, 1979.

Lupton, Robert D. *Compassion, Justice, and the Christian Life: Rethinking Ministry to the Poor.* Ventura: Regal, 2007.

247

Luz, Ulrich. *Matthew 8–20*. Translated by James E. Crouch. Hermeneia. Minneapolis: Fortress, 2001.

Martyr, Justin. *Dialogue with Trypho*. Vol. 1. Ante-Nicene Fathers. Peabody: Hendrickson, 2004.

Mason, Rex. "The Use of Earlier Biblical Material in Zechariah 9–14: A Study in Inner Biblical Exegesis." In *Bringing Out the Treasure: Inner Biblical Allusion in Zechariah 9–14*. Edited by Mark J. Boda and Michael H. Floyd, 1–208. New York: T&T Clark, 2003.

Maximus the Confessor. "Four Hundred Chapters on Love." Pages 33–98 in *Maximus Confessor: Selected Writings*. Translated by George C. Berthol. New York: Paulist Press, 1985.

Mazar, Amihai. *Archaeology of the Land of the Bible; 10,000—586 B.C.E.* Anchor Bible Reference Library. New York: Doubleday, 1992.

McIver, Robert K. "The Parable of the Weeds Among the Wheat (Matt 13:24–30, 36–43) and the Relationship Between the Kingdom and the Church as Portrayed in the Gospel of Matthew," *JBL* 114 (1995): 643–59.

Melito of Sardis. "A Homily on the Passover." In *The Christological Controversy*. Translated and edited by Richard A. Norris, Jr., 33–47. Philadelphia: Fortress, 1980.

Miller, J. Maxwell and John H. Hayes. *A History of Ancient Israel and Judah*, 2nd ed. Louisville: Westminster John Knox, 2006.

Moltmann, Jürgen. *Theology of Hope: On the Ground and Implications of a Christian Eschatology*. Translated by James W. Leitch. New York: Harper & Row, 1967.

Newbigin, Lesslie. *The Gospel in a Pluralist Society.* Grand Rapids: Eerdmans, 1989.

Nietzsche, Friedrich Wilhelm. *Thus Spoke Zarathustra: A Book for All and None*. Translated by Adrian Del Caro. Cambridge: Cambridge University Press, 2006.

Nogalski, James D. "Zechariah 13:7–9 as a Transitional Text: An Appreciation and Re-evaluation of the Work of Rex Mason." In *Bringing Out the Treasure: Inner Biblical Allusion in Zechariah 9–14*. Edited by Mark J. Boda and Michael H. Floyd, 292–304. New York: T&T Clark, 2003.

Paul, Shalom. "A Technical Expression from Archery in Zechariah IX 13a," *VT* 39 (1989): 495–97.

Perkins, John M. *Beyond Charity: The Call to Christian Community Development.* Grand Rapids: Baker, 1993.

_____. *Let Justice Roll Down.* Ventura: Regal, 1976.

_____. *With Justice for All.* Ventura: Regal, 1982.

Plöger, Otto. *Theocracy and Eschatology.* Translated by S. Rudman. Richmond: John Knox, 1968.

Potok, Chaim. *In the Beginning.* New York: Alfred A. Knopf, 1976.

Poythress, Vern. *The Shadow of Christ in the Law of Moses.* Phillipsburg: P&R, 1991.

Pratt Jr., Richard L. "Hyper-Preterism and Unfolding Biblical Eschatology." In *When Shall These Things Be: A Reformed Response to Hyper-Preterism.* Edited by Keith A. Mathison, 121–54. Phillipsburg: P&R, 2004.

Provan, Iain, V. Philips Long and Tremper Longman III. *A Biblical History of Israel.* Louisville: Westminster John Knox, 2003.

Purves, Andrew. *Reconstructing Pastoral Theology: A Christological Foundation.* Louisville: Westminster John Knox, 2004.

von Rad, Gerhard. *Old Testament Theology.* Vol. 2, *The Theology of Israel's Prophetic Traditions.* Translated by D. M. G. Stalker. New York: Harper and Row, 1965.

_____. "The Origin of the Concept of the Day of Yahweh," *JSS* 4 (1959): 97–108.

Radner, Ephraim. *The End of the Church: A Pneumatology of Christian Division in the West.* Grand Rapids: Eerdmans, 1998.

Rainey, Anson and R. Steven Notley. *The Sacred Bridge: Carta's Atlas of the Biblical World.* Jerusalem: Carta, 2006.

Reiner, Erica. "Thirty Pieces of Silver" *JAOS* 88 (1968):186–90.

Roberts, J. J. M. "The Davidic Origin of the Zion Tradition," *JBL* 92 (1973): 329–44.

Rudman, Dominic. "Zechariah 5 and the Priestly Law," *SJOT* 14 (2000):194–206.

Ryken, Leland, James C. Wilhoit and Tremper Longman III. *Dictionary of Biblical Imagery.* Downers Grove: InterVarsity, 1998.

Ryken, Philip Graham, ed. *The Communion of Saints: Living in Fellowship with the People of God.* Phillipsburg: P&R: 2001.

de Sales, Francis. *Introduction to the Devout Life.* New York: Random House, 2002.

Schaefer, Konrad. "The Ending of the Book of Zechariah: A Commentary," *RB* 100 (1993): 165–238.

Schaff, Philip. *History of the Christian Church.* Vol. 7, *The German Reformation, The Beginning of the Protestant Reformation up to the Diet of Augsburg, 1517–1530.* 2nd ed. Peabody: Hendrickson, 2006.

Schaper, Joachim. "The Jerusalem Temple as an Instrument of the Achaemenid Fiscal Administration." *VT* 45 (1995): 528–39.

Schmemann, Alexander. *For the Life of the World: Sacraments and Orthodoxy.* Rev. ed. Crestwood: St. Vladimir's Seminary Press, 1973.

_____. *The Journals of Father Alexander Schmemann 1973–1983.* Crestwood: St. Vladimir's Seminary Press, 2002.

Sider, Ronald J. *The Scandal of the Evangelical Conscience: Why Are Christians Living Just Like the Rest of the World?* Grand Rapids: Baker, 2005.

Smith, Mark S. *The Early History of God: Yahweh and the Other Deities in Ancient Israel.* Grand Rapids: Eerdmans, 2002.

Stark, Rodney. *The Rise of Christianity.* New York: Harper Collins, 1997.

Stronach, David. *Pasargadae: A Report on the Excavations Conducted by the British Institute of Persian Studies from 1961 to 1963.* Oxford: Oxford University Press, 1978.

Thielicke, Helmut. *Notes from a Wayfarer: The Autobiography of Helmut Thielicke.* Translated by David R. Law. New York: Paragon House, 1995.

_____. *The Silence of God.* Translated by G. W. Bromiley. Grand Rapids: Eerdmans, 1962.

Thomas, D. W., ed. *Documents from Old Testament Times.* London: Nelson, 1958.

Tiemeyer, Lena-Sofia. "The Guilty Priesthood (Zech 3)." In *The Book of Zechariah and Its Influence.* Edited by Christopher Tuckett, 1–19. Burlington: Ashgate, 2003.

Tollington, Janet E. *Tradition and Innovation in Haggai and Zechariah 1–8.* Vol. 150. Supplements to the Journal for the Study of the Old Testament. Sheffield: JSOT Press, 1993.

Tov, Emanuel. *Textual Criticism of the Hebrew Bible*, 2nd ed. Minneapolis: Fortress, 2001.

Tuckett, Christopher M. "Zechariah 12:10 and the New Testament." In *The Book of Zechariah and Its Influence.* Edited by Christopher Tuckett, 111–21. Burlington: Ashgate, 2003.

VanderKam, James C. *From Joshua to Caiaphas: High Priests after the Exile.* Minneapolis: Fortress, 2004.

_____. "Joshua the High Priest and the Interpretation of Zechariah 3," *CBQ* 53 (1991): 553–70.

Vassady, Béla. *Limping Along . . . Confessions of a Pilgrim Theologian.* Grand Rapids: Eerdmans, 1985.

Waltke, Bruce K. *An Old Testament Theology.* Grand Rapids: Zondervan, 2007.

Watts, Rikk E. "Mark." In *Commentary on the New Testament Use of the Old Testament.* Edited by G. K. Beale and D. A. Carson, 111–249. Grand Rapids: Baker Academic, 2007.

Weinfeld, Moshe. *Social Justice in Ancient Israel and the Ancient Near East.* Publications of the Perry Foundation for Biblical Research in the Hebrew University of Jerusalem. Minneapolis: Fortress Press, 1995.

Wilken, Robert Louis. *The Spirit of Early Christian Thought.* New Haven: Yale University Press, 2003.

Williamson, H. G. M. *Ezra, Nehemiah.* Vol. 16. Word Biblical Commentary. Waco: Word, 1985.

Wright, N. T. *The Climax of the Covenant: Christ and the Law in Pauline Theology.* Minneapolis: Fortress, 1992.

_____. *For All God's Worth: True Worship and the Calling of the Church.* Grand Rapids: Eerdmans, 1997.

_____. *Jesus and the Victory of God.* Vol. 2. Christian Origins and the Question of God. Minneapolis: Fortress, 1996.

_____. *Surprised by Hope: Rethinking Heaven, the Resurrection, and the Mission of the Church.* New York: HarperCollins, 2008.

_____. *What Saint Paul Really Said: Was Paul of Tarsus the Real Founder of Christianity?* Grand Rapids: Eerdmans, 1997.

INDEX OF SCRIPTURE